At the Court of an African King

by the same author

*

THE SACRED STATE OF THE AKAN
THE AKAN TRADITIONS OF ORIGIN
THE AKAN OF GHANA, THEIR ANCIENT BELIEFS
THE DIVINE KINGSHIP IN GHANA AND ANCIENT EGYPT

AT THE COURT
OF AN AFRICAN KING

Eva L. R. Meyerowitz

FABER AND FABER LIMITED

24 Russell Square

London

First published in mcmlxii
by Faber and Faber Limited
24 Russell Square London W.C.1
Printed in Great Britain by
Latimer Trend & Co Ltd Plymouth

Preface

This book was written to commemorate the heroic fight of Nana Akumfi Ameyaw III, King of the Bono-Tekyiman State (now called Tekyiman-Brong) and his people, for independence from Ashanti and the restoration of nine villages which they had lost to Ashanti, for the second time, in 1935. This act of aggression on the part of Ashanti was confirmed when, in that year, the Gold Coast Government, following its policy of indirect rule, revived the Ashanti Kingdom as a great power by founding the Ashanti Confederacy. This meant that all the former vassal states again came under the domination of the King of Ashanti. Tekyiman-Brong was one of them.

I met King Akumfi Ameyaw III when in the spring of 1944 I strayed by accident into Tekyiman town. This meeting was a fateful one for both of us as it had far-reaching repercussions. I realized with astonishment that I had stumbled on the survivors of an ancient, highly developed civilization, enormously interesting from various points of view. Capt. R. Rattray, who had been in this part of the world some twenty years before me, saw only a poor and primitive people. Poor the Bono-Tekyiman certainly were, owing to a succession of misfortunes which befell them when, after their defeat in 1740, they became vassals of Ashanti.

I was determined to get all the Bono-Tekyiman traditions relating to their former civilization and this I was promised if, in return, I would help them in their struggle against Ashanti and the British Gold Coast Government. I was prepared to support them after I had convinced myself of the justice of their case, but for the moment I did not see my way clear. I was at that time Art

Preface

Supervisor at Achimota College near Accra and had to return there; then I had undertaken to accompany my husband, then Acting Director of the Institute for West African Arts, Industries and Social Science, to Nigeria, and after that to South Africa on leave. In February 1945 we went to London where in June he died.

Thanks to Mr. N. F. Hall (now Sir Noel Hall), whom I had met during the war when he was the development adviser to the Resident Minister in West Africa, and to whom I had spoken of the ancient civilization of Bono-Tekyiman, I was awarded a study grant from the Colonial Development and Welfare Fund. This made it possible for me to return to Nana Akumfi Ameyaw III and his people in January 1946.

In my book *The Akan Traditions of Origin* (Faber and Faber 1952) I have a chapter on the history of the Bono Kingdom of which Tekyiman had been originally the second largest town. In my third book *The Akan of Ghana, Their Ancient Beliefs* (Faber 1958), there is a long chapter on the reigns of the Kings and Queenmothers of Bono. *The Divine Kingship in Ghana and Ancient Egypt* (Faber 1960), which I wrote next, gives an account of the civilization of ancient Bono. The present book is concerned only with the struggle of the Bono-Tekyiman people for their rights, and my part in it. In the Prologue and Chapter I, I sum up the historical events before 1949, including my activities on Bono-Tekyiman's behalf from 1944 onwards. The main part of the book is based on the diary which I kept from October 1949 to March 1950 when I once more returned to Tekyiman, having been awarded a research grant for further studies from the Academic Board of the University College of the Gold Coast. The Epilogue describes events in the years 1950–61 when, after a renewed struggle, Bono-Tekyiman's independence from Ashanti was finally acknowledged by the Ghana Government and the nine villages were restored to Nana Akumfi Ameyaw III.

I started to write this book in the beautiful home of the late Dr. Louis Mirvish and Mrs. Hilda Mirvish in Cape Town. They both took a great interest in it and I am especially indebted to Dr. Mirvish for his encouragement and criticisms. Dr. Louis

Preface

Herrman, himself a writer, also read the first chapters and commented on them, for which I am grateful.

When I returned to London, I again had good and helpful friends. My gratitude is due to Eva Gutfeld for her thorough perusal of my manuscript and her most valuable suggestions. I am deeply grateful to Mrs. Beatrice Hooke for the improvement of my style, and I wish to record my thanks to Mr. Patrick Raymond for reading the manuscript and giving me help with its presentation.

In the text I refer in places where I am dealing with the Bono Kingdom to one or other of my books for readers who are interested in greater detail. I have shortened their titles as, for instance, *Sacred State* for *The Sacred State of the Akan*, my first book, which was published by Faber and Faber in 1951, and so forth.

EVA L. R. MEYEROWITZ

Contents

Contents

Illustrations

Illustrations

MAPS

Prologue

Meeting Nana Akumfi Ameyaw III, King of Bono-Tekyiman

Easter 1944. I had a month's vacation from Achimota College and decided to spend it searching for the ruins of Beeo-Nsoko. Beeo-Nsoko had once been the capital of the Banda Kingdom, one of the earliest kingdoms in the country now called Ghana, and had played an important role in the gold trade with the western Sudan; the town was totally destroyed by civil war in the first half of the seventeenth century and never rebuilt.[1] However, after a three week's search south of the elbow of the Black Volta River I had to give up; I did not find the ruins, as I discovered too late that I had looked for them some thirty miles too far north. Finally at Fugula a knowledgeable old man advised me to go to Tekyiman, some seventy miles to the south-east, and make inquiries there. This was sound advice, as I learnt in Tekyiman that the kings of Bono, predecessors of the kings of Tekyiman, had ruled Banda for roughly a hundred years after the destruction of Beeo-Nsoko.

I did not know at the time (1944) that the Tekyiman people were in trouble with the Gold Coast Government and reputed to be unfriendly to Europeans. The British District Commissioner at Wenkyi, who administered the State, was therefore most uneasy when I proposed going to Tekyiman-town. But when I insisted, he telephoned to the Tekyimanhene (King of Tekyiman) that I would arrive in an hour and that he and his people were to receive me with all courtesy.

[1] See *Akan Trad.*, pp. 45–8.

13

Prologue

I went to Tekyiman with Kofi Antubam, one of my students—now the best-known painter in Ghana—whom I had taken along to act as my interpreter. We found the Tekyimanhene Nana Akumfi Ameyaw III (Pl. 1) and his elders (ministers and high court officials) already waiting for the meeting with us in the audience-courtyard of the palace. Kofi and I were given a seat facing the assembly. It was soon obvious from the manner of the people that all were sullen and resentful.

After the customary greetings had been exchanged I was asked by the royal spokesman what my mission was. I explained through Kofi that I had been searching for the ruins of Beeo-Nsoko but had failed to find them. I would be grateful if they could tell me where they were and if they could relate to me the historical events which led to the destruction of the town.

The spokesman replied that they could not help me; it was not the custom to divulge other people's history. Seeing that I did not get any further, I asked them about their own history; when Tekyiman was founded for instance. Nana Tekyimanhene (as he was addressed) thereupon replied coldly that they did not tell a stranger about the history of their State. So I asked what I could do to cease to be a stranger and become a friend. There was a long discussion. Finally the King said: 'The Europeans and the Ashanti call us Brong, but our name is Bono. We wished to be called Bono again, Bono-Tekyiman. If you could give us back our proper name we would regard this as an act of friendship.'

I thought for a moment. I had heard the name Bono before. But where? Suddenly I remembered. I asked: 'Are you the people whose ancestors knew the art of making cloth of gold?' There was silence, a silence which never seemed to end. Everybody looked at me until I began to feel uncomfortable. After what seemed ages Nana Tekyimanhene broke the silence: 'Yes,' he said, 'we are these people. But how do you know?' I explained that about three hundred years ago a French trader visited the Gold Coast and wrote down everything he saw and heard. In this book he mentioned the Bono people and the cloth of gold.[1]

[1] Barbot, *A Description of the Coasts of Northern and Southern Guinea and Ethiopia Inferior*, Paris 1732, p. 188. Barbot speaks of weaving fine

14

Prologue

I was then asked whether the Tekyiman State could have this book. I replied that I did not think so, as the book was in London in the British Museum but on my return to England I could copy the passage referring to Bono and send it to them. The meeting then closed and the King asked me to go to the rest-house. He would consult his elders about my request.

About an hour later a royal messenger came to see me. He asked me in the name of the King if I wished to see the battle-field on which the Bono had been defeated by the Ashanti and had lost their independence (about 1740). Of course I wanted to see it, and taking Kofi with me, we drove at once to the palace, where a royal spokesman and a guide were already waiting for us. We set off in my car on the road to Wenkyi.

After travelling a few miles I was asked to turn left. I was surprised, as there was no road, only a clearing in the forest overgrown with high elephant grass. It turned out, however, to be the road to the village of Asueyi. I had no idea how to get the car over a deep ditch that ran along the main road at this spot; but we had luck. Just then two women came along carrying heavy loads of firewood and I bought the wood which was just enough to fill the ditch. With some trouble we got the car across and drove blindly into a sea of green, mowing down the high grass before us. After a short while the road became visible. It led us to Asueyi and then further to the Tano River. There we stopped, and stepped out of the car.

The Tano River, at this point near its source, was not very wide. A huge tree-trunk served as a bridge; it was worn smooth by the tramp of many feet. We crossed it and walked along a narrow path till we came to a valley. It was the most extraordinary valley I had ever seen, small and completely circular. It was here that the fateful battle had taken place over two hundred years ago.

The valley had only two entrances, one opposite the other. On the one side the warriors of Tekyiman had entered, on the other side their enemies, the Ashanti. The battle was fought round the

stuffs with gold in Vanqui (then a town in Bono). However, the people thought that I referred to the loin cloth woven of gold thread which the kings used to wear on New Year's Eve.

Good Morning Rock, which looked like a giant pillar thrown
across the valley and was so called because the first rays of the
morning sun shone on it. It was hollow, and I was shown the
passage that led into it, but declined to crawl in on the soft white
sand for fear of snakes, scorpions and poisonous spiders. The
rock had changed hands many times in the course of the battle
till, when night fell, the Tekyiman declared themselves beaten
and asked for a truce to bury their dead. This was granted by the
Ashanti who had also sustained heavy losses. By the light of
torches the Tekyiman carried their fallen nobles into a large cave
in the side of a cliff which, during the battle, had served as the
headquarters of their general, the governor of Tekyiman. The
cave was then walled up. Warriors of common descent were
thrown into the seemingly bottomless pit in front of the cave. The
Ashanti buried their dead in another cave facing the valley.

While I was being shown these places, with amazement I heard
for the first time of the power and splendour of the Bono Kingdom. It had been founded about 1300, and was the first great
civilization in what is now called Ghana. It came to an end about
1740. The capital Bono-Mansu had been burnt down during the
war by its own desperate inhabitants after the defeat in the valley
of Asueyi, and Tekyiman, Bono's second largest city, became the
capital of a new state, the Bono-Tekyiman State. A prince of the
old Bono royal lineage was permitted by the King of Ashanti to
rule over it as a vassal of Ashanti. His successor today is the
Tekyimanhene, Nana Akumfi Ameyaw III.

When I returned from the scene of the old battlefield I thanked
Nana Tekyimanhene for the great favour he had shown me by
taking me to the battlefield, never seen or heard of by Europeans.

Next morning a royal messenger announced to me the visit of
the King, who soon afterwards arrived in his car. Apparently I
had behaved well and to the satisfaction of his people, for Nana
Tekyimanhene told me that he wished to show me something
else. This time we went in his car along the road to Nkoranza,
then got out and walked in single file along a completely overgrown path. Men with cutlasses preceded us, slashing through
the bush and making a passage. They were followed by a priest,

who was in charge of the most sacred cave that was our destination. I walked behind the priest with Kofi. Then came Nana Tekyimanhene, accompanied by a royal spokesman and two or three of his elders.

We must have walked a mile or two when we arrived at a glade in the tropical forest—on the left of which was the dark mouth of the secret cave. Nana Tekyimanhene explained that the cave was the dwelling-place of the spirits of his Royal Ancestors, the Kings of Bono and Bono-Tekyiman. Then he asked me to enter the cave with him.

It was a strange experience. The cave was shaped like a small cinema. In place of the screen there was a solid sheet of sunlight which streamed through a cleft in the ceiling. On our entrance hundreds of bats started to fly about, filling the air with an eerie sound. The ground of the cave was smooth rock, so smooth that I constantly slipped. The King, seeing my plight, courteously gave me his arm. Then we walked slowly towards the sunlight—or was it the 'altar' below it, the slice of rock which had fallen from the ceiling of the cave? The priest walked beside but slightly ahead of me, kneeling every second step on one knee, and beating his chest all the while with his fists to announce our arrival to the spirits of the Royal Ancestors. He chanted a language which Kofi did not understand, probably an archaic form of the present Akan language (Twi).[1] Shortly before we reached the 'altar' we stopped in silence blinded by the sunlight. Bats were flying all around us, but did not molest us. Then we turned back.

At the entrance to the cave Nana Tekyimanhene asked Kofi and me to wait in the glade as he had a small rite to perform. I sat down on a tree-trunk. The morning sun streamed through the trees; orange-throated lizards came to play around my feet. After a while we heard the voice of the priest coming from the cave. Kofi, standing next to me, translated as much as he could catch. It seemed that the priest was invoking the spirits of the Royal Ancestors, the Kings of Bono and Bono-Tekyiman. When contact was established with them Nana Tekyimanhene apologized

---

[1] Dialects of Twi are spoken by the various Akan people to which among others the Tekyiman and Ashanti belong.

Prologue

to them for having brought me, a white woman, to their dwelling-place; but it was most important for him to know whether I could be trusted. The Royal Ancestors, it seemed, were most enthusiastic about me and assured him that I could be fully trusted and should be told everything I wished to know of their history and culture. They prophesied that I would restore the glory of the Bono Kingdom and would relieve the Tekyiman State from all its troubles with Ashanti and the Gold Coast Government.

When Nana Tekyimanhene reappeared he said nothing about what had happened. He only pointed to the ornaments which he wore across his forehead and told me smilingly they symbolized 'union' or 'unity'. From now onwards his State would regard me as a friend and he and his people would tell me all about the reigns of his predecessors.

On my return in 1946 and in 1949 to Tekyiman, Nana Tekyimanhene and I made a solemn pact that he and his people would help me with my anthropological work and I in turn would help the State by being their spokesman with the Gold Coast Government. This pact was honoured by both parties.

Nine Villages in Dispute

The cause of Tekyiman's trouble with the Gold Coast Government were nine villages of which the Ashanti had robbed them in 1935. In order to understand the people's determined struggle to regain them (which forms the main story of this book) it is necessary to have some idea of the historical background.

After the destruction of the Bono Kingdom (1740) the Ashanti gave the heart of the country to Chief Baafo Pim, the traitor, who had played the powerful State into their hands, and made him King of Nkoranza; like Bono-Tekyiman it had to recognize the suzerainty of the King of Ashanti.

Sixty years later a rebellion broke out in Nkoranza and the Asantehene (King of Asante or Ashanti) Osei Bonsu Panyin asked the Tekyiman to fight the war for him. This they did, eager to avenge themselves, and when the Tekyimanhene Kyereme Kofi (1782–1830) took Wiafe, the successor of Baafo Pim, prisoner, against the wishes of the Asantehene he sacrificed him over the stool, the shrine of the last King of Bono. This action had disastrous repercussions for Tekyiman; though not immediately, for the Asantehene was engaged in wars in the south and unable for the moment to punish Kyereme Kofi and his people for their disobedience.

In 1818 the Ashanti-Gyaman war broke out and Tekyiman was forced to send troops in support of Ashanti as well as seven priests, who were renowned for their power with the gods Tano and Ntoa, the ancient national deities of the Bono Kingdom. The Tekyiman casualties in this war were enormous, since the Asantehene used the Tekyiman contingents as shock troops. After the victory Osei Bonsu Panyin expressed his great satisfaction with the Tekyiman war effort and invited the Tekyimanhene Kyereme Kofi and his seven priests to take part in the victory parade in Kumasi, the capital of Ashanti.

All went well, and the Tekyimanhene and his seven priests went home in due course. After their return to Tekyiman, however, the Asantehene informed Kyereme Kofi that from that time onwards his powerful priests, and the towns and lands which each ruled as a chief, would be no longer his. That meant that the Tekyimanhene lost the seven most prosperous towns in his kingdom; for their taxes were now to be paid into the Ashanti treasury, and jurisdiction over them passed to Kumasi chiefs, who administered these towns according to the wishes of the Asantehene.

A rebellion was out of the question, owing to the terrible losses that Tekyiman had suffered in the war, and protests were useless. The Tekyimanhene Owusu Amprofi (1830–7), who succeeded Kyereme Kofi and the Tekyimanhene Amyeaw Kyereme (1837–51), and Bafuo Twi (1851–64), who demanded the return of the towns, were given evasive replies. Finally when, in 1877, the reigning Asantehene Bonsu Mensa demanded troops from Tekyiman to quell a rebellion in Juaben, the Tekyimanhene Kwabena Fofi (1864–86) refused, with the result that war broke out between Ashanti and Tekyiman. This war was to last almost twenty years but ended with the victory of Tekyiman.

Prologue

In this war Tekyiman-town was destroyed, and the Tekyiman Government thereupon moved to the Kingdom of Gyaman (now in the Ivory Coast) to continue the war from there. Guerrilla forces were left behind under a chief Yeboa to harass the Ashanti; the guerrilla fighters were stationed in the hills and lived in the caves which are so plentiful in this region and were supplied with arms and men from Gyaman. In course of time several attempts were made by the Ashanti to bring the war to an end, for the country was useless to them. Ashanti settlers were murdered by the guerrillas and their farms burnt down, trade was at a standstill and little tax revenue reached Ashanti from the devastated and denuded country.

When, in 1895, the Anglo-Ashanti war broke out the Asantehene Prempeh I, unable to fight on two fronts—against the English in the south and the Tekyiman in the north—offered peace once more, demanding the return of the Tekyiman people from Gyaman, and this time promising the return of the towns in dispute. According to Tekyiman traditions the Tekyimanhene Gyako II (1886–99) asked for an official delegation to be sent to him at Bondugu in Gyaman and this the Asantehene subsequently sent. But by the time the Ashanti delegation, accompanied by representatives of the Tekyimanhene, returned to Kumasi to tell the king that the peace offer had been accepted, the Anglo-Ashanti war was over and Prempeh I was a prisoner. He was exiled in January 1896 to the Seychelles Islands and there was no king to succeed him. When the Tekyimanhene Gyako II living in Gyaman heard this he sent his spokesman Kwabena Fofi and three other Tekyiman representatives to the British Government in Accra. They were accompanied by a representative of the King of Gyaman Agyeman, who was to certify that the Tekyiman Government and its people were actually living in Gyaman and that they wished to return to their country. The British Government in Accra referred them to their officer in Kumasi, and it was agreed that the Tekyiman people should go back to Tekyiman and that the seven towns should be returned to them. The Tekyiman people then returned, and in 1897 Tekyiman-town was rebuilt close to the ruins of the old town.

Prologue

In 1925 the Asantehene Prempeh I returned from exile and was allowed to rule again in Ashanti proper. He died in 1931 and was succeeded by the present Asantehene Nana Sir Osei Agyeman Prempeh II. In 1934 the British Government planned to restore the old Ashanti Confederacy of states, and by the end of 1935 all the preliminary work was done. The Tekyiman State, which had been requested to join Ashanti again, still refused. Pressure was then brought to bear on the people, on the one hand by the British Government, which for the purpose of indirect rule and administration wanted Ashanti as large an area as possible, and on the other by the Asantehene and the Kumasi chiefs who wanted Tekyiman again under their rule and to avenge their defeat of 1896. The District Commissioner at Wenkyi, who knew nothing of the history of Tekyiman and its desperate twenty years' war against Ashanti,[1] had the Tekyimanhene Yao Ameyaw destooled for 'maladministration', a charge which was not difficult to make on account of the unrest in the State. There was nothing left to the succeeding Tekyimanhene Kwasi Twi but to submit.

The first meeting of the Committee of Privileges of the Ashanti Confederacy took place in November 1935 and, like other heads of states, the Tekyimanhene Kwasi Twi, accompanied by a number of elders and chiefs, went to Kumasi. Like all the others he swore there the oath of allegiance. The moment he had done so the Asantehene turned to him and informed him that the seven towns[2] were his no longer. (Today these towns are no more than villages, although the most flourishing in the State; and now there are nine, as two more villages, Agwase and Subinso, had been founded on land belonging to one of these former towns.)

In vain did the Tekyimanhene Kwasi Twi protest to the Gold Coast Government; in vain did he refer to Tekyiman's Treaty with Queen Victoria (1897). He was unable to secede from the

[1] I met him in 1946. It is not surprising that he did not know, as the Tekyiman people had not given him an account of their historical past as it was the custom to keep historical traditions secret. They did not realize that it might have made a difference.
[2] Their names are: Tanoso, Tanoboase, Tuobodom, Boyem, Nkiyraa, Offuman and Branam.

21

Ashanti Confederacy, and when he refused to go to the next meeting in Kumasi the people were forced to destool (dethrone) him. His successors Ameyaw II (1936–7), Berempon Kwaku Kyereme (1937–41), and Kwaku Gyako (1941–3), were also destooled when they continued to worry the Government about the villages. Following the principle of Indirect Rule, the Government regarded the dispute as a matter to be dealt with by the Ashanti Confederacy Council; but the Asantehene refused to restore the villages to Tekyiman on the grounds that they had always belonged to Ashanti. In 1944 the present Tekyimanhene, Nana Akumfi Ameyaw III, was elected to succeed after he had sworn an oath to his people that he would do everything in his power to regain them. When I met him in April 1944 Nana Akumfi Ameyaw III had been reigning for two months.

CHAPTER I

Tekyiman 1946-9

Tekyiman-town

The Bono-Tekyiman State, referred to simply as Tekyiman (Techiman) by the Gold Coast Government (now called Tekyiman-Brong) covers a tiny area. As far as I know its square miles have never been counted, as Tekyiman was regarded by the Gold Coast Government as part of Ashanti; but I should say that its length is roughly some 70–80 miles, and its width, taken at its widest point, no more than thirty-five. In 1944–50 there were about 20,000 inhabitants, of which Tekyiman-town, the capital, may have had about 4,000: that is to say, it was an African village. It had no drains, electric light or gas.

The heart of the capital was at the cross-roads; in the centre a signpost on a round platform pointed north to Wenkyi, the capital of the Wenkyi State, at a distance of 22 miles; east to Nkoranza, the capital of the Nkoranza State, 32 miles; south to Kumasi, the capital of Ashanti, 78 miles; and west to Sunyani, a town then in Ashanti, 40 miles (Pl. 2). On the road going north to Wenkyi on the right hand, with the entrance facing an open square, was the Queenmother's house, and next to it, at a right angle, the palace of the King. The word 'palace' is an exaggeration, as the building, small and single-storied, in swish (mud) and covered with a sheet-iron roof, was as simple as could be. A leopard, crudely painted and half effaced on the whitewashed wall alone indicated that here lived the King. Guards were unknown; whoever wished to see the King went into the office; its two small windows next to the wooden entrance door were the

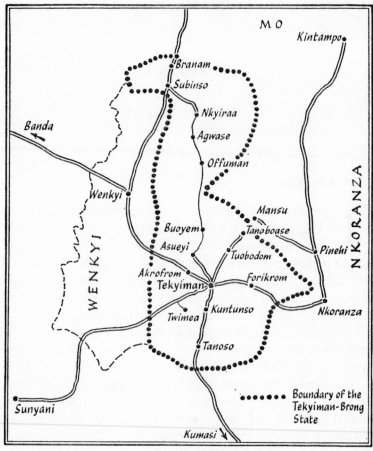

The Tekyiman-Brong State Borders

main feature of the façade that faced the square and beyond it the main road with its line of trees.

None of the cross-roads had many houses; a few minutes' walk and one was out of town. The houses, many had small shops, were built mostly in European style: single-storied and usually sheet-iron roofs. But in the angle between the Kumasi and the Sunyani roads there was a whole quarter inhabited by the poorer people of the town; the houses were built in mud and covered with thatch (Pl. 3). Goats, sheep and chickens strayed through a maze of alleys. On the other side in the angle formed by the Kumasi and the Nkoranza roads there was another quarter behind the houses that lined the streets. Here among some green, and a palm tree here and there, were the houses of the well-to-do; the whole gave the impression of a residential area.

On one end of the Kumasi–Wenkyi road was the Methodist Mission with its school and chapel, on the other the Roman Catholic Mission with its school and fine church. The market was on the other side but much farther down at the very end of the town. The temple of the State god Taa Kese was situated opposite the palace not far from the post office but invisible from the main road; a lane led to it. The temple was a modern structure and surrounded by the rooms of the priests.

Building was forbidden on the ruins of the old town which was destroyed in the Tekyiman–Ashanti war of 1877–96. But it had a small cocoa plantation which bordered on the Nkoranza road more or less next to Cadbury and Fry's where cocoa was bought, weighed and despatched to the coast. The former houses of the aristocracy, generally two-storied, are said to have been well kept and beautiful; they were decorated with symbolic designs in relief arranged in large patterns.

The present town of Tekyiman, which was founded in 1897, had no splendours from the beginning. The Gold Coast Government abolished slavery in 1901, which made it impossible to keep in repair two-storied houses built of swish which suffered damage after heavy rains. Craftsmen, who could have decorated the walls of the houses, had moved away during the Tekyiman–Ashanti war to find work in other states. Moreover, the prosperity for which the people had hoped after they had freed themselves from the yoke of Ashanti, did not materialize. In the past the gold and cola-nut trade with the Sudan and North Africa had brought wealth to Tekyiman, but when the British introduced their currency, which ousted the gold-dust currency of the Gold Coast, and the French did the same in the surrounding territories, gold was no longer in demand. Nor were the cola nuts (however, some twenty or thirty years later cocoa took their place). About 1920, rinderpest wiped out the cattle and horses in which the people's wealth was invested and, in order to stamp out sleeping sickness and prevent soil erosion, the Gold Coast Government made it illegal to import stock from the western Sudan. Many people emigrated at that time. By 1944, when I first came to Tekyiman, the region was a backwater, further impoverished by the cold war with Ashanti and the Gold Coast Government.

All that was left to the people were their memories of the past —the memories of the splendour and power of the Bono Kingdom. The King's town alone, it is said, had several thousand inhabitants more than has Tekyiman today. It had two palaces, that of the heir-apparent and co-ruler, who in the eyes of the public *was* the king; and behind it the palace of the divine ruler, the real king, who lived hidden as his main duty was to give 'life' with his solar *kra* or soul. Everything he used was made of gold, the metal of the sun, and he was venerated like a god. Behind his palace was the harem of his wives of whom 3333 was the desired number, and they were supervised by over a hundred eunuchs.[1]

All the people in the King's town—the household officers and the palace staff, sword-bearers, gun-bearers, palanquin-bearers, heralds, executioners, minstrels, musicians, the royal bodyguard, and so on—were fed by the hundreds of cooks under the command of the Chief of the cooks, a courtier, and his heir-apparent and were called together for their meals twice daily by a bell.

Next to the heir-apparent's palace, which was situated, like the present palace of the Tekyimanhene, behind a square on the main road, was that of the Queenmother's heir-apparent and co-ruler. The real divine Queenmother—whose soul was that of the moon—lived at Amona, a few miles from the capital. She lived surrounded by her daughters and small sons, the princesses of the royal lineage, and unmarried royal daughters, apart from the hundreds of young girls who were given to her for education. These were the daughters of the 'queenmothers', the head women

---

[1] The kings married the daughters of most noble families in the country in order to tie by blood the people to the dynasty. Thus the blood of the Bono and Bono-Tekyiman kings runs in most Tekyiman people today.

of towns and villages, and were to succeed them one day, and the daughters of vassal chiefs. The Queenmother's household officers, who were all women, had the same titles as those of the King. She never went out, but her heir-apparent and co-ruler did, and then she was preceded by 300 selected beautiful girls, many of them of slave origin.

The capital, Bono-Mansu, is said to have been a big town. Excavation of the site now overgrown with bush might one day give us an idea of its size. It was as international as a modern capital today; at the time the town was destroyed (1740) eight languages were spoken; the *lingua franca* was Twi, the language of the ruling class.

When the Ashanti conquered the country thousands of people fled leaving the country denuded; Bono's 'intelligentsia'—the craftsmen, goldsmiths, weavers, carvers, the musicians, the organizers of the great market which was visited annually by caravans from North Africa—went into captivity at Kumasi, the capital of Ashanti, to teach the king and his court the civilized way of life. Tekyiman, Bono's successor state, was left with nothing and the Ashanti consuls stationed in the country made a recovery impossible; all went in the form of taxes to enrich the Ashanti. The loss of the most prosperous towns in 1819 was the last straw, and resulted finally in the Tekyiman–Ashanti war of 1877–96.

My Return to Tekyiman in 1946

In January 1946 I returned to Tekyiman to start my anthropological research, sponsored by the Colonial Office and financed by the Colonial Welfare and Development Fund. During the few weeks I stayed in Tekyiman some events took place which have to be recorded here.

One morning I went to the palace to greet Nana (I shall from now on call the Tekyimanhene 'Nana' as everybody refers to him thus). He informed me sadly that something very serious had happened. It had been discovered that during the night the Queenmother Nana Akua Dapaa had received two men, well known in Tekyiman, who had bribed her with £200 to destool him so that a king more amenable to the Government and Ashanti could succeed him. The Queenmother was in consequence confined to her house, and if she could not clear herself at the coming trial, she would be forced to abdicate.

The trial took place two days later, starting at ten o'clock in the morning. All the State elders were in court, only Nana, having constitutionally no say in the matter, was absent. Kofi Mosi, the High-priest of the national god Taa Kese, then a young man of barely thirty, defended the Queenmother so brilliantly that several times he nearly got her off. But the elders were convinced of her guilt, partly because she was always short of money, partly because she led the opposition in the State. She had always advocated appeasement and reconciliation with Ashanti and the Government, believing that Tekyiman could not possibly win, for by that time their struggle had already lasted more than ten years.

The trial continued without a pause till about five o'clock when the Queenmother, exhausted, gave in and admitted her guilt. She placed her sandals on the table as a sign of relinquishing her office, for neither a king's nor a queenmother's feet may touch the ground. Then she signed the paper that had been prepared for her, confessing to high treason, and her willingness to abdicate. After that she went barefoot to her house and fetched a snow-white sheep. The animal was sacrificed on the spot to purify her from her sin. She was then told that she would be banished from Tekyiman-town and would have to live till the end of her life in a small village in the northernmost corner of the State; the particulars of her sentence would be told to her after a conference with Nana. Meanwhile she could return to her house but was under arrest.

On the next day the Queenmother had to surrender her regalia and everything she had acquired during her term of office. I went to see her before she left to say good-bye. She was a woman in her forties; I was sorry for her because she was gay and lively, and exile would be hard on her. I thought how happy she had been on the day, about a month or two earlier, when I had gone to her house to greet her, but found nobody there except an old retainer. He had led me to the Queenmother who was asleep in a hammock in one of the open-walled rooms facing the entrance court. He wanted to wake her up, but I shook my head; it was a pity to wake her, she slept so peacefully. But then I saw her right foot sticking out of the hammock, just where I stood, and I could not resist tickling it. With a cry she woke up. When she saw me, she threw both her arms round my neck. I quickly put my arms around her waist, because the hammock did not seen to have been fastened very well. She hugged me, and laughed, and talked endlessly. I did not understand a word. She then let me lift her out of the hammock and place her on her sandals on the ground. She was about my own height and slim, with fine bones. Then she ran lightfootedly away, beckoning me to follow her, to a corner of the court where she had started to prepare beans for her supper. She loved cooking. I sat down next to her and helped her sort the good beans from the bad. While we were thus busy one of Nana's messengers had appeared on the scene to take me to the palace, and I had left her reluctantly.

A month or two later the new Queenmother Nana Afua Abrafi was enstooled. Meanwhile Nana had taken the opportunity to find suitable husbands for all those princesses who had taken lovers from among the tall-legged Songhay from the Middle Niger. The aristocratic Akan women seem to like these handsome strangers.

I was not in Tekyiman for the enstoolment as I had work in the Northern Territories, in Gonja and Dagomba. On my way back I stopped at Wenkyi, however, in order to see the District Commissioner, who resided in Wenkyi as it was a much bigger place than Tekyiman. The District Commissioner was busy but I could hear his voice. He was having a first-class row with somebody. The somebody, the African clerk told me, was Nana Tekyimanhene. I took the key of the rest-house and begged the clerk to tell Nana Tekyimanhene that I was in town.

I was still unpacking when Nana stormed in, accompanied by his retinue. For a moment he was too upset to speak, but by and by I got the whole story. In order to tell it, I must revert to the beginning of my trip.

Tekyiman 1946–9

On my way up from the coast, I had spent a few days in Kumasi in the Residency as a guest of Mr. G. Hawkesworth, and in my conversation with him begged him to do something for Tekyiman. If the villages could not be restored to Tekyiman at least the Government could show them other favours and not treat the people as outcasts, continually harping on their disobedience and rebelliousness. Mr. Hawkesworth, after he had listened patiently, promised me that he would do what he could; and three months later, when a Durbar was due, he managed to persuade the Governor of the Gold Coast to hold it in Tekyiman instead of Kumasi. When the Tekyiman learnt this, they were overjoyed and did everything to make the Durbar a great success. It took place while I was in the north. The Governor and the Chief Commissioner of Ashanti (Mr. Hawkesworth) were received with jubilation and all went well till His Excellency made his speech.

First the Tekyiman thought that they were not hearing aright as they listened to the Governor's words. Then they realized that the speech had been written by the District Commissioner of Wenkyi, who had tried for the past few years to break their resistance. For they had to hear from the Governor's mouth that they were an obstinate people, making difficulties all the time, obstructing the administration and so forth. And to crown it all they were advised to destool their king, the source of all trouble. Nana, when he told me about it in the rest-house at Wenkyi, said that he had to smile bitterly, but his people were stunned.

When the Governor had left the District Commissioner came to Tekyiman and demanded a letter to the Governor, in which Nana was to apologize for his insolent behaviour. The District Commissioner had thus interpreted Nana's bitter smile. This was refused by the whole people with indignation. Shortly afterwards Nana had to pass through Wenkyi to visit some of his villages in Tekyiman's northern districts. There was no road at that time passing through his State. According to custom Nana, although in a great hurry, called on the District Commissioner. The District Commissioner, however, let him know that he was busy and left him and his chiefs to wait outside, like people of no account, on a bench in the sun. After two hours Nana was called in. By that time he was so furious that he, a king, who was to be respected by his people, had been treated like a beggar, that he told the District Commissioner exactly what he thought of him. Hence the dispute that I had overheard.

I was upset to hear from Nana that the Durbar had been such a disaster. I tried my best to cheer him up and promised to come to Tekyiman the following day. We would then discuss what best to do in the matter of apology to the Governor.

Nana had hardly left when the District Commissioner came to see me. He told me about the annoying encounter which he had with the Tekyimanhene and said that he could not understand why I was on the side of these wretched people who made unconstitutional demands and constantly defied authority. I asked him how he, an Englishman, would feel if England's most prosperous towns were under the jurisdiction of France and paid taxes to it—moreover, towns which the English had won back in battle in a twenty-year's war and lost again through pressure of, let us say, the United Nations. I do not remember what he replied, but I did all I could to calm him.

He had hardly gone when I received a third visitor. It was the African chief clerk of the District Commissioner who had interpreted the conversation between the District Commissioner and Nana. We knew each other well, so he gave me the details of the talk, including those bits which he had not dared to translate. He was uneasy about it because, as an interpreter, he was bound by oath to translate as precisely as possible. Since he had left out only the insulting words used by both sides, I told him not to worry, that as a matter of fact he had been very wise and diplomatic and had prevented a much worse situation from arising.

In the afternoon of the following day I was back in Tekyiman. When I got out of my car before the palace I met Nana's secretary who asked me to come to his office as Nana was in a council meeting. He then told me what had happened on Nana's return from Wenkyi the day before.

Nana, apparently still furious, immediately arranged for a council meeting in which he told his elders and chiefs about the insult he, that is to say the State, had suffered at the hands of the District Commissioner. It was then immediately agreed that the people should be told about it and should gather in the square for a ceremonial purification of the State. At six o'clock when the sun went down, three hours or so after Nana had returned, the State drums were carried out and were beaten right through the night. Sheep were sacrificed, while the people stood for hours praying that no evil might befall the State. Then they filed past Nana where he sat on his dais to express their sympathy. Finally they all swore a spontaneous oath of allegiance that they were ready to follow him unto death, if death it had to be. If there had been people who had criticized Nana's policy, they were now also on his side. The whole of Tekyiman stood solidly behind the King.

While the secretary and I were still talking a messenger arrived from Nana asking me to come and greet him. I found him in the audience-courtyard with his elders and, after I had greeted him and the assembly, I was allowed to sit down and be present at the discussion, although in order not to disturb the proceedings nothing was translated to me. I soon realized, however, that everything turned on the letter of apology to the Governor which the District Commissioner of Wenkyi had demanded following Nana's behaviour at the Durbar. Everybody present gave his opinion. Nothing could have been more democratic. In the end an agreement was reached: to do nothing until the District Commissioner put such pressure on them that there was no other way out.

When I first came to Tekyiman in 1944 it had only two schools, both only up to Standard III. Almost everybody was illiterate, which shocked Kofi Antubam, who was then my interpreter. He talked to Nana about this lack of education and frightful back-wardness, and begged me to assist him in convincing Nana that schools were absolutely necessary. Nana saw this point, but in conversation with me complained that the teachers lacked respect and that none of them had come to greet him in the two months that he had been king. I replied that the teachers, mostly young men from the coast, were perhaps too shy to do so. In any case he could soon change this. Why not give prizes to the best pupils, for instance? The teachers would soon come running after him. Knowledge, the art of reading and writing, is a great asset. Look at the white man, I said, the power he has got, and all because he can read and write and study.

Nana said nothing, but my speech and Kofi's efforts were not lost on him. The progress made in education in the one and half years I was away was surprising. On the day of my arrival one of the schools gave a concert—Nana had meanwhile founded several schools—to which the people of the town were invited, and two days later I was to witness a performance by Boy Scouts. But the Standard VII school for boys and girls from thirteen upwards, which Nana wanted to have for his people, was refused by the District Commissioner of Wenkyi on financial grounds. There was one in Wenkyi only twenty-two miles away and Tekyiman children could go there to school till there were enough children for Standards VI and VII. But at that time Tekyiman and Wenkyi were, so to say, at war on account of the land cases between the two states, and Nana would not hear of it. So the people decided to build their own school without Government assistance. For months every man, woman and child in Tekyiman came to build the school in the native style, of mud but with large rooms, and more beautiful than any house. One day the school was ready except for the roof, which the people did not want to be of thatch but of sheet-iron. As there was none in Tekyiman Nana ordered it from Kumasi, and this was when the District Commissioner heard of it. He immediately rushed to Tekyiman and forbade them to roof the building; firstly to punish them for having done something without his permission, and secondly for not having written the letter of apology to the Governor. All entreaties to be allowed to use the school for other purposes were in vain. They suggested a community centre where the newly acquired brass bands could practise, where dances could take place and so forth. The building had to remain unroofed. The District Commissioner knew full well that it would not survive the rains. In 1949 I was shown the heap of earth, all that remained of the school that had been built with so much

C

love and enthusiasm. The letter of apology to the Governor had to be sent after all.

The Years 1947–9

And so the fight for the nine villages, in the form of passive resistance, went on right through 1946–9. Letters sent to me regularly in London informed me in detail of the state of affairs. In July 1947 things became so bad that Nana, his elders and village chiefs sent a petition, signed by all, to the Chief Commissioner of Ashanti, once more requesting the return of the nine villages. They were answered in December with a blank refusal and were warned that if Tekyiman continued to obstruct the peaceful progress of the administration all the powers and privileges invested in the Tekyiman Stool would be withdrawn by virtue of the Native Authority (Ashanti) Ordinances. In other words the Tekyimanhene and his elders would be relieved of their offices and the State would be administered directly by the Gold Coast Government.

In February 1948 things came to a head. On February 16th Nana wrote to the Secretary of the Ashanti Confederacy Council that he was unable to comply with the summons to attend the next meeting in Kumasi. The State elders, chiefs and sub-chiefs of his villages forbade him to do so. Their reason (which was not stated) was that Nana and his delegation had not been treated with the respect due to them, either in the house of the Ashanti chief with whom they had to stay in Kumasi, or by the Asantehene.

On the same day another letter was sent to the Governor of the Gold Coast. It stated that the Tekyiman State had broken off all communication with the Ashanti Confederacy and from now on would not pay the one-third share to the Ashanti National Fund. The letter was signed by the Queenmother and eighty-four chiefs and sub-chiefs including Nana's elders. Copies of the two letters were sent to the Chief Commissioner of Ashanti and the District Commissioner at Wenkyi.

The Government retaliated by punishing this act of open rebellion. It was impossible to destool Nana. All attempts so far had failed, and there was no party in the State which was willing to support the Government in this matter. So Nana was suspended from office together with his State elders, the so-called 'Native Authority' in Tekyiman. Those chiefs of the nine villages who had dared to declare themselves openly for Nana—the chiefs of Tanoso, Tuobodom and Offuman (II)[1]—were also suspended from office. Nana's suspension and that of the members of his State Council was to last for one year. Nana thereupon commissioned Dr. J. B. Danquah, the lawyer and well-known politician, to write a Petition to His Excellency the Governor asking:

1. That Order No. 115 of 1948 suspending the Tekyimanhene and his Elders from acting as a Native Authority be rescinded. *2.* That Order No. 5 of 1948 suspending the Tanosohene, Tuobodomhene and the Ohene of Offuman II as members of the Tano-Subin Native Court[2] be rescinded. *3.* That the declaration of the Committee of Privileges (Ashanti Confederacy), in so far as it refers to the nine villages claimed by the Tekyimanhene, be set aside; and *4.* That a Committee of Inquiry be appointed to determine the issues between the Asantehene and the Tekyiman Stool.

On December 8th Dr. Danquah received the reply that His Excellency was not prepared to authorize under the present circumstances the rescinding of Order No. 115, or any of the other Orders. Nor was His Excellency prepared to intervene with regard to the return of the nine villages, since the Ashanti Confederacy Council at its meeting in 1936 accepted the findings of the Committee of Privileges. His Excellency, moreover, was unable to accede to the request for a Committee of Inquiry, as 'this would serve no useful purpose'. Fearing some such reply Nana had, the previous August, appealed to me for help, and I then wrote to the Secretary of State for the Colonies, Mr. A. Creech-

[1] There were Offuman No. I and Offuman No. II. See, for details, p. 232.
[2] On my return from my first visit to Tekyiman in 1944 I went to see Mr. Hawkesworth, the Chief Commissioner of Ashanti, and told him about the hardships of the nine villages in dispute. Mr. Hawkesworth then created the Tano-Subin Native Court which freed the villages at least from the jurisdiction of Ashanti.

Jones, a letter giving the whole historical background to the Ashanti–Tekyiman dispute, and making suggestions as how to come to an agreement which would be accepted by both parties concerned. This letter was sent to His Excellency but apparently did not influence the Government's policy. This was evident from his reply.

Two days after the Governor's letter had been received in Tekyiman, Nana wrote me a letter voicing the complaint that, although his people had paid all the taxes, he had received no money from the District Commissioner (who, since Nana's suspension, was the treasurer of the State) to pay for the libations and offerings to the spirits of his Royal Ancestors and the national god Taa Kese, Tano the Great. On account of this the usual customs had not been performed for the past six months, which had brought ill-luck to the State: the death of the Adontenhene Kwaku Fah, and that of the new Korontihene[1] and others among his elders. A day earlier I had an unexpected letter from Nana's stool wives (royal wives of noble birth) in which they told me that they had not received for months the allowance due to them and their children, although the levies had been paid by the people of Tekyiman. The elders had approached the District Commissioner but he had replied that all such allowances had been suspended when Nana was suspended from office.

Nana had forty wives but the great harems did not exist any longer. A boy of seventeen was the last eunuch; he died in 1946. When I heard of the plight of Nana's wives and that there was not enough money for the religious services, although the taxes for both had been paid, I wrote a letter to the Governor, and enclosed copies of the two letters which I had received from Tekyiman. At the same time I sent copies of all three letters to the Secretary of State for the Colonies.

I am sorry to say that the Gold Coast Government did not do

[1] The Tekyiman State, like most Akan states, had seven prominent elders who were the heads of the seven great clans. At the same time they were, in the past, generals in the army and to this day have military titles. The Adontenhene commanded the main body of the army; the Korontihene together with the Nifahene, the Right Wing. The Korontihene was also the administrator and governor of the capital.

any thing to redress these just complaints. Nana and his people were reprimanded for having appealed to me and not to their District Commissioner, which they had—but had omitted at the time to do so in writing through the newly established Managing Board with the functions of which they were still unfamiliar. The affair dragged on till May; meanwhile a number of disastrous events shook the Tekyiman people to the bone.

The whole of January 1949 Nana spent in Accra in order to discuss with his lawyer, Dr. Danquah, the refusal of the Governor to grant an inquiry into the Ashanti-Tekyiman dispute. At the same time he consulted his other lawyer, Mr. Larbi, to see what could be done about the various land cases in which Tekyiman was involved and the confiscation of the property of the three suspended chiefs of Tanoso, Tuobodom and Offuman II: a loss which ran into thousands of pounds. Then on February 6th Nana left Accra in order to perform in Tekyiman the funeral customs for the deceased Adontenhene Kwaku Fah, whose death he had mentioned in his letter to me in December. There an accident occurred, which was reported to me by the Queenmother and ten Elders of the State Council in a letter dated February 24th:

Dear Mrs. Eva,

We are deeply sorry to report an incident which occurred here on the 7th instant involving the Omanhene[1] *with the accidental shot of one of his subjects. The* Omanhene *returned from Accra on a short visit after his long absence from home, arriving on the eve of the 6th instant. There was a great jubilation through the State all the night. On the 7th the Aworowa Brass Band came to welcome their dear King who has returned home. The music went on throughout the day and about 4.30 p.m., the* Omanhene *went with the troops of the late* Adontenhene's *house to sympathise with the bereaved family as it was during his absence that the* Adontenhene *died. When he entered the house it was his duty to perform a custom by firing a gun. He sent a messenger to bring a gun from his house.[2] He*

[1] *Omanhene* means King (*hene*) of the State (*oman*).
[2] Usually the old-fashioned Dane guns were used for this purpose, but to honour their King the people had bought him a modern double-barrelled gun. The Dane guns received their name from the Danish

had loaded the gun himself in accordance with the demands of custom when any of his principal chiefs die. He did not know that the messenger had already loaded the gun before giving it to him to dance by way of Royal display, so congested to such an extent that some people pushed him and the gun dropped from his hand and instantly exploded. His own niece received bullets and subsequently died at Kumasi Hospital after three days time. One of the Stool-carriers also received two bullets and he is fully recovered now.

The Omanhene *was arrested about mid-night by two Super-intendents of Police from Kumasi with a number of Mobile Police to Kumasi* without the knowledge of his Elders, Chiefs and subjects. *The* Omanhene *was illy treated that he was not offered the oppor-tunity of placing a ward in charge of the Palace. Up to now we do not know how to manage the Palace. He has been bailed and has been ordered to stay outside Ashanti until the case is tried. That is the situation in Tekyiman now. Our loyalty to our* Omanhene *will never be unsavoured, we shall never forsake our dear* Omanhene. *It was only an accident but because of this our case the Government has taken such steps against him in order to harass and suppress us. We vow we shall never retreat from this case until justice is done.*

May Allmighty God give you long life to fight for justice for us as you are doing. Once more we sent you our vote of thanks for the interest taken in the case coupled with sincere greetings to you.

We remain yours,

(their marks)

for and on behalf of Tekyiman State.

This shows very great restraint in view of the fact that Nana had been treated with such extreme discourtesy by the police. After all, he was a king, and to kidnap him in the middle of the night while the townspeople including his guards were asleep from emotional exhaustion and fear (or praying dully in a stupor) was not the fair thing to do. According to native custom the police officers should have got in touch with the Gyaasehene, who is in charge of the palace as chief of the Royal Household.

traders who from the seventeenth century onwards bartered guns for slaves at Christiansborg Castle near Accra.

African policemen, who stayed behind in Nana's bedroom while he was escorted to the car, stole everything they found in the way of valuables—the gold nuggets and gold dust with which Nana's pillows and part of the mattress were filled and gold jewellery and ornaments belonging to his regalia. A king has to sleep on gold, which is believed to refresh his life-giving powers[1] during the night. They stole also large sums of money, as Tekyiman had no bank; the nearest was in Kumasi. I was furious, because I would have taken action, but Nana's people had been afraid that if they lodged a complaint about the stolen goods either directly or through me, the police would give evidence against them and would be believed; for the people were unable to prove their case. Nana, who was away, first in prison and then in exile in Accra, was too crushed at that time to worry about his personal loss.

Nana was subsequently accused of 'manslaughter by negligence', and for 'discharging a gun in town'. The case came first before the Magistrate's court in Kumasi. Bail was granted but he was to stand his trial at the Assizes in Kumasi. As Kumasi, the capital of Ashanti, was too much of a humiliation for Nana, who was after all in rebellion against the Asantehene, his lawyers tried their best to have the case transferred to the Divisional Court in Accra, but failed. However, on April 2nd I got the news that Nana had been acquitted and, as he wrote to me happily: 'At the close of the case for prosecution His Honour the judge and the assessors did not even call me to defend.'

On account of the shock of hearing that her 'dear husband' had been taken away by the police to an unknown place, one of Nana's wives gave premature birth to a baby daughter. Nana reported it to me and then went on:

I consider and have decided with all my Elders to name her after you for the fine things you are doing for Tekyiman. I desire to obtain your consent before doing so, and therefore be good enough to inform me, if I may. She will be educated thoroughly since she is named

[1] The King's *kra* or soul had the life-giving powers of the sun.

after you. This will make the State remember forever your kind
deeds and efforts on behalf of Tekyiman.

Needless to say I accepted this living medal and this is how I
came to have little Eva for a daughter. For it meant more than
just my name. I would have to take her over when she was five
years old, so that 'she could model herself on me'. As it happened,
a year later the child's mother Akosua Ankomaa died. But since
I had no home of my own and when the child was five was back
in South Africa and then in other parts of the world, the child
(now ten years old) is still with her father.

The cold war between Tekyiman and the Ashanti was resumed
immediately after Nana's acquittal. On April 19th the elders informed me that:

Just after the acquittal the Asantehene, in the name of the Con-
federacy Council, requested that the Tekyimanhene be arrested. This
was narrowly avoided by a good friend who timely informed the
Tekyimanhene of the impending danger. The Tekyimanhene left
Kumasi immediately and the house was afterwards surrounded by
Ashanti N.A. Police.

They closed their letter asking me to intensify my efforts and
help them further.

In May Nana learnt through his intelligence service that the
Chief Commissioner of Ashanti intended to renew Nana's suspension from office for another year. He begged me in a letter
dated May 20th to get in touch with the Colonial office and protest to prevent a second suspension for,

if it materializes, it will endanger the unity of the Tekyiman people
because, although the majority of them are behind the struggle, it is
quite probable that such a suspension will automatically disturb the
understanding of some of them about the position of things. I do hope
that you will do your best to help us. Meanwhile I will do well to
explain matters to my people. By the foregoing, I do not mean to say
that my people are not one. I say, it may trouble the minds of them,
and if it does not happen by your assistance, I will be pleased.

Tekyiman 1946–9

On June 13th the second suspension from office as dreaded by Nana was announced in the *Gold Coast Gazette*. Nana reported it to me with the following words:

Enclosed please find Gazette No. 50 of the 13th June 1949 being Order issued against Tekyiman as written to you. I am very pleased to tell you that my State is strongly backing me: no one has flinched an inch.[1]

On June 24th the people of Tekyiman resolved to take things into their own hands. In a letter addressed to the Chief Commissioner of Ashanti, the Senior District Commissioner at Sunyani and the District Commissioner at Wenkyi, they wrote that, seeing that they had paid the levy and other taxes for the period of 1948–9 and had expressed their willingness to continue to pay, and that the Government had not fulfilled its financial obligation and was furthermore withholding the Grants-in-aid to all schools in the State—

Now therefore the whole people of Tekyiman at a meeting on the 24th day of June, 1949, at the Ahenfie (palace) Tekyiman, with view of utter dissatisfaction the inconsistency as grossly unjust and detrimental to the progress and welfare of Tekyiman as a whole, and it was agreed to resolve and it is hereby resolved as follows:

1) . . . that the Tekyiman State should and do hereby register a

---

[1] What is entailed by the suspension from office of a king in a native state is clearly expressed by Dr. J. B. Danquah in a letter dated June 4th 1948 to Michael Foot, M.P., House of Commons:

'The position is that the Government of the Gold Coast is empowered to make and unmake a Native Authority or a Native Court. As a rule the chiefs of the districts are constituted into such Native Authorities and Native Courts, for without them the Administration could not carry on without strain in the particular district. When the Tekyimanhene was suspended as a Native Authority both his administration over his people and his authority over the Treasury of his State were taken over by the District Commissioner. As well, he and his chiefs were stopped from participating in the Native Court in their headquarter town, Tekyiman, and in fact, the people have thus been deprived of any civil court for local cases, the District Commissioner as a magistrate taking only the criminal cases in the town in his Magistrate's Court.

The African knows his chief as the head of the administration and of the Court. The position as it now exists tends to undermine the traditional prestige and authority of the Tekyimanhene and his chiefs and elders.'

protest against the preparation of Estimates for the period of 1949/50 or thereafter, nor would the people of the State agree to pay any tax or levy over which the District Commissioner should have control unless and until the misunderstanding prevailing as between the Government and the people of Tekyiman, upon which bank the progress of Tekyiman, had been settled.

2. That the Estimates for the period 1949/50 should be prepared by the people themselves and to run a treasury of their own, the sources of revenue being a yearly taxation on a voluntary basis.

Then followed a detailed account of how the people wished to spend their tax money: remuneration for the Tekyimanhene, elders, chiefs and sub-chiefs; allowance for the stool wives and for the propitiation of the Royal Ancestors; Grants-in-aid for all schools in the State; allowance for the construction of a lorry park and a hospital; to name just the most important items.

At about the same time a Petition to His Majesty King George VI was prepared by Dr. J. B. Danquah for Nana and his State, after the Petition to the Governor had failed to produce any results. This Petition, according to local custom, was sent first to the District Commissioner in Wenkyi, to the Senior District Commissioner at Sunyani and to the Chief Commissioner of Ashanti. After each of them had made his comments it was forwarded to the Governor of the Gold Coast, who carefully studied the document and sent it, with his comments, to the Secretary of State for the Colonies, who in turn made suggestions and handed it over to His Majesty the King. Seeing that the process was a long one, Nana sent me two copies to make use of as I saw fit. They were accompanied by the following letter:

Dear Mrs. Eva Meyerowitz,

APPEAL TO YOU TO INTERCEDE WITH GOVERNMENT OF THE GOLD COAST ON BEHALF OF TEKYIMAN STATE.

I, Akumfi Ameyaw III, Tekyimanhene, and the undersigned Elders of my State, Tekyiman, have the honour most respectfully to appeal to you to help or we perish. We have been most unfairly treated by the local Government. The attached papers will give you the full picture of what has transpired in the past and of late between Kumasi (Ashanti) on one side, and Tekyiman (Bono) on the other side. We dare not lay the blame on anybody. But nevertheless we have a strong feeling that it has all come about because of the complete prevalence of the lack of a deep knowledge and understanding of the cultural values, history and institutions of the Akan peoples on the part of the Officials of our local British Government.

Now, judging from the success with which you worked with us during your Ethnological Research two years ago, you, Madam, are the only person who can best present, and fight, our case. We therefore request, that you help officially, that you intervene in the matter and intercede with Government both locally and in England, so that we might find some justice in our cause.

May God give you strength and courage to fight out the good cause of a humble people.

We have the honour to be,

Your humble friends,

Their marks

1. Akumfi Ameyaw III, Tekyimanhene,
2. Yaw Aboah, Gyaasehene,
3. Kwaku Fan, Adontenhene,
4. Kwafi Tabri, Akwamuhene,
5. Kwafi Wusu, Twafohene,
6. Yaw Donkor, Ankobeahene,
7. Kofi Yeboa, Kyidomhene,
8. Yaw Nwinim, Nifahene,
9. Kwaku Agyepong, Benkumhene,
10. Kwaku Ankameh, Akyeampenhene,
11. Afua Abrafi, Queenmother.

W/W/to marks:
for Private Secretary.

N.B.: You will find that the attached papers include a Petition to His Excellency, the Governor, to which I

*have not got as yet a reply. I shall
let you know as soon as I get a reply
from him.*

*Akumfi Ameyaw III.
Tekyimanhene.*

This was on the 28th August. In September everything was quiet. The cold war was not resumed before November. Meanwhile on October 3rd I arrived in Tekyiman.

CHAPTER II

October 1949

On the Road to Tekyiman and Arrival

While I was still in Accra I had wired to the District Commissioner at Wenkyi to book me the rest-house at Tekyiman, where I was expected on October 3rd, but had not received a reply. I wired a second time from Kumasi, for if the rest-house was occupied, I would have nowhere to stay. Nana I knew would have been only too pleased to put me up in the finest house in town. I preferred the rest-house, however, where I could be independent and private. Moreover, it was situated a mile out of town and was less plagued by malaria-infected mosquitoes.

On the morning of the 3rd the District Commissioner had still not replied; not even to a third wire from me. I finally decided to leave Kumasi after lunch—I stayed in the old rest-house there—whether I got a reply or not. About eleven o'clock I had started to pack some of my personal belongings when I was interrupted by Santos, my cook-steward, who announced the visit of three strangers. I asked him, 'Do I know them?' He shrugged his shoulders and replied, 'Black men, Madame' ('Madam' he pronounced—like most West Africans—the French way, with the accent on the second syllable) 'with English flag for car.' This must be a chief, I thought, although I knew that nobody except high Government officials was permitted to fly the English flag. 'All right', I said, 'show them into the dining-room.'

When my visitors came in I was sure that I had never seen them before. Assuming that there had been a mistake, I asked them whether they had really come to see me. They laughed, amused—I smiled, puzzled. After they had seated themselves we shook hands across the table. Then I asked, according to local custom, 'Will you tell me please who you are and what your mission is?' One of the men got up and introduced himself as Mr. Afwireng, secretary of the Tekyimanhene Nana Akumfi Ameyaw III. Pointing to the young man sitting next to him, he introduced him as Mr. D. K. Owusu, grandson of the Tekyiman Stool,[1] which means in English a prince (Pl. 10). The third man was Sergeant Ayerttey, the driver of the royal car. Their mission —to take me to Tekyiman without delay. Nana and all the people in the town had been waiting for me since early morning; my visitors had been sent by Nana to meet me on the road so that I might enter Tekyiman in style. Hence the English flag to honour me. Unable to find me on the road, they had drifted into Kumasi in search of me.

After I got over my surprise I asked Mr. Afwireng, 'Is the Tekyiman rest-house free?' He replied amused, 'Yes, of course; do you not know that nowadays Tekyiman is regarded as an unsafe area for Europeans? The Government regards us as rebels,' and they all laughed heartily. I then told them that I had telegraphed to the District Commissioner for permission to stay in the rest-house but had not received a reply. This did not surprise them much, as all the wires were down owing to a succession of heavy thunderstorms and it was not worthwhile repairing them until the weather improved. Much relieved, I then asked them what I should have asked first: about Nana's health and that of the Queenmother. The news being good I then inquired about little Eva. Princess Eva was well too. All was satisfactory.

We drank gin and chatted excitedly. After a while Sergeant Ayerttey excused himself tactfully and I asked the questions which I had been burning to ask from the beginning. What had happened politically during the fortnight I was at sea? Any new developments? No. It was then their turn to ask me whether I

[1] Royal sons are not princes, seeing that the succession is matrilineal. But the grandson of a king, whose mother is a princess in the line of succession, is a prince and can succeed to the stool or throne. As the child has the status of his mother Mr. Owusu was a prince.

had any news. What was going to happen to their Petition to the English King? I told them that, as far as I knew, it was still in the hands of the Governor in Accra. And the Treaty, their Treaty with Queen Victoria, which I had discovered at last? Would that help? I shrugged my shoulders.

Suddenly we became aware that time was flying and that we should leave for Tekyiman. As I was sure that my visitors would like to see some of their friends in Kumasi, and I wanted my lunch, I suggested leaving about half past one. They agreed readily and promised to return at the stipulated time.

At one o'clock my car was ready packed; Sergeant Kwei, my driver, stood beside it smoking a cigarette, waiting for Sergeant Ayerttey to return with Nana's car. They had both been in the army during the war driving lorries in Burma, and were friends. Both were Ga and their home was Accra. Santos was not ready yet, he was still cleaning the kitchen and getting his own things together. Finally my visitors arrived, and shortly afterwards we were off.

After two and a half hours drive through the tropical forest we reached the outskirts of Tekyiman; the car in front of mine stopped and Mr. Afwireng asked me to get into Nana's car so that I might enter the town with Nana's ambassadors. When I had done this Sergeant Ayerttey announced my arrival by joyously sounding the horn. People rushed out of the houses towards the car, waving and cheering. At the crossroads, a traffic policeman complete with white gloves was on duty for the occasion. He stopped the car and saluted me in military fashion, but grinning all over his face, and waved the car on in the direction of the palace.

When we arrived at the entrance to the palace I got out of the car, and Mr. Afwireng and Mr. Owusu took me through the cheering crowds into the narrow forecourt and from there into the audience-courtyard, where, after mounting a few steps on the right, we were in the small reception room of the King, furnished in European style. Nana was there all alone, dressed in a snow-white cloth which he wore like a Roman toga. Among the Akan white is the colour which symbolizes joy and happiness. He came

47

towards me and embraced me, and then, unable to say anything, kept my hand in his for a long time. Finally he pointed to a chair and made me sit down next to him. Everybody who had followed me left, except Mr. Afwireng who remained to act as interpreter.

Before we started talking politics and Tekyiman affairs, attendants brought some Dutch Sherrywine for me. Nana, a devout Moslem,[1] did not drink. The bottle and glasses were placed on a small table covered with a white cloth. Some flowers stood on the table in a vase. It is known to be a European custom that flowers must be on a table whenever an occasion is celebrated. The flowers came, as I knew, from the garden of the Roman Catholic Mission school, the only place in Tekyiman which had a garden.

After we had talked for about half an hour some of Nana's Elders came to greet me, but left again immediately. Then the African District Police officer from Wenkyi, who happened to be passing through Tekyiman, begged to be allowed to meet me. Nana let him enter, for he knew that the policeman would give the District Commissioner in Wenkyi a minute description of how I was honoured. In police fashion he immediately opened his notebook to take down my name, the exact moment of my arrival, the time of my intended departure, and so on. When he had finished he gave me a charming smile, his name and particulars about himself, so that I, in turn, could give a favourable report of him to the District Commissioner.

A little later, Nana informed me that his Elders were now ready to welcome me in the audience-courtyard. He led me out of the room and into the courtyard and courteously took me to my place. It was a European chair covered with a white cushion under one of the smaller state umbrellas. The umbrella among the Akan is a sign of rank, only kings and chiefs had the right to own one. Mr. Afwireng then posted himself next to me. When Nana had seated himself on his throne chair on a dais I got up, following native ceremonial, and walking from one to the other from right to left greeted everybody with a handshake. Then I

---

[1] Nana had been converted to Islam, see p. 59. Most members of the royal house were Christians.

sat down again and all the assembly including the King filed past me and greeted me in their turn.

When the greetings were over the royal spokesman got up and asked about 'my mission'. I explained to the people—Mr. Afwireng translating sentence by sentence—that I had been given a grant by the University College of the Gold Coast to do further research among the Akan with regard to their religion and customs, and that I had chosen Tekyiman because the Tekyiman people were the descendants of those who once ruled the powerful Bono Kingdom and creators of the earliest civilization in the Gold Coast. Also I wanted to find out more about their historical background so that I could help them more effectively in their struggle against the Government. I emphasized that I was sure that, if the Government knew more about their past, there would be fewer misunderstandings, and the Government would realize that the nine villages, of which the Ashanti had robbed them in 1935, were truly theirs and would be restored to them.

Nana thanked me and replied that everything would be done to assist me in my work. Then he gave a short speech reminding all assembled what I had done for the State since 1944. He then thanked me in the name of his people and at the same time begged me to support his State further in its struggle for its rights. At the end of his speech he said that now I must go to the rest-house, for I must be tired after all the travelling.

The rest-house was situated on the Nkoranza road right out of town and in the middle of elephant grass at the foot of a small hill. Santos had been busy unpacking my things and it already looked quite homely; I was happy to be back. The rest-house, built like a bungalow, had three rooms: a bedroom at the back, containing a bed, a wardrobe and two dressing-tables; a dining-room which prided itself on a long table, a number of chairs and a small netted cupboard for drinks and foodstuffs; and an empty front room which served as a store room. Since there was no boys' room, Santos and Sergeant Kwei slept in the front room on their mats which they spread out on the floor each evening. A veranda went right round the house, and closely packed shuttered windows opened out on an area of short-cut grass on which grew

D

a few shrub trees. A kitchen house was opposite the entrance door on the other side of the drive. It contained an old stove, bundles of firewood, a drum of water and a rickety table. The rest-house-keeper with his two wives and children lived in two huts built near the road.

I had hardly sat down when a number of visitors arrived, first one of Nana's N.A. (Native Authority) constables with a letter from Nana.

My dear Mrs. Eva,

I have asked my police to guard you day and night till you depart from us.

Many thanks, in anticipation,

Yours faithfully,

Tekyimanhene.

It was signed with his cross and the signature of his clerk who had translated his message into English.

The N.A. constable, an old man who in former times had been a member of the Royal Bodyguard, then posted himself before the entrance door covered by a roof where he remained until six o'clock. He was relieved by another member of the force. As I disliked being guarded in day-time, and also found it unnecessary, I asked Nana the following day to send me a constable for the night only; to which he agreed.

The constable, my first visitor, was followed by Nana's chief spokesman, Kwabena Adjaye, and the spokesman of the Queen-mother. They arrived in a car which they had borrowed from the Co-operative Society. They drank a half-bottle of my gin and took the empty bottle with them to show Nana how well I had received them. (At that time a bottle of gin cost 12s. 6d. in Accra but was sold in Tekyiman at the black market price of 27s. Nana had forbidden the open sale of liquor in his kingdom to discourage drinking.)

An hour later Nana came himself, accompanied by Mr. Afwireng and the Korontihene Kwaame Abankwa his second in command, and the Tanosohene Yaw Mensa, the chief of Tanoso (Pl. 8), who lived in exile in Tekyiman (Tanoso was one of the villages in dispute). The conversation was entirely devoted to politics not only Tekyiman's political affairs but those of the country in general. It was a time of unrest, the time when the Coussey Report was written, the acceptance of which brought a great measure of self-government to the Gold Coast people.

It was late when they left. Nana left his handkerchief behind and the Korontihene his sandals. This pleased me greatly, for I took it as a sign that they had felt much at home in my place. I delivered both articles next morning to an attendant in the palace, who tittered with amusement.

The attendant then passed me on to another attendant who led me into Nana's presence. I thanked Nana once more for his kindly reception on the day before, as is the custom. Nana ordered that his daughter Eva should be brought to me so that I could see my child. Sergeant Ayerttey brought her in, as the child's mother could not be found. He placed her gently in my arms. She was a lovely baby, seven months old, and dressed for the occasion in a brand-new white woollen dress, with woollen socks and a white bonnet. Poor darling! She could hardly breathe in this outfit in the heat, and was wet with perspiration. As she immediately started to cry, frightened by my white and unfamiliar face, I returned her to Ayerttey, who took her tenderly in his arms with that wonderful gentleness towards children one so often finds in African men. Nana then suggested that after my visit to the Queenmother I should take little Eva with me to the rest-house. I agreed with pleasure, because I wanted to give her my presents; a whole baby's outfit suitable for the climate and the indispensable rattle.

I then went over to the Queenmother's house, accompanied by Mr. Afwireng who acted as interpreter. The Queenmother Nana Afua Abrafi, a young and charming woman, received us in the courtyard where she sat with her husband, Nana Kodjo Kuray, who was her and Nana's cousin, and two women elders who served on her council of women.[1] After a while she called in her

[1] The Queenmother in the Akan state used to rule the women and had her own council of elders and a court where she judged cases—disputes over marriage payments, divorces, charges of rape, seduction, intercourse in the bush, and other matters in which women were involved. She had

two children to meet me: Kwabena, a boy about three and a half years old, and Afua, a girl a year old who could not walk yet (Pl. 5 and Pl. 4). Both were naked, as is only proper in that heat. Kwabena immediately took a liking to me, which delighted the Queenmother, especially when he said, taking my hand, 'When I am big I am going to marry you'. A few days later the Queenmother with her retinue paid me a return visit and brought the two children along. Kwabena took the doll which I had meant to give to his little sister and amused everybody when he once more declared that he was going to marry me and, pointing at the doll, said that that 'was our child'.

On the way back from the Queenmother's house to the rest-house I met Nana's people on the road, loaded with gifts for me: live chickens, eggs, yams, pawpaws, oranges, limes and bananas. I was truly grateful for them, because it was difficult to obtain most of these things at that time on the local market and the quality of the fruit was so much better than that of the market produce. These gifts were repeated every three days.

The Durbar in my honour

Early the following morning a royal messenger informed me that I was going to be given an official reception by the State at one o'clock. I was also told that Nana wished me to stay at home until that time so as to be fresh for the occasion. I therefore spent the morning quietly reading, undisturbed by visitors. Then I dressed myself in a pale-blue linen frock and took a sun helmet instead of a hat.

When I reached the main road in my car, crowds of people barred the way, so that it was impossible to progress at more than snail's pace. Everybody cheered; many tried to shake my hand through the window of the car, some women shouted *medofo*, which means 'beloved' or 'darling'. When I arrived at the en-

her own police and her own treasury. 'Queenmother' is a European term chosen probably because constitutionally the Queenmother is the mother of the king whether she actually is his mother or not; more often she is his sister or cousin. The word *Ohemmaa* for 'queenmother' means literally 'female king'.

trance to the square in front of the palace I was met by Mr. J. K. Ankomah, the Inspector of N.A. Police, and Mr. Afwireng, who told me that the reception would not take place in the palace but in the square, so that the people could witness the ceremony.

I had to get out of my car; policemen used their batons to clear a path for me and my companions. Finally, with the crowd behind me, I stood alone facing a great assembly. For the moment I was too surprised to move. I saw Nana and his court and the Queenmother with her ladies sitting at the far end of the square; looking to my right I saw lined up all the chiefs of the State, surrounded by their retinues, while to the left were cordoned off the teachers of Tekyiman, the schoolchildren and the traders and clerks of the town. I was overwhelmed; then I became aware that the surging and cheering mass behind me had become silent and were waiting expectantly for the proceedings to begin. My entrance was announced by the playing of 'God save the King' by four brass bands. I suddenly realized the tremendous significance of the occasion. This was no ordinary reception; it was a Durbar to which only the Governor of the Gold Coast had a right.

Mr. Ankomah and Mr. Afwireng then led me round the square. A herald preceded us, calling out the name of each chief as I greeted him with a handshake. Many I knew from former visits; many kept my hand in theirs for a little while, smiling in affection. In their colourful cloths, adorned with gold ornaments, under their large umbrellas of rank, they formed a brilliant spectacle.

Though my face by now seemed to have frozen into a perpetual smile, and my arm was limp from all the handshaking, I had to go through the same procedure with Nana's elders and court officials and with the ladies of the Queenmother. As I paid my respects to Nana he whispered that he was happy to have me here. He sat under the enormous double state umbrella of his ancestors, the Kings of Bono. He wore full regalia; a purple cloth of heavy velvet richly embroidered with the royal emblems, necklaces, armlets, bracelets, finger-rings, anklets and toe-rings of gold, and round his head a chaplet covered with triangles of gold. I had never seen him looking so handsome and young; he was forty years old. On his right the Queenmother, in a group apart, was also beautifully dressed but wore no gold or silver ornaments. She had with her little Kwabena, who may—for the succession is matrilineal—one day be the king.

The teachers and the schoolchildren, the traders, clerks and others on the left side of the square I greeted by inclining my head. Then Mr. Ankomah and Mr. Afwireng led me to my place under one of the smaller state umbrellas in front of them. The bands, which had played, after 'God save the King', a variety of English songs 'to make me happy' (I had to smile, because I am not English), now played again a few bars of 'God save the King'. I sat down on a chair covered with a white cushion while Mr. Ankomah posted himself next to me. Mr. Afwireng took his seat on the other side of a little table on which stood a vase of flowers. There was silence.

Then the Akyeamehene, the chief of the royal spokesmen, and five spokesmen planted themselves in front of the sword-bearers who sat in two rows on the ground before Nana, holding in their hands the ceremonial gold-hilted state swords. The spokesmen held in their hands long golden staffs, the symbol of their office. Heralds shouted 'Silence' and the Akyeamehene turned to me and asked me what my mission was.

So I told them of my mission again for all the people to hear—Mr. Afwireng translating sentence by sentence: that I had come to write down their religion and customs and their historical traditions in order to put them in a book, and thus preserve for all time the things of the past. I pointed out to them that, as now more and more people became westernized and children went to school to learn European ways, they no longer troubled to learn the old lore. The result was that much precious knowledge was lost. I was sure that their children's children would be grateful one day that they had given this information to a person who could write down their ancient history and traditions before it was too late.

Nana replied to me through the Akyeamehene, in the name of the State, that I would be given every help so that the world could learn about their great civilization that had unfortunately come to an end when the Ashanti conquered the Bono Kingdom. Then he begged me to tell him and his people about their 'case'; what the Colonial Office in London thought about the matter and when His Majesty the King of England would reply to their petition.

This question found me rather unprepared and for a moment I did not know what to say. Then I got up again and told them as well as I could of my dealings with the Colonial Office on their behalf and of the difficulties of the British Government in finding a solution that was just to them and to the Ashanti. I explained that the Government still wanted proof that the nine villages which the Asantehene Nana Prempeh II took from Tekyiman when the Government re-established the Ashanti Confederacy in 1935 had belonged to Tekyiman before 1901 when the Ashanti Kingdom had ceased to exist. The Ashanti claimed that these villages had always been theirs and denied that Nana Prempeh I returned them to Tekyiman in 1895, following a war of about twenty years. Without any written evidence, it would be difficult for the Government now to demand from the Asantehene, who had always been helpful to the Government, the handing over these villages to Tekyiman. All the Tekyiman State could do was to continue to demand the villages and to fight, united under Nana. In South Africa they have a device: 'Unity is strength'. Have patience. Do not give up hope. Victory there must be in the end.

When I sat down Nana thanked me and assured me that his people would continue to fight for their rights or die. He then asked me to describe in detail how I found the treaty, their treaty with Queen Victoria. So I got up again and related how I searched for it, first in Accra and Kumasi and then in England, till at last I held it in my hands, the very paper on which the ancestors of Nana and some of his elders had made their mark. I told them I found it in the Public Record Office in London, a very big building, much bigger than any building in the Gold Coast, in which treaties were stored, the thousands of treaties England had made in the course of her history with many peoples on this earth. Nothing, I said, could show better the might of England than this house full of documents. And among all these thousands there was *their* treaty, the treaty they had concluded with Queen Victoria in 1897, in which they had placed themselves under British rule, which had guaranteed them peace. Thereupon Nana thanked me, still through the Akyeamehene, for all I had done for his State, and assured me that everybody here loved me. The Akyeamehene then prayed for my long life and good health so that I could continue the struggle and help them further.

When the Akyeamehene had finished, Nana got up and took the place of the royal spokesman, for he wanted to tell his people in his own words what I had done for them. He greeted me as the true daughter of Queen Victoria, her re-incarnation; and just as Queen Victoria had given peace to them and let them keep the villages, after they had won them back in battle from the Ashanti, so, Nana said, he was sure that I would bring peace to Tekyiman and make it possible for the villages to be theirs again, this time for ever. After this speech Nana began to dance, a slow cere-monial dance with mincing steps, to express his joy that I was again among them. Page boys ran towards him to hold up the ends of his cloth like a train. After a little while the Queenmother with her ladies joined him, dancing together in a group, while Nana continued to dance alone in front of the assembly but now throwing handfuls of coins into the crowds. Not only pennies but also sixpenny pieces; one happened to fall at my feet. I wondered whether I could pick it up and keep it as a reminder of the great day. Looking round I saw a nice little boy standing with his father behind me; he had his eyes fixed on it but neither he, nor any other of the children dared to take it. So I said to him, 'Come take it, it is yours,' and like a hawk swooping down on its prey he took it and held it up triumphantly. Of course Nana's generous gesture resulted in a general scramble for the money as the crowds broke through the cordon, and the police had the greatest trouble in bringing order out of the chaos. When the middle of the square was clear of people Nana declared the day to be a day of happiness and a public holiday in honour of my arrival. Amid tremendous cheering I returned to my car while the brass bands played 'God save the King' for all they were worth. I could still hear them when I arrived at the rest-house.

October 1949

Later in the day Mr. J. K. Ankomah, the Inspector of the N.A. Police, came to see me (Pl. 11). He reported that Nana had commissioned him to act as my interpreter, Mr. Afwireng being too busy in the office. We had a long talk in which I outlined to him the nature of my work. I was pleased to find him so intelligent, eager, pleasant and—what was amazing—gentle; not at all what one imagined a police chief to be. I came to appreciate his gentleness when I had occasion to see him at work, interrogating arrested persons and taking finger-prints.

After him another visitor called, the British District Commissioner from Wenkyi. He was a newcomer; a young man, who, as I found later, tried his best to understand the people with whom he had to deal. Before he left he asked me whether I knew why so many brass bands were in town playing in the streets, and why people were dancing. I smiled and said lightly, 'Because I am back'. He looked at me sideways, but said nothing.

The Day after the Durbar

The morning following the Durbar, Sergeant Kwei drove me to town together with Santos, my cook-steward, dressed in his best. I left him at the palace as Nana had desired to see him. I had the car parked under the trees in the main road, so that Kwei could have his breakfast in the local bar, while I picked up Ankomah from his room in town—he was a bachelor—to wander round the town with me.

Tekyiman-town had not changed since I saw it last three years before; no new buildings had sprung up—the lack of funds made this impossible. But people when they talked to me were cheerful enough and confident that they would win their struggle. Passing houses of the State elders and friends from former times, I went in to greet them. Ankomah and I were received, as was usual, in the three-walled room facing the entrance courtyard and given chairs. Mine, for some reason or other, always had a plush cushion. The conversation invariably centred on politics: Gold Coast politics in general and Tekyiman affairs in particular. All promised me a return visit within the next few days.

October 1949

Coming out of the Nifahene's (one of Nana's elders) house, Ankomah and I went over to the temple of Taa Kese, Tekyiman's national god, and found the High-priest Kofi Mosi, his male relations and all the priests gathered in the temple courtyard. The High-priest's old mother, the Tanohemmaa, the only woman among them, was so happy to see me again that she hugged me in front of all the men. She was small and slim, in contrast to her son who was tall, young and exceptionally good looking (Pl. 16). He was the same High-priest who, in 1946, had defended the former Queenmother when she stood trial for high treason and had nearly got her acquitted by his brilliant speeches.

As I saw the priests busy counting funeral donations—a priest had just died—I wanted to leave, but the High-priest and his mother would not hear of it. It would only take a few more minutes. So I sat down again and watched the proceedings.

One of the priests who could read and write—he had served in the army in Burma during the war—wrote every penny down in a notebook and deposited the coins in a brass box. I contributed what is called *saabodie*, three shillings and sixpence, which pleased them very much because it was the correct amount to give for a person who was not related to the deceased. When they had finished, the High-priest called for two bottles of beer, one for a libation, the other for me to take home, because it was not proper for me to drink in their presence. While the bottle was being handed over to me, one of the hornblowers in the service of the god placed himself behind my chair and played a tune in my honour. Then the libation was poured out by the High-priest, who wished me a long life, health and success in my work. A little was left in the glass which was then passed round for everybody to take a sip. A drop of it was given to me in a second glass to be used solely by me, for which I was grateful. I should have drunk of course from the same glass, but they remembered from my visit three years ago that this was 'tabu' for me. Not all the people in the Gold Coast had been so considerate. When I had taken down the history of Elmina on the coast, the chief and his elders there insisted that I drank the libation of gin together with them from a tiny cup carved of coconut wood which must have been generations old. Nine or ten old men had drunk already from it, they had been coughing and spitting during the interview and there was not a dry place left on the cup's rim. I refused, embarrassed, but it was the custom, and the chief and elders insisted. So I did drink from it and the people were so delighted that they clapped their hands and cheered me. We parted great friends—which, after all, was all that mattered.

On the way back from the temple to my car I met the exiled Tanosohene, who had visited me with Nana on the day of my arrival. He wore a trench coat (Pl. 8)—he had been in the army during the war. When he heard from Ankomah, in the course of the conversation, that the Tano priests had blown a horn in my honour, he said: 'If you get the villages back for Nana and I am chief again in Tanoso, then I will compose a tune which will commemorate your great deed.' I was very pleased, of course, at the thought of becoming part of the local tradition, for tunes blown on the ceremonial horns keep historical events alive.

When I reached my car Santos, who had waited for me, told me that he had had his audience with Nana: Nana had given him ten shillings and he was going to buy some khaki shorts with it. At home—he was an Ijaw from the Niger delta—he would tell all his relatives and friends that 'a king has given them to me'. He reported that Nana had told him to look after me well, because I was a very precious person and must have good food so that I should remain strong and healthy.

In the afternoon I went with Ankomah to the Songo, Tekyiman's twin town (inhabited by Moslems, mostly of foreign origin) to pay my respects to the chief of the Songo, Gariba Adjaji, Nana's great friend who had converted him to Islam. I knew that they saw each other daily to read the Koran together and to visit the little mosque, built in Sudanese style, to pray. He was an exceptionally fine and nice old man, a Hausa by birth, and he and his wife, the head woman of the Songo, welcomed me warmly. They introduced me to the chief of the Mossi people (from Mossi, situated north of the Gold Coast) who lived next door to their compound and was in charge of Nana's white horse, sacred to the Royal Ancestors, the Sun kings of Bono. It was the only horse in Tekyiman. In the times of the Bono Kingdom everybody who was of any account owned a horse. Men, women and children used to ride (as they still do in Basutoland today) and gallop along the one-way streets into which the main road was divided by a line of trees. Nana had entrusted the care of his horse to the chief of the Mossi as his own people, owning horses no longer, had forgotten how to do it. But the chief of the Mossi, overanxious, overfed it, and not daring to ride it too often, gave it no proper exercise. When he heard from me that I loved horses he got Nana's permission for me to ride it and came the following day to the rest-house with it. But I refused, to his great disappointment, because I felt that the horse, whose legs were swollen, was in pain and still had to do another three miles back; also I feared that its trot was horrible.

From the Songo we went to Kenten, a mile or so farther on, as Ankomah wished me to see his cocoa trees there. Strolling through the village we came to a house where divorce proceedings were in progress in the courtyard, and we stopped to listen. Nana was represented by an elder and one of the spokesmen handled the case. The husband was a quiet young man, an ex-serviceman who had fought in Burma; the wife was a noisy, quarrelsome woman who objected to his having married a second wife. She yelled at him and used abusive language; he just sat unmoved and did not trouble to reply. We had to leave before the end, but we heard later that the couple were divorced on grounds of incompatibility of temperament.

At the rest-house visitors were waiting for me—the Tuobodomhene Kwaame Frimpon (Pl. 12), his sister the Tuodobomhemmaa Afua Fosiah, Queenmother or head woman[1] of Tuobodom, her husband, and some of their elders, to greet me. I knew them well from 1946 and was delighted to see them all. We sat down round the table in the living-room and drank some

---

[1] There is no term for 'head woman'; the suffix *hemmaa* can either mean 'queenmother' or 'head woman'—Tekyimanhemmaa, Queenmother of Tekyiman; Tuobodomhemmaa, Queenmother or head woman of Tuobodom. Also Tekyimanhene, 'King of Tekyiman'; Tuobodomhene, 'Chief of Tuobodom'; Akyeamehene, 'Chief of the Royal spokesmen', and so forth.

gin while we talked animatedly, recalling the time when I came to Tuobodom and went with them to see the Golden Pool at the source of the Tano River. I particularly liked the Tuobodomhemmaa, as she was a lively woman and generally full of fun. But now she was sad, as she and her brother had to live as exiles in Tekyiman and were poor; the revenues of Tuobodom—which was one of the villages in dispute—went to Ashanti and to the chief and Queenmother who had usurped their places. I promised to see a great deal of them and so I did; the Tuobodomhene was always eager to give me information, especially with regard to the god worshipped at Tuobodom, Tano Twumpuduo, the former State god of the Bono Kingdom.

The N.A. Police Dance

I was invited the following day by the N.A. police force—the card was signed by the Inspector Ankomah—to a dance in my honour in the yard of Cadbury and Fry's on the Nkoranza road. I accepted, of course, with pleasure, and Nana again ordered me to rest—no visitors in the afternoon—so that I would have enough strength to dance through the night. The invitation said eight o'clock and, not knowing that, as a person of honour, I was expected to arrive late, I turned up punctually—much to the embarrassment of Ankomah, who was still busy organizing the crowds. He asked some teachers to entertain me till he was able to devote himself to me.

One of the teachers was a youth; he could not have been more than sixteen as he told me that he had passed Standard VII the year before and had got his appointment at the Infant School only on account of Tekyiman's shortage of qualified staff. His English, as could be expected, was far from good and he tried to impress me by spicing his sentences with quotations from the Bible and old-fashioned books. I listened to him while I was looking round watching the people streaming in: the elderly persons sitting down on chairs, or on the low stools, all along the yard; while the young people placed themselves behind them, talking and greeting newcomers. In the centre of the yard was the only light provided for us: a petromax lamp resting precariously on a stand.

After a pause in the conversation the young teacher came out with a request: would I please open the ball with him? I looked at him surprised; what book could he have got this from? I shook my head; the brass band was playing but I did not much like his suggestion. But he persisted and pleaded with me. As it obviously meant a great deal to him, I gave in reluctantly; I did not wish to disappoint him. He was so young.

How does one open a ball? I had only a hazy idea on the subject. I had some vision of an elegant waltz but how was one to do this well on Cadbury's cement floor? And then I remembered that the waltz was a funeral dance in this country. This seems strange, but the waltz had been adopted by the people perhaps at the beginning of the century, and was incorporated in rites connected with the dead. I have seen it performed. One day I took Mr. H. J. Braunholtz, who was then the curator of the Ethnographical Department of the British Museum in London, to Bisease near Kumasi to show him one of the few remaining old Ashanti houses. To my great disappointment the house was closed because the woman who owned it had just died. In front of her body, laid out in state on a bed in an open courtyard of a house in the centre of the village, young people joyfully danced a waltz, a magic rite to help the dead woman to 'life' in heaven.

No, I mused, a waltz would not do; besides, an opening dance should be stately; some steps of a quadrille might be more suitable, but I did not remember them very well. Still I decided on it, and so we made our appearance on the 'dance floor'.

The brass band played a slow tune to which one could adapt the steps. I showed my partner what to do and to my delight he quickly understood. Soon we were engrossed in it, turning slowly round one another, separating, taking the arm . . .

Suddenly we were interrupted, and my young friend was shaken out of his dreams. One of the N.A. police constables, in civilian clothes, on the command of Ankomah, grabbed him and shouted something to him. Hotly the youth answered back but was arrested and led away. Bewildered I went back to my place. Ankomah then came to me and explained that I had honoured the least worthy of the teachers, the least worthy of the assembled partners for me, and that there had been an outcry. He could not do otherwise than to arrest the youth to make it clear to the people that he was to blame, not I. I protested, as I felt that I was also to blame. While we were still arguing the youth, who had managed to escape, threw himself at my feet and begged me: 'Please, please, Mother, tell him that I did not make you dance. Please, please, Mother, say that I was not disrespectful!' The constable, who had followed him, took him roughly by the arm and dragged him away. Ankomah, to prevent further mistakes on my part, placed me firmly in the care of two elderly teachers. They talked Education Department with me and teaching conditions in Tekyiman—not the kind of conversation to accompany dance music.

However, my dancing had broken the ice. My young friend and I had opened the ball after all. The band played quicker now: 'Highlife', the favourite dance all over the country. It was of West Indian origin, a dance with which I was not acquainted at the time, and thus deeply disappointed the Agricultural Officer from Wenkyi, a tall well-built African, who had learnt it in Accra. He had meant to give a fine performance with me and could not understand that I, a European, did not know this 'European' dance. All the same I learnt the basic steps quickly enough with Ankomah, who had the patience to teach me. Much encouraged I soon hopped about with other partners, dancing, in addition to 'Highlife', a variety of foxtrots, one-steps, and rumbas.

As late as half past ten Nana's representatives appeared. I should have come after them if Ankomah had not forgotten to let me know. The band immediately blew a fanfare. All dancing stopped till they had seated themselves; the ladies next to me, the two Chiefs and their retinue opposite us on the other side of the yard. They were the Tuobodomhene and the Offumanhene Kwaame Gyamfi (Pl. 13). The three ladies were the Tuobodomhemmaa, her young daughter, and the Offumanhemmaa Kromah.

They were all most beautifully dressed; especially the Tuo-bodomhene, who wore a cloth of heavy white silk like a toga and with it a turban of the same material.

Before the music started again, attendants of the Chiefs brought me Nana's presents for the evening: a bottle of Dutch Schnapps, much appreciated in this part of the world, two bottles of beer and a tin of fifty Players cigarettes. I was expected to entertain; so much I had learnt from previous trips. I therefore at once sent over half a bottle of Schnapps to the two Chiefs; the other I presented to the band. One bottle of beer I gave to my retinue, consisting of Sergeant Kwei, who was somewhere in the crowd, and one bottle I kept for the Queenmothers of Tuobodom and Offuman and myself. The cigarettes I distributed to people who came to our table. The two Queenmothers smiled, seeing me so busy, and I smiled back. We could not talk much as my Twi was limited and they did not speak English. The Tuobodom-hemmaa was radiant because she loved music and dancing, as she let me know through Ankomah. The Offumanhemmaa I only knew slightly. She was, like her brother, quiet and kindly.

Then the dance really started. The yard by now was so crowded that one could hardly move. The two Queenmothers constantly encouraged me to accept partners and there were many who wished to dance with me. When, hot and tired, I returned to my seat, they assured me each time that I had done well and laughed, amused. They treated me like a daughter at her first ball. They did not dance themselves; at least as long as I was there.

I also had the honour to be asked for a dance by the Offuman-hene, who was the older man, and then by my old friend, the Tuobodomhene. We must have looked strange together, he a prince from *A Thousand and One Nights* in his white silk robe and turban, and I in a pencil-slim white, grey and blue striped evening dress which I had bought in Paris. Looking at him I could not believe that this young, handsome and elegant prince was the same whom I had visited three years ago in Tuobodom. He was at that time, although a chief, a priest in training, haggard, emaciated from long fastings and going into trances, bearded and looking much older. He only spoke of his god to me. And now we

64

danced a Highlife in Cadbury's yard round and round the petromax lamp.

Gradually the dance became wilder and wilder—drums had joined in to accentuate the rhythm, drowning more and more the brass instruments—and presently a transformation took place: one after the other the couples separated and the young people, without a command being given, arranged themselves in single file, forming a spiral around us. There was a far-away look in their eyes, as if they were in a trance, and the character of their dance was unmistakably African. The spiral enclosed the prince and me and came nearer and nearer, leaving us less and less room to dance in, but the dance went on and on and became a nightmare to me. When I almost dropped with fatigue the prince called a halt and the spell was broken; slowly the young people dispersed. It had become dark, as the moon, which had shone so brightly in the early evening, had disappeared behind a cloud and the petromax lamp needed pumping up. There was for a moment an atmosphere of general exhaustion.

I was too tired to go on, and begged the Queenmothers to leave. They were much upset and so were the Chiefs, for they had thought that I would stay as long as they. So I had hoped. But everything I did beyond my strength was likely to produce a bout of malaria, and I could not afford to get ill. When Ankomah came to our table I told him about my decision and he at once took me to the band and told the bandleader that I was going to leave. The music was stopped immediately and I had to make a speech in which I thanked the band publicly for having played so well. The bandleader in turn then thanked me in the name of the band and expressed the wish to play a dance in my honour. I chose my host Ankomah for a partner, but begged for no drums this time. The young people danced again in couples and a kind of cheerfulness returned. Then I said good-bye, telling everybody how much I had enjoyed myself. Soon I was back in the rest-house where Santos, more than half asleep, was anxiously waiting for me.

October 1949

Visit to Okyeame Pong's Daughter Eva

The day I arrived in Tekyiman, October 3rd, one of Okyeame Pong's wives gave birth to a daughter. Okyeame Pong, Nana's senior spokesman and cherished adviser (Pl. 14), asked to be allowed to name her Eva after me, to which I agreed with pleasure. He came to see me in the rest-house with his wife and newborn child (Pl. 15) when it was ten days old and invited me to Bonkwae, his village, to take part in the festivities of the patron god of his lands, Buruma.

Bonkwae is situated a few miles from Tekyiman-town on the Sunyani road. When I got out of my car I was delighted to see numerous small monkeys swinging from tree to tree opposite the entrance to Okyeame Pong's compound. The monkeys were unmolested and knew it.

After Okyeame Pong and his large family had welcomed me, I was shown round, for there were a number of new buildings under construction: small houses for the family, and sheds for drying and storing cocoa. I was made to sit down in front of a two-roomed house, roofed with corrugated iron, which served him as reception room and office. Little Eva II was brought to me by her mother and lovingly placed in my lap. She slept peacefully, having just been fed. In every respect she was a fine baby and I could be proud of her.

By and by other visitors arrived, among them the Queen-mother, the Tuobodomhene and the Tuobodomhemmaa, and the High-priest of Taa Kese accompanied by his retinue. After a while we all went to a grove in the nearby forest where the priest of Buruma was already dancing, accompanied by drummers, precariously balancing the shrine of the god on his head (Pl. 17). We sat down on chairs on one side of the grove, while the villagers stood opposite us, next to the drummers, and also behind us. It was a beautiful morning; everybody was in a happy mood and enjoying the outing. At last the priest sacrificed an egg by throwing it against the trunk of a huge silk-cotton tree. When the rites were over the priest was introduced to me and, after I had given him the traditional three shillings and sixpence for his god, he embraced me with fervour. I was not particularly pleased about that, because the sweat of his partly naked body and some of the white clay with which he was painted came off on my newly laundered dress. The village women laughed, and said that I should feel honoured because it was the god in him which made him do so; it was the god who wished to show his love for me. Priests had the right to embrace any woman their god fancied.

Then our whole party went to Buruma's sanctuary, a small hut in a corner of Okyeame Pong's compound, and sat down on low stools, forming a circle in front of it. The shrine of the god was uncovered by an old priest and placed on a five-columned stool whitened with clay. The outside of the shrine, a brass basin filled with sacred objects which symbolized the power of the god, invisible because a layer of a hard black material covered them, was then rubbed with the yolk of an egg and thus sanctified. The egg is the symbol of birth and creation; the rites centred on the rebirth of the god, *Nkotoba*, a number of short knotted branches, symbol of the god's authority, were placed on top of the shrine and before it, and pieces of boiled yam, the first offerings to Buruma. Then Okyeame Pong came, holding in his hand a bowl of holy water containing *adwera* leaves for consecration; he blessed us all by sprinkling some of the water over us or over our hands. More offerings were prepared, but I could not wait for the conclusion of the rites. It was already three o'clock and I had promised Nana to call on him as he wanted to show me something.

Nana talks of Himself

I found Nana with Mr. Afwireng in the office of the palace; the latter was busy translating to him the Coussey Report, which had just come in from Accra. Nana showed it to me and requested me to read it, so that later I could discuss it with him and his elders. The Coussey Report, when it became reality, was to give the Gold Coast people a large measure of self-government: universal adult suffrage from the age of twenty-five, local government and regional administration, a House of Assembly, corresponding to the House of Commons, with a speaker to direct the procedure of debates, and an Executive Council composed of six ministers with portfolios headed by a Prime Minister.

While we were talking about it Nana's little Eva was brought in by her mother. Nana thought that the child was sick; but seeing that a string of beads was cutting right into her fat little tummy, I took it off and she stopped crying at once. Instead she started to babble and, as seeing me for the first time, grasped my nose in wonder and pulled it. Nana was much amused and asked for the child; and, after having seated little Eva on his lap, gave her a volley of kisses on her left cheek. She did not seem to mind.

Nana had time and was in a good mood, so he took me to his reception room in order to tell me about himself. He was born in 1909; his mother had been the beautiful princess Abena Abrafi, who had so many suitors in her youth that she could not make up her mind whom to marry. Finally she fell in love with Nana's father, the great hero of the last phases of the Tekyiman–Ashanti war, and was willing to marry him. This pleased King Gyako II (1886–99) greatly, as he was thus able to honour a man who had rendered great service to the State. The marriage proved to be a happy one; there were eleven children, and all grew up strong and healthy.

Nana's birth—he was the tenth child—gave his mother great pain; for three or four days she was unable to deliver him. Nobody dared to tell King Yaw Kramo (1907–27) about it, for a difficult birth in the royal lineage signified that the child to be born, if it was a boy, would be his successor. Only when Nana's mother nearly died was the King told; he at once rushed to her and placed his sandals on her body, thus acknowledging the child as the future king. Nana was given the name Gyako Badu; when he was elected king the High-priest of Taa Kese saw in a trance that his reign would resemble that of the Bono king Akumfi Ameyaw I (Akumfi means 'slayer', i.e. of enemies) and Nana accepted this as his royal name.

King Yaw Kramo, owing to the circumstances of Nana's birth, took a special interest in the boy, who was his nephew, and, when Nana was still small, requested his mother to let him live in the palace. Thus Nana became familiar with state affairs and life at court at an early age. As he had a love for weaving, he was taught this craft and became accomplished in it. When he was eighteen his uncle was assassinated (1927) and Nana, shocked and unhappy, fled from Tekyiman and went to the Northern Territories of the Gold Coast. There he took to trading, exporting sheep and smoked fish to Tekyiman and other places.

After a few years he went south to Akwapim and taught weaving to seven young men and worked with them for four years. Homesick, he then returned to Tekyiman. But he left the town again after three years and went to the Fante country on the coast to teach fifteen young men the making of the *Adinkra* printed cloth. Still restless, he gave it up after some time and started to travel. When he came to the French Ivory Coast and saw the need there for British goods, he opened a store at Bondugu. Soon dissatisfied and longing for home he returned once more to Tekyiman, but, unhappy about the conditions there, left shortly afterwards and went to Kintampo, a town situated in the neighbouring Nkoranza State. Still interested in trade, he became a food supplier to the Gold Coast Regiment which was stationed there. A few years later the Tekyimanhene King Kwaku Gyako, who had succeeded his uncle, was destooled (1943), and the then reigning Queenmother Nana Akua Dapaa recalled the prince and enstooled him as king early in 1944.

Nana's family was a very old one, as he explained to me. Before A.D. 800 his Royal Ancestors ruled the Diadom Federation in the eastern Sahara; from A.D. 800–1000 the Diala Kingdom in the Timbuktu region on the Niger; and when this also was conquered, they moved south to found the First Bono Kingdom in a region now called Mossi. The Second Bono Kingdom was founded by them roughly three hundred years later (c. 1298) with the capital Bono-Mansu. He also told me that his ancestors who had lived in the 'White Desert', the 'Country of the Sand', had been a white or light-skinned people and that through intermarriage with their subject Negro peoples they had finally become 'black Africans'.

Nana then emphasized once more that he shared the same

ancestors with the Asantehene; they were Dia by origin and falcon clan people. But whereas Nana's Royal Ancestors had founded the Diala Kingdom on the Niger, the Asantehene's had founded the neighbouring Diara and after that the Bona Kingdom (in the Ivory Coast). When this was conquered by Moslem Mande about 1600, a princess and her followers went to the Bono Kingdom and were given land in Bono's most southerly province, the Kumasi region. About 1690 Osei Tutu, a great-great-grandson of the Bona princess, founded the Asante or Ashanti Kingdom, which soon became powerful through conquest and in 1740 destroyed the Bono Kingdom.

I was surprised that Nana, when he had finished talking about himself and his Royal Ancestors, did not ask me about myself, my home, my background. Thus he never learnt that I was not English, of my upbringing in Germany and my life in South Africa. I could also have told him that by profession I was a sculptor and, had it not been for his Royal Ancestors, who had decreed that I was to be told of Bono's history and culture, I would not now have been in Tekyiman collecting material for future books.

When I had returned to the rest-house and had just settled down reading, Santos announced a Songhay trader, who wanted to sell me some rugs. As I love the Sudanese rugs, especially those from Timbuktu and Niafunke on the Niger, which closely resemble the Berber rugs of Morocco and Algiers, I immediately got up to see his wares. There were several really beautiful ones, and I finally selected one with an unusual pattern. When I paid the trader the two pounds he had asked, he returned ten shillings to me with the words: 'It is a custom with us that when we meet a person with so fine a face as yours, we do not trade with this person; we reject all profits—one gives, and praises Allah.' I thought that I had misunderstood him and turned questioningly to Santos who had translated from Hausa into English. But to my surprise he said: 'It is true Madame, it is true!' with so much emphasis that I could only look at him astonished. For Santos was usually grumpy and found fault with me in many ways. I held the ten shillings in my hand not knowing what to do, but when Santos urged me: 'Take it, Madame, take it,' I took it and thanked the trader as graciously as I could. And I smiled, for I thought that I understood now why the Akan princesses showed such preference for the Songhay men from Gao; there was more to them than their long legs and good looks—they knew how to pay a woman a compliment.

The Battle at Tanoso

On the morning of the battle between Tanoso people and the Ashanti Police I received a visit from the Akwamuhene Tabiri Kwasi, one of Nana's important elders. While he was sipping my gin he told me that he was unhappy and worried, because his cocoa farm had been destroyed by fire a few days before, and the day before his corn farm had been devastated by black monkeys. He hoped that I would be able to help him by getting him a modern gun. The District Commissioner at Wenkyi refused to give any Tekyiman a licence for guns and ammunition, and the old-fashioned Dane guns were not powerful enough to keep the monkeys at bay. I told him that unfortunately I could not get a licence either, and explained to him the reason why. Knowing from my life in South Africa what monkeys can do to a farm, I sympathized with him and, to show him how much I understood his worry, told him about an experience of mine with baboons.

One day, I said, my husband—he died a few years ago—and our son, aged four, were camping in the Valley of Death, in the south of Africa. The valley was so called because it was swarming with yellow cobras, poisonous snakes—which we did not know at the time, otherwise we would not have camped there. It was very hot; and after our midday meal we rested under a tree not far from our tent. I could not sleep, and suddenly noticed a troop of baboons coming towards us. They approached the tent gingerly, pretending to play, but all the time closing in on it. When they had nearly reached it, a farmer, luckily for us, appeared on the scene with his hunting dogs. His maize field on the other side of the valley had just been destroyed by these baboons, as they pluck much more than they wish to eat. He shot at the baboons and they ran, and, shooting as he went, chased them up the stony hill opposite us. Two of the animals were mortally wounded. In a flash the dogs were upon them tearing them to pieces. They were ferocious dogs, experienced in fighting baboons, their bodies scarred from the wounds they had received in battle with them. One of the wounded was a young male, the other a female with a baby clinging to it. When the dogs got at her, she gave a horrifyingly human cry. Then the farmer turned back with his blood-dripping dogs and told us that for some time now we would be safe.

The monkeys round Tekyiman were not baboons but were about the same size. They had black, glossy fur and a patch of white on the chest. The tip of the long tail was also white. The Tuobodomhemmaa once made me a present of three skins to use as floor mats. I never saw one of these creatures alive, but occasionally came across their dead bodies tied to poles barring paths leading to farms, to scare live ones away. Their meat, by the way, is smoked and sold on the market. The Tekyiman do not eat it, but it is eaten by some of the Nigerians in the Songo who regard it as a delicacy.

In the early afternoon Ayertee brought me little Eva and a boy of twelve or thirteen who acted as her nurse. I took a photograph of the two children (Pl. 7) and amused little Eva with a celluloid fish. She soon began to cry, however, and after half an hour I sent her back. Then I settled down to work again.

About five o'clock that afternoon Ankomah unexpectedly appeared in a torn shirt, with a bump on his forehead and an injury to his leg. He was too excited to give a proper account of what had happened but so much was clear: that he came from Tanoso, one of the nine villages in dispute, about ten miles from Tekyiman on the Kumasi road.

According to his story a battle had taken place there when Ashanti police came to confiscate the year's crop of cocoa from the farms of the exiled Tanosohene, and the people resisted them. There were some killed and over a hundred wounded. Ankomah had then gone with a lorry full of wounded to take them to hospital in Sunyani, about forty miles from Tekyiman, for the

Tekyiman State had no hospital, dispensary, or doctor. On the way, the lorry—which was going too fast—collided with another lorry, and there were fresh injuries. As Ankomah was in no fit state to be questioned further, and still had to report to Nana, I let him go and patiently waited for the morning to hear from Nana himself the truth of the whole affair.

Next day, as early as it was decently possible, I drove to the palace and arrived just in time to have a few words with Nana, who was about to drive to Sunyani. He asked me to come back in the afternoon. When I called later Nana was sitting in a State Council meeting, for it was to be expected that this battle would have serious repercussions. He allowed me to be present and himself told me briefly what had happened. The Ashanti police, a party of five men, came to confiscate the cocoa of the Tanoso-hene and the people, angered, assaulted them and thrashed them. The police then sent to Kumasi for reinforcements, and the Tanoso people sent an urgent message to Tekyiman for help and instructions. Luckily Nana was at home and received the messenger, who was accompanied by excited Tanoso exiles and Tekyiman people. They all clamoured to be allowed to go to Tanoso to fight the police and chase them off the lands of the Tanosohene. Nana, seeing that he would not be able to keep the people back, agreed on condition that only Tanoso exiles should go, to assure themselves that their relatives were safe. Ankomah, as the Inspector of N.A. police, was to accompany them, but in civilian clothes. They must go unarmed. Two lorries full of people then went to Tanoso.

When the Ashanti police returned, a 'battle' took place. The police were armed with batons and knives. As far as I could ascertain, the Tanoso armed themselves with sticks and stones and clubs, and some with cutlasses. There were eight seriously wounded, five on the Ashanti side and three on the Tanoso side. The rest were slightly wounded and received treatment in Sunyani and were sent home.

A few minutes after my return to the rest-house from the State Council meeting, the District Commissioner of Wenkyi, passing through Tekyiman, came to see me about the 'battle'. He took a very serious view of it, as Nana had not told the Tanoso people to submit to the Ashanti police but, on the contrary, had sent reinforcements under Ankomah. I explained to him that Nana could not have acted otherwise, as the people, angered beyond control, would have gone anyhow. By making Ankomah responsible that no blood was shed, some restraint was placed on the people, and only eight were seriously wounded and needed to be detained in hospital. It was just a flare-up of tempers in Tanoso. After all, the Ashanti had no right to confiscate the property of the exiled Tanosohene. Unfortunately the District Commissioner was not convinced by my arguments. The Tanoso people had defied authority and Nana had supported them. Moreover when he came to Tanoso he had met three constables of Nana's N.A. police force who were just about to arrest the chief and he would not believe that this had been done without Nana's knowledge.

Nana's popularity grew considerably after the 'battle'. His wisdom was praised by all and earned him the thanks of his much tried people. His prompt visit to Sunyani Hospital to cheer up the three wounded was much commented on and repaid with love.

A Day in the Life of a Divine King

Two days later Ankomah was taken ill with fever; this was rather unfortunate for me because, at ten o'clock in the morning, Nana had called a number of people together to answer all those questions of mine which could not be answered by any one person alone, as the responsibility for divulging information of the type I desired had to be taken collectively. As it happened, something else interfered and the meeting was postponed to the afternoon.

When I arrived punctually at 3.30 the people selected by Nana had already assembled in the audience-courtyard, but the meeting could not begin because some of the princes had not appeared. By 3.45 they still had not come and the Ayokohene, the chief of the royal clan who had charge of the princes, exercised his authority and imposed on each of them a fine of £5, two sheep for sacrifice, and two bottles of rum for libation to the Royal Ancestors. He also demanded that the meeting should be postponed for fifteen days.

Nobody offered any comment on this, but Nana, eager to have the meeting, seeing that so many people had come, suggested that those questions could be answered which did not definitely require the presence of the princes. The elders at once agreed to this; whereupon I was invited to pose my first question. I asked: How did the divine kings of the ancient Bono Kingdom spend their day?

There was a shocked silence; for a time nobody spoke and I felt deeply embarrassed. Then the Ahenemahene got up. He was the chief of the royal sons whose mothers were commoners and who therefore were also commoners. Most of these royal sons served the king in the household (cooks, stewards, cup-bearers etc.) or in the palace (palanquin-bearers, sword-bearers, body-guard etc.). The Ahenemahene, always the eldest royal son of a commoner mother, was the only person who, in the past, was authorized to enter the king's bedroom when the king was there, and the present Ahenemahene was therefore the only person who knew, through the traditions passed on from one Ahenemahene to his successor, what the room of the kings of Bono looked like, the bed in which the king slept and what happened when the king got up.

The Ahenemahene Kwasi Twi, who gave me the information, was a pleasant and intelligent man who knew the traditions well, and without more ado he proceeded to tell me what I wanted to know. I think that most of those present also heard for the first time about this aspect of their historical past, since traditions of this type are kept absolutely secret and are only known to the king, the princes, and the holders of the office concerned. Nana Kwasi Twi spoke as follows:

The king of Bono slept on the top floor of his three-storied palace under a flat roof which was covered with *okro*, a tropical vegetable, which not only made the roof watertight but also symbolized the king's generative force. The window of his room opened to the east to catch the rays of the rising sun, for the kings of Bono, like the Pharaohs of Ancient Egypt, were the sons of the Sun-god. The bed was built like a seven-tiered pyramid, each tier being covered with material of a different colour of the rainbow. The rainbow was envisaged as a ladder by which the sleeping king's *kra* or soul could ascend to his father the Sun-god, and by which the Royal Ancestors who lived with the god could descend to visit the king at night. The counterpane and sheet of the bed were of brocade[1] or yellow silk embroidered with gold, the metal of the sun. The king's mattress and pillows were stuffed with gold dust that would renew his life-giving force while he slept.

The king's reveille was sounded by the Ahenemahene when the sun rose. On reaching the presence of the king the Ahenemahene slipped off his sandals as a sign of respect and three times rang a bell which hung above the bed. He then turned away to avoid the king's first glance, which might be dangerous if the royal ancestral spirits, with whom the king had communed during the night, were still occupying his body. The king would then invite the Ahenemahene to sit down and would ask him what was going on in the capital. After giving the latest news the Ahenemahene might take the opportunity of apologizing on behalf of any of the king's sons who had incurred his displeasure, or of asking favours in their name.

When the king was ready to rise the Ahenemahene again rang the bell three times and a number of men entered the room and threw themselves on the floor, allowing the king, who might never touch the floor with his bare feet, to walk on their naked backs into the ante-chamber. There the king was received by the Adwarefohene, the chief and the attendants in charge of his morning toilet, who made him sit, facing east, on a low stool decorated with solar symbols, his feet on two elephant tusks. The attendants bathed, dried, and perfumed the king with lime juice —limes are yellow like the sun—using a sponge made of the bark of the plantain tree (the plantain is a sexual symbol and alludes to the king's generative force).

When the morning toilet was finished the Asarefohene and his

---

[1] Brocade was imported from the north and came probably from Italy.

attendants entered to grease or oil the king's skin. He was then dressed by the Manwerehene and his attendants who kept the king's wardrobe; the Manwerehene decided what robe the king was to wear on that day and also chose the sandals and gold ornaments. Next the Nsafiesohene and the drink-bearers were called in to offer the king palm wine or other refreshments. Breakfast, a substantial meal, was served in another room on the second floor by the Sodoohene and the stewards; there the jester had to amuse the king. A group of small boys, the sons of nobles on the palace staff, were also present, because a king must always have subjects round his feet. After the meal the king was given a cold water massage and was required to rest.

When the king got up he was carried—that is to say, supported under the arms—to his reception room on the ground floor. There usually awaited him some of the State elders and royal sons in high office, from whom he received information about any political events or developments. The king, being divine, had to lead a secluded life in his palace which he only left once a year to take part in the ritual purification of the State on New Year's Day. The real ruler and king in the eyes of the public was the heir-apparent and co-regent, the head of the State Council; only the final decisions were made by the king. As he himself had usually been an heir-apparent he was well acquainted with state affairs and was therefore able to decide on all matters.

The king's next meal was served to him at four o'clock and was followed by another massage and a rest, after which he was free to amuse himself. Sometimes the princesses or royal daughters would dance before him, their bare arms and bosoms powdered with gold dust; sometimes his young sons would sing to him, or play the lute, or join him in a game of *warri*, played with gold nuggets. On Fridays, the day of rest in the Bono Kingdom, the royal sons whose mothers were of noble birth would ride on white horses into the great courtyard to salute him. Sometimes tournaments were arranged, the participants being armed with spears.

But when the sun sank below the horizon it was time for the king to withdraw. Then, when the golden lamps on their tall golden stands had been lit in his private apartment, one or other of his 3,000 wives would come to him. The wives for the night were chosen by the Odabenhene, guardian of the harem—he was always an elderly prince, grandson of a king and son of a princess. The king was not allowed to have a favourite wife but was expected to sleep if possible with a thousand wives a year.

When the Ahenemahene Kwasi Twi had finished giving me this account, there was a long silence. Then the Korontihene rose to say that in the past, for speaking about these matters, a slave would have been sacrificed to inform the Royal Ancestors in the Upper Kingdom that the disclosure was necessary. Since human sacrifice had been abolished, he proposed to make a libation of six bottles of gin. Nana impassively gave immediate orders for the gin to be brought. When it came the herald called for silence and a bottle was then handed to the Adumfohene, the chief of the executioners of human sacrifices, who poured out half of the contents on to the ground while the Twafohene (formerly the general of the advance guard) said a prayer. The rest was poured into a libation cup to be passed round. The other five bottles were handed to the chief of the stool-bearers who took them into the Chapel of the Stools to pour their contents over the black stools of the Royal Ancestors. Then a violent argument arose among the assembled people; some got so excited that they wept—remembrance of the glory of the past brought home to them the ugly present, with its poverty, humiliation, and possible ruin. I was greatly embarrassed that my inquiry had caused so much pain and had proved so expensive to Nana. I begged to be allowed to pay for the gin, but this he refused.

Nana, annoyed by the uproar, then took my arm and led me into the reception room, leaving the people to quieten down. He ordered beer for me and then put a record on the gramophone, some silly American song long out of fashion. When the music stopped, he started to give me some more information on his Royal Ancestors.

When I returned to the rest-house I thought of the kings of Bono, who had acclaimed me so enthusiastically in the sacred cave five years ago and thus had made all this research possible for me. They were great kings and, from the seventeenth century onwards, obsessed with gold. I learnt from another source that part of their morning etiquette was to dip their hands deep into a bowl filled to the brim with gold dust that was every night fetched from the nearest goldfields[1] by a court official on horseback. Gold, the metal of the sun, was believed to restore to the full the life-giving power of the King's soul (*kra*) on which the State depended. He then went to the 'Golden Tree' before his palace; it was a bare tree-trunk with three branches cut short encased in gold to hold a golden basin of sacred water from the Golden Pool, the source of the Tano River. He sprinkled some of it into the sky and then on himself in order to bless his soul. He thanked the Supreme Being for his good health and prayed for long life and prosperity for himself and his State.

The civilization of the Bono Kingdom was basically a Bronze Age one. This is evident from the political structure of the State, which was a confederation of chiefdoms ruled by a divine king, and from its religion which centred on fertility cults with their dying and rising gods, the Lord of Growth. But the main achievements of the Bronze Age—architecture in stone, writing and the wheel—were lacking.

Architecture in stone was not possible as the country lacked suitable stone. But writing? Bono-Mansu had, almost from its beginning, a twin city, the Songo, exclusively inhabited by Moslems, many of whom were literate. There was also the trade contact with Moslem people in the western Sudan and North Africa. Moreover, Mohammedan influence was strong in Bono, certainly from the sixteenth century onwards. The Queenmother Ameyaa II (1564–6), for instance, married a Moslem, and the Queenmother Aferanowaa (1598–1604) twice married mallams (priests) who certainly knew how to read and write. Her daughter Aferakommaa (1604–10) is reputed to have had many Moslem lovers, especially among the foreign envoys. She was well versed in Islamic matters and did much in her reign to smooth out the quarrels which arose in the palace because so many of the princes

[1] They are said to have been situated NW. from Bono-Mansu near the Twi and Tain Rivers.

and princesses had been converted to Islam. This barred them from the succession, to which they objected, and also from being buried in the royal cemeteries. Nana Ankomaa (1680–1707), the daughter of a converted princess and a Moslem father, had to renounce Islam to become a queenmother.[1]

Why then did the Bono kings and queenmothers never introduce the art of writing into the State as did the kings of other Bronze Age states in the Ancient East and Egypt? One may assume that they had no interest in preserving in writing the records of their history, descriptions of their country, stories or poems and songs for which prizes were offered by them every New Year festival.[2] The preservation of oral traditions was well organized; it was the duty of certain officers who held hereditary posts at court to remember, and on occasion recite correctly, the events of the past: the royal minstrels, for instance, recounted the outstanding events in a king's reign; the *abrafo*, masters of ceremonies in the cult of the Royal Ancestors, proclaimed the warlike exploits of each king; the mortuary priest and custodian of the royal cemetery recalled the personal appearance and character of the dead kings and queenmothers; the royal treasurer preserved the traditions concerning gold (gold mining, Bono's gold dust currency), while the overseer of the great market had to remember all the events connected with the trade with foreign countries. The chief royal spokesman had to know about the land and under which king the clans and sub-clans had acquired it, and so forth. Every Friday since the founding of the kingdom, the royal princes had received instruction in its history from the Ankobeahene, the chief of the royal bodyguard, whose duty it was to be acquainted with it. The priesthood also kept the hymns and songs which had been composed in honour of their deities, and every noble family handed on from generation to generation the story of its origin, the deeds of prominent members and important events in its history.

The animal which represented the Bono Kingdom was the

[1] For the reigns of the Bono Queenmothers see *Ak. of Ghana*, Chapter V.

[2] Though they had pictograms which expressed religious beliefs, *Sacred State*, pp. 198–202.

parrot, a bird that symbolized eloquence. With eloquence or oratory the nation tried to gain its ends, and the passion for oratory may have had something to do with the people's lack of interest in the written word.

Bono's way of living was conventionalized; the behaviour of the people was traditional and uncritical. The habit of experiment did not exist, nor did they engage in reflection for intellectual ends. Their conception of the world prevented it, for the belief in spirits constantly surrounding them—the spirits of the Royal Ancestors and of the greater and lesser gods who dwelt in trees, plants, rivers and hills—blurred the distinction between fantasy and reality. Logical thought was valueless so long as people believed that their very existence depended on the goodwill of these spirits and their power to act as intermediaries between them and the supreme deities. Even Islam when accepted could not oust these beliefs.

The wheel must have been known, at least to the far-travelled Bono traders, and certainly the potter's wheel, which may have been used by some of the foreign Moslems in the capital, would have been familiar to them. It was not generally used, owing no doubt to the power of the queenmothers, who supported their potteresses and the traditional work they produced with their hands. They would never have allowed men to compete with them by using the wheel; moreover, the potteresses, conservative and proud of their craftsmanship, might have rejected it. The cart, two or four-wheeled, was useless in Bono when so many of the roads were sandy and slaves to carry loads were plentiful. The horse was used for general transport; the whole nation rode. Oxen may have been used as draught animals, though nobody seems to remember this in Tekyiman. But it is remembered that pack-oxen were used by Nana's ancestors and their people when they left the eastern Sahara and made their way to the region of Timbuktu, where they settled and founded the Diala State some time before A.D. 800.

Bono's standard of living was high, thanks to the export of gold[1] and the highly priced cola nuts grown in plantations. The

[1] See for gold trade *Sacred State*, pp. 202–6.

Ashanti in the Kumasi region still refer to it with admiration and wonder; slaves, when carrying loads, would use as head-pads material good enough for everyday clothing. Gold, on which the prosperity of the country depended, was mined according to the latest available techniques certainly from the early seventeenth century onwards;[1] the gold mines in the Banda hills, which came into the possession of Bono after the destruction of Bee-Nsoko, are evidence of it.[2]

On account of the Bono people's passionate interest in trade,[3] they had little liking for war, unlike their conquerors, the Ashanti. Bono, at the height of its power, included all the open country between the Black Volta River and the tropical forest, and for a short period extended into the forest which included the Kumasi area. This territory had been acquired for the most part by inducing the small city states and tribes on its frontiers to accept the Bono king as suzerain in exchange for security and the advantages of belonging to a powerful nation. The vassal states retained self-government although their kings or chiefs had to marry royal daughters whose sons succeeded; if they were matrilineally organized their queenmother married royal sons to tie them to the royal house of Bono. An interesting case, which bears witness for Bono's unwarlike character, is that of the ancestors of the present Atebubu people. About 1600, these migrants from the north, most of them probably Tuaregs, settled in an arid and uninhabited part of the Bono Kingdom. The Bono requested them to come to the capital to have their position legalized, but the people refused, not wishing to become subjects of the Bono kings. The Bono could have driven them out or subjugated them by force, but instead granted them the land and

---

[1] King Ati Kwaame (1609–18) is said to have travelled as a prince to the Wangara country in the western Sudan, then one of the richest gold-bearing regions, to study gold-mining techniques.

[2] For the mining of gold see *Sacred State*, pp. 198–202.

[3] Bono's second king, Akumfi Ameyaw I (1328–63), sent Prince Obunumankoma to the Sudan and North Africa to advertise his country's wealth and to study the gold trade. So did the above mentioned Ati Kwaame (see n. 1) and his successor Ameyaw Kurompe (1618–33). The Queenmother Akua Gyamfiwaa (1643–56) when a princess travelled to many courts of Sudanese kings for the same purpose.

guaranteed their independence as long as they lived peaceably and traded with them. This arrangement lasted till the fall of the Bono Kingdom.

The Ashanti could never have conquered Bono if the State had been sound and internally strong, but from about the end of the seventeenth century internal conditions were becoming increasingly unstable. Trade had created a wealthy section among the people, which wanted a voice in the Government, but this the kings and queenmothers were not prepared to give. The result was a growing discontent which the government tried to keep in check with the help of Sakrabundu. Sakrabundu, an antelope god, and originally a sky-fertility deity of the same type as Tano, developed into an evil god, when the priests, foreigners from the Wangara country, unable to secure an important place for their god, had recourse to black magic and the smelling out of witches. In the past, not only in Bono but according to tradition in other Akan states also, such priests were expelled, but Sakrabundu gained the adherence of the kings who hoped to derive advantage from his support; for anyone who was politically unreliable or had become too wealthy and influential could be declared a witch and subjected to the poison ordeal; if he died his wealth was confiscated by the State. Owing to the power of Sakrabundu political reforms were impossible.[1] In the reign of the last king, Sakrabundu had become so murderous that a section of the people supported the Nkoranza chief Baafo Pim who, cherishing a personal grievance, was prepared to oust the dynasty with the help of the Ashanti. Thus Bono was conquered without bloodshed, except for the battle the Tekyiman fought in the circular valley near Assueyi.

Unfortunately for Bono, the Asantehene Opoku Ware believed in the ruthless and forcible exploitation of conquered territories. Bono was divided into a number of vassal states and the heavy taxation levied by successive Ashanti kings reduced the once prosperous state to penury. Large numbers of Bono people moved away to other countries and further emigrations took place after the outbreak of the Tekyiman–Ashanti war in 1877. When the

[1] See *Ak. of Ghana*, pp. 124–5.

British occupied the Bono or Brong States, as they are now called, the country was thinly populated and poor; no traces remained of what had once been a wealthy and highly civilized kingdom.

The Ashanti had always been a military power, interested in warfare rather than trade; such luxury the ruling classes enjoyed was derived from the exploitation of conquered states. Bowdich, who visited Kumasi in 1819 to obtain a trade treaty with Ashanti, wrote:[1] 'They (the Ashanti) are as little commercial as the Romans were in their infancy and the Government would repress rather than contenance the inclination (believing no state can be aggrandized but by conquest) lest their genius for war might be enervated by it, and lest, . . . from the merchants increasing to a body too formidable for their wishes to be resisted, . . . break the spell of their conquests, and undermine their power.'

The excavation of Bono-Mansu, especially of the kings' and queenmothers' palaces, might perhaps give us an idea of Bono's former greatness. It might shed light on an African civilization that may rank with that of ancient Ghana, also founded by Dia (Diagha or Diaka) people from the region of the Niger bend, and thus sharing the same ancestors with the founders of Bono (Diala) and Ashanti (Diara).[2]

The Party in the Rest-house

For a long time I had been interested in beads—especially the stone beads of antiquity which had found their way south from North Africa and the Sahara, as well as ancient glass beads of Phoenician and Venetian origin. I had already been twice to the market to see the bead sellers, venerable-looking old men from Northern Nigeria, who turned out on to their mats old cement bags full to the brim with beads. So far I had managed to get an antique barrel-shaped carnelian, a white alabaster bead cylindrical in shape, and a bead which might have been jade. I was also very interested in the old locally-made beads. Among these

[1] *A Mission to Ashantee*, p. 235.
[2] See 'The Akan and Ghana' in *MAN*, vol. LVII (1957), pp. 86-7.

were the much priced *bota*, *bodom* and *teteaso* beads, whose manufacture was introduced into the Bono Kingdom by the Queenmother Gyaasewaa (1656–79). In order to provide a basis for the study of beads, Nana had been good enough to collect some for me from families in Tekyiman. That day the Queenmother and some of her ladies, who were reputed to know about the subject, were to come to the rest-house to give me information.

The party arrived: the Queenmother, her husband, her two children and their nursemaids, her spokeswoman and four ladies from her council of women. Ankomah had arrived earlier. There were not enough chairs and some of my boxes and suitcases had to be fetched by Santos to seat us all. To get the party going I offered my guests Dutch brandywine and was pleased to see that soon everybody felt at home. When we came to the subject of beads the Queenmother unexpectedly presented me with a necklace, for which Tekyiman-town and the villages in the region had each given a bead. I was overjoyed by the present; nothing could have pleased me more. I looked lovingly at the beads and then inquired from which village each bead had come. I was more interested in that for the moment than in the name of the bead and its origin. As the envelopes in which each bead was enclosed had been kept, Ankomah read out their names.

The beads were of all colours and shapes. Among them was one of my favourites: an opaque blue glass bead, an old one, which might have come from Djenne on the Niger, where this type of bead was first manufactured in western Africa some centuries ago. It is said that originally this bead came from China. There were also six others of the same type but of more recent date, some of them European copies. Their blue was much less beautiful, harder and brighter. Then there was a collection of *bota* and *bodom* beads and one *teteaso* bead, but not from the seventeenth or eighteenth century as the family do not part with them; they are worth their weight in gold. A bead I liked very much, and unfortunately said so, was called 'Love your husband'; my liking it amused everybody. It was of a dull black, cylindrical, but larger round the middle, with a number of uneven yellow circles of which each contained—in fine blue lines on white—a moon symbol.[1]

Then we drank some more brandywine. But when I thought that it was time for work the Queenmother's cheerful spokeswoman got up and started dancing. She was fat, but a most graceful dancer, and she accompanied her dance with a song '*Teteaso man nynnaa nim, Oman Tekyiman, oman dada*'. When she sat down Ankomah translated it to me: '*Teteaso* (the name of the bead) is as old as the State, the Tekyiman State.' The *teteaso* beads, the designs of which vary, are usually long and four-sided, sometimes spherical and always in three or four colours. I had to learn the *teteaso* song, and when I managed it, the spokeswoman sang it again and I had to join in. When we came to the second line, the Queenmother sang the first, and when we reached the third line, her ladies sang the first while the Queenmother sang the second and so on. Then we started all over again, this time accompanied by the dance in which the spokeswoman was joined by some of the other ladies. I tried too, as everybody insisted, but had to drop out. I just could not do it; the African rhythm is almost impossible for a European to learn.

When the dancers sat down again, I made a renewed attempt to do some work, as I understood it, but the spokeswoman cut me short, telling me that there were more songs about beads, for instance the song about the *amankwatia* bead and the *apupuo*. And before I could say anything she started singing: '*Apupuo nsobodie*'—'Creator of water that is used and thrown away. Is that gratitude?' And so we sang and drank and danced till it was dark and the Queenmother suddenly said that the children must be fed and put to bed. Little Kwabena did not want to leave. He had enjoyed himself too, but, with another piece of chocolate, he was persuaded to go. Afua was already asleep in the arms of the Queenmother's husband.

When the Queenmother said good-bye I begged her to tell Nana that, although I had said that I would not accept a present before the return of the nine villages to Tekyiman, I could not refuse a necklace of beads given me by the villages of the State.

[1] See for beads *Sacred State*, pp. 50, 156, 207 and Pls. 95-7.

The mention of the nine villages made the Queenmother sad. For a moment she said nothing. Then she made a short speech referring to the nine villages and the political situation. Her speech—she spoke very well, used as she was to speaking—ended with the plea: 'There was sorrow when I came to the stool. Please do not let sorrow alone be connected with my reign. We put all our trust in you. Do relieve us from all sorrow.'

The Accident of the Chief of the Songo

Kwabena, the little son of the Queenmother, suffered badly from sores on his thighs and legs which I had started to treat with iodine, cleaning them with a solution of Dettol, because I thought that they were mosquito bites which the child had scratched with dirty fingers. But when deep areas of raw flesh remained which would not heal, I consulted the dispenser from Nkoranza when he passed through Tekyiman. The dispenser was certain that Kwabena was suffering from yaws (*frambesia, pian*) and that three injections of penicillin would be enough to cure him. Yaws is a common disease in West Africa. It is caused by a spirochete, somewhat similar to the syphilis bacillus, and is highly contagious; but it is not a venereal disease.

Tekyiman-town still had no dispensary as the Government had withdrawn all grants-in-aid after Nana's suspension from office and Tekyiman could not afford (the estimate for the building alone was £4,500) to build one with two or three rooms for hospital cases. A travelling dispenser therefore still came once weekly on Fridays, to treat the sick in the prison which was cleared of its inmates for the purpose. As it was Friday and I wanted to see how Kwabena was getting on I went to the prison but the dispenser was not there and hardly any patients; they had all rushed to the office in the palace as there had been an accident.

I could hardly get into the small office as it was crowded with people commiserating with the victim of the accident. He was the Chief of the Songo and he was receiving first aid from the dispenser. He had been knocked down by a lorry, but luckily his injuries were slight; the right side of his face was swollen and

87

scratched and he appeared to be suffering from shock, but otherwise he seemed all right.

The old man was quite overwhelmed when I expressed my sympathy and sat down opposite him on a chair. He got up again and again to shake my hand for coming to support him in his plight. I did my best to calm him down and amused him with the few Hausa words I knew, which made him smile but also brought tears to his eyes. But all these pleasantries came to an end when Nana stormed into the room and demanded to see the culprit. The culprit was a young boy who had been crying but was soothed by Ankomah who was now taking his finger-prints, name and address. Nana, full of wrath that his beloved teacher and friend had been hurt, and perhaps also that a commoner had injured a chief, slapped the boy's cheeks right and left, then let his hands fall on the boy's shoulders and spoke to him first harshly then gently, his voice gradually dropping till it was no more than a whisper. He then admonished the boy, saying 'You are young, you must obey your elders; having disobeyed them by trying to drive a car, which you had been forbidden to do, you have caused this accident to happen.' The trembling boy promised everything; whereupon Nana forgave him, and turning to Ankomah dismissed the case. The boy could hardly believe that he was to receive no punishment and the assembled people cheered Nana, deeply impressed by his wisdom and magnanimity.

Nana then turned to the Chief of the Songo, inquiring about his injuries, but the Songohene, still overwhelmed that I had come and stayed to console him, only pointed to me. Nana, who till then had not been aware of my presence, thanked me warmly for having sympathized with his friend. The Chief of the Songo was then led out and taken home in Nana's car. Soon everybody had left and Ankomah and I were alone in the office. He collected the finger-prints of the boy and filled in forms and put them away in the big rickety cupboard in the now silent room. Each time he passed me we looked at each other and smiled without saying a word. And smiling again to each other we left the office together. Ankomah like myself saw the amusing side of things; there was no need to discuss the event, we understood each other perfectly.

The Opening of the Football Club and the first Football Match

Once more I was invited to a dance. This time it was given by
the members of the newly founded football club. I had learnt my
lesson and decided to be late in order not to repeat the mistake I had
made at the N.A. police dance. However, when at half past eight
I had not arrived, Nana, worried, sent his car and a message that
I was to come at once. In this case I ought to have been punctual
because Nana had to open the club before the dance, a fact that
I did not know. Ankomah had once again failed to enlighten me
and to give me proper instructions.

When I arrived in the town I found the streets full of people
and had some difficulty in getting through to the Co-operative
building where the opening ceremony and dance were to take
place. I found Nana seated on the open veranda of the building
which overlooked the 'dance floor'; that is to say, the open
ground before the building which was covered for the occasion
with army ground-sheets. He welcomed me warmly and then
asked me to sit down at a little table next to his. As soon as I had
done so, the brass band played 'God save the King', and Nana
addressed the hundreds of people who stood along the ropes
around the 'dance floor'. Thus the club was opened. Then the
band played a few tunes to give chiefs and elders and members
of the football club an opportunity to leave their tables and greet
me. Nana sent me a tin of cigarettes and some beer so that I could
entertain whom I wished, and the football club made me a present
of a bottle of brandywine. I asked the Offumanhene, who was
sitting between me and Nana, to join my table; I also asked
Ankomah and Kwei, who were regarded as my retinue and, according to custom, should share the beer and the brandywine
given to me.

When the dancing began I sat back thinking with shame of my
behaviour at the N.A. police dance where I 'opened the ball' with
the young teacher and had so scandalized the women. But this
would not have been wrong on this occasion, and I only became
aware of it when Nana expressed his disappointment at my not

dancing. Everybody had told him how beautifully I danced, and now I had not given him the pleasure of seeing for himself. Ankomah thereupon hurriedly fetched the agricultural officer from Wenkyi, the best dancer present and the one with whom I had also danced at the N.A. police dance. But alas, the dance was a blues and the ground most uneven. To dance well was simply impossible. Still the people who had watched us clapped delightedly and Nana was satisfied and begged me from now on to dance every number.

For the next dance, a Highlife, I chose Ankomah as a partner. Unfortunately the band remembered my preference for Highlife and played on and on till I simply could not dance any more. The ground-sheets were laid over grass and stones and proved to be very tiring for the feet. Also, on account of these obstructions, one danced out of time, which, after a while, I found unbearable.

For the next two dances I remained in my seat to rest, as I explained to Nana, who could not understand why I was tired already. Then followed another long Highlife, and then another, and this completely exhausted me; and it was only ten o'clock and the whole night was before me! However, relief came unexpectedly. Suddenly there were thunder and lightning and such a downpour that within minutes the whole 'dance floor' was under water. Everybody ran for shelter. Umbrellas were fetched for me but by the time I reached my car I was wet through and my evening shoes were caked with mud. Thus ended the dance which had started with so much enthusiasm.

On the following afternoon the first football match took place on the new sports ground in front of the Methodist School, Tekyiman versus Konongo. I was invited, of course, and left the rest-house in my car at two o'clock. When I arrived in the little lane which led to the sports ground I found myself behind Nana, whose car had been stopped by Corporal Kusi, one of the N.A. police force (Pl. 9). The brass band was playing 'God save the King' and when Nana's car was waved on, my car moved forward and was also stopped by the Corporal. He saluted me smartly and then gave a sign to the band to play 'God save the King' for me also. I did not quite know how to behave in this situation but thought that I could not go wrong if I saluted military fashion—my right hand at my sun helmet. When the music stopped I flashed a smile to Corporal Kusi, who thereupon ordered a second verse to be played. When at last I arrived at the sports ground I found Nana waiting for me in the so-called car park, so that we could enter together, cheered by the crowds.

Nana and I had hardly seated ourselves—he under one of the larger state umbrellas, I under a smaller one—when the brass band started to play 'God save the King' once more. Then the game began. The team from Konongo, a mining town in eastern Ashanti, wore faded blue shorts and grey jerseys, while the Tekyiman wore brand-new uniforms—white shorts with green stripes at the sides and green shirts with red collars and lapels. Since the Konongo were for the most part Ashanti, the Tekyiman fought them with terrific passion and every gain made by the Tekyiman was greeted with tremendous cheers by the people who surrounded the playing-field. The Offumanhene, whom I had asked to sit at my table, an experienced footballer himself—he had learnt the game in the streets of Accra before he became a chief—explained to me what went on, as my knowledge of football was nil. Ankomah, who followed the game excitedly, interpreted. Once he ran away from us, and following the example of others, threw two shillings to a footballer who had scored a goal. The Tanosohene, the third at my table, showed equal interest. Only Nana, alone under his umbrella, seemed bored. He chewed cola-nuts or smoked; he did not even listen to what we were saying. By six o'clock the game was over; Tekyiman had beaten Konongo.

While the victorious Tekyiman were carried off the field and cheered as heroes by the people, Nana gathered the beaten foe around him and gave them an address. His speech was fairly long and vibrated with feeling. He told them not to mind the defeat and not to be bitter about it; after all they had been at a disadvantage. Whereas his own people had rested and eaten well before the game, they had travelled and, as it happened, had arrived in Tekyiman only an hour before the match. This was not fair and he, Nana, hoped that soon they would return to Tekyiman for another fight, but this time as his guests, when he would see that they were well fed and rested before the match. The Konongo, much cheered by Nana's speech, thanked him with shining eyes and accompanied him to his car cheering. Walking next to Nana I asked him why he had not addressed his own team and congratulated them on the victory. Nana, much surprised, replied: 'Why, they have done their duty!'

CHAPTER III

November

The Purification Ceremony at Forikrom

It was the season of spring festivals (*Apo*) which celebrated the death and rising of the gods, the Lords of Growth, so that they could give renewed life to the earth. I had witnessed such a festival at Bonkwae, Okyeame Pong's village, and at Kuntunso. Now it was the turn of Forikrom, a village on the Nkoranza road four miles from Tekyiman. There the chief, the Forikromhene Kwaku Agyepon (Pl. 18), one of Nana's important State elders, celebrated the rebirth of the god Baako, the patron god of his lands. Unfortunately I came too late for the ceremony, but was told all about it.

From early morning onwards men, women and children of Forikrom and the outlying farms had thronged round the large brass basin in the street before the chief's house to rub their naked bodies with Baako's medicine, which had been produced by boiling in holy water hundreds of different roots and herbs. The medicine was believed by the people to cleanse them from all evil and to give them strength, and in olden days had protected the warriors from bullets and sword cuts. In the medicine there was the activity of the renewed power of the god who had died and had been reborn to the mother goddess.

By the time I arrived Baako's shrine (consisting of two calabashes in which some objects packed in leaves were visible—two calabashes because one was the shrine for his male life-giving soul, the other for his female life-giving soul) had been taken back to the sanctuary. It had been paraded through the streets. I was asked, however, to pay a visit to the deity and entered the sanctuary with Baako's priest. As Baako's worshippers have to approach him naked, the priest standing next to me let his trousers down and took off his shirt; I, luckily, was exempted from the rule. Then he reverently looked at the shrines and explained to me in broken English the powers of the god.

The next afternoon I returned to Forikrom to take part in the *Asubo* ceremony, a yearly purification rite for the Forikromhene and the Forikromhemmaa and their ancestors represented by the stools, the shrines for their souls. I was late because Ankomah was unable to come at the last moment and I had to wait till Nana found another interpreter for me, the treasury clerk, Mr. Ampomah. The Chief was already seated in his palanquin when we arrived, and the procession was ready to go to Baako's sacred stream. As the rite was secret Mr. Ampomah was not allowed to come with me and, seeing that nobody assigned a place to me, I walked next to the Chief.

Soon the executioners of human sacrifices, who in the past killed the people who had to go with the chiefly ancestors to heaven, went into trances and started to dance around me, brandishing their swords, while the Chief's gun-bearers shot wildly into the air from their old Dane guns. I did not feel very comfortable, and moved up to the stool-bearers who carried the stools, the shrines of the chief's predecessors. The priestesses who accompanied them were by that time also in a trance, and when they espied me embraced me so violently that I almost lost my balance. I then decided to join the Forikromhemmaa and her ladies ⌐† the head of the procession. To my great joy I found there the Tuobodomhemmaa and the Offumanhemmaa who greeted me affectionately without leaving the single file. As I still had no special place assigned to me I soon found myself walking all over the place, for the sword-bearers, gun-bearers, executioners, priests and priestesses all wished to perform dances in my honour, which caused me to stop to witness their antics.

Finally we arrived at the sacred grove where the Forikromhene had to leave his palanquin and walk on foot, under his big umbrella, to the sacred stream. There the procession split up, the women remained near the bank of the stream, the men walked a bit farther away to a place closely surrounded by trees. I was asked by the Chief to come with him. Chairs were put down for us and his elders, and the remaining retinue grouped themselves around us in a semi-circle according to rank. Before us in a row sat the stool-bearers with the sacred stools of the chief's ancestors. Then one of the elders and the chief stool-bearer went to the stream and uprooted some *summe* plants (their snow-white cone-shaped flowers on long slender stalks are symbols of the mother goddess). They were dipped in the sacred water and then carried back to us. The stools were uncovered on one corner only, sprinkled with the water thus purified, blessed, and then covered up again. Then the Forikromhene and I were sprinkled with the holy water and I got an extra blessing from an old priestess, who, kneeling before me with her arms round my legs, said a long prayer, calling the gods to grant me long life. When everybody else had been purified and blessed, we got up and joined the ladies who had already formed themselves into a procession. The same rites had been performed over the stools of the deceased queenmothers. The offerings for the god Baako which the women carried with them had also been blessed and purified.

When we reached the place where the Forikromhene had left his palanquin he performed a ceremonial dance in honour of his ancestors before he sat down in it again. He danced gracefully and looked handsome in his white cloth, the gold ornaments on his headband glittering as he turned. The procession waited. Then, when he was seated in the palanquin and lifted up, the large *fontomfrom* drums behind him began to boom, the gun-bearers fired again in all directions into the sky, and the people shouted '*Asubo, Asubo*' (cleansed, cleansed). The village people far away responded with rejoicings.

This time I walked next to an elder who explained the rite to me. Suddenly it began to rain, a good omen, and a chief called me to come under his big umbrella in order not to get wet. He then excused himself, as, for some reason or other, we could not both walk under the same umbrella. I, horrified, wished to leave again, as it was against all rules for a chief in a ceremony to walk without his sign of rank. He laughed; and before I could say more, disappeared from view. I walked on in his place, enjoying my impersonation of a chief, my head held high, but in a second all the gun-bearers, sword-bearers, and executioners crowded around me, and hell was let loose. They performed a war dance in my honour. Their drummers drummed in a frenzy; executioner women with knives between their teeth passed me, and the white-faced priestesses fell into trances. I only saw their faces bobbing up among the brandished swords and the flashes of the guns. I was glad when we reached the village and the Forikromhemmaa's ladies got hold of me and led me into the Chief's house, to the *pato*, an open-walled room from which I could watch the stools being carried into the stool-house opposite. There the Forikromhemmaa supervised the cooking of the ceremonial food offerings to her ancestors on the stool and the Chief's ancestors. From time to time she joined me to tell me what went on in the stool-house as I was not permitted to enter it.

When it became dark and a thunderstorm threatened I begged to leave, although the rites had not been completed. I thanked the Forikromhemmaa and the Forikromhene for having allowed me to take part in the *Asubo* ceremony, and also said good-bye to the Tuobodomhemmaa and the Offumanhemmaa and all the assembled village elders. I was still on the road when the storm broke, lightning lit up the sky continuously, the thunder deafening.

The Birth of a God

Passing the palace early next morning I saw Nana standing before it all alone. I got out of my car to greet him and talk to him. He was pleased to see me and said that he was waiting for Ayerttey to drive him to Akrofrom (a village on the Wenkyi road, six miles from Tekyiman) to witness there the birth of a god.

I must have looked puzzled for he explained to me that a priest had recently been possessed by the spirit of a god, who wished to be worshipped on earth and have a shrine at Akrofrom. But the god's spirit had first to be called down from the sky by the priest, an event which had been predicted to take place on Friday or Saturday. Today was Tuesday, but in order to give status to the priest and to show the people that the new god was welcome in the state, he had to go to Akrofrom. Nana then expressed the wish that I should be present at the great event and said that he would send a message in due course.

The message came early on Friday morning. It was a beautiful morning, ideal for the birth of a god. I set out at once for Akrofrom. I found Nana in the courtyard of the house belonging to the Gyaasehene Yaw Atoa who was also the chief of Akrofrom; it was thronged with people. Nana sat on the raised platform of one of those three-walled rooms, so characteristic of Akan houses, opposite the entrance door. He was surrounded by the village elders and some of the State elders. Somebody made room for me so that I could sit down next to him. Nana at once informed me that a nearby house belonging to the spokesman of the Gyaasehene had been evacuated so that I could go there when I was tired; he said that he knew that I got tired soon and usually left festivals before their conclusion. I thanked him warmly for his consideration and promised that I would stay in Akrofrom as long as he wished.

Then I looked round and waited for things to happen. Some priestesses, deep in a trance, danced in a corner, but nobody paid much attention to them. Among them was one of the priestesses who so passionately embraced me at Forikrom. When she espied me she made her way through the crowd and threw herself on the ground before me. When she got up she seemed dazed, only the whites of her eyes could be seen and she trembled all over. Suddenly, as if she had only now become aware of my presence, she bent forward and embraced me gently and, to my embarrassment, seated herself on my lap—a great honour. Then she slid down and, embracing my legs, muttered something, probably the prayer for long life. Then she left me, only to return, hurling herself violently against me. To soothe her I caressed her naked back. In the end she left and disappeared in the crowd.

As time passed Nana became noticeably impatient and openly showed that he was in a bad mood. After another quarter of an hour, he imperiously ordered the priest, who was to give birth to the god, to show himself.

G 97

November

Immediately the priest entered the courtyard followed by two of his spokesmen. There was a dead silence while he slowly walked towards Nana with downcast eyes. I did not know what I had expected to see but certainly not this man of sorrows, haggard from long fastings and visibly in pain under the strain of the heavy objects which hung from his head and the back of his neck. These were largely *nkotoba*, the clubs of authority of the gods, of the same type as those of Buruma at Bonkwae (p. 67), and knives and daggers. A python skin crowned his head, a knife shaft covered his nose and one framed his face on each side, which gave the effect of a medieval helmet. In his right hand the priest held a spear, in the left a spear and a dagger. He was dressed in a long white tunic and a short white skirt; his feet were bare (Pl. 22).

The spears, knives and daggers symbolized his god as a giver of life and death, the *nkotoba* his power to kill transgressors, above all witches, and in war, the enemy. The python skin was the symbol of the god's annual renewal. The Akan gods of this type, called *obosom*, of which there are scores, are believed to be the sons of the Supreme Being and act as intermediaries and deputies of the deity. They are the 'little gods' but each is treated in daily practice as though he were omnipotent, omniscient and omnipresent.

When the priest had reached the middle of the courtyard he stopped timidly. He was afraid to go closer to Nana and with good reason, because Nana was angry and showed his displeasure; he bluntly told the priest that it was a disgrace that the spirit of the god had not yet been caught and if he could not produce the god soon, he had better leave it altogether. He (Nana) had state affairs to see to and could not waste more time on him. The priest trembled and muttered something to his spokesmen, who then informed Nana that if the event did not take place today, it would certainly take place next Friday. Nana replied curtly that he would not wait and would be returning today to Tekyiman.

The Gyaasehene, much disturbed, and the village elders begged Nana that the villagers might be permitted to assist the priest for another week with drumming, dances and sacrifices.

Nana then exempted them from work on the farms for that week. But he told the priest that if the god was not born next Friday, he would have to go into exile in the bush, where the spirit of the god evidently was, and remain there. The priest hung his head meekly and with downcast eyes left the courtyard, while the Gyaasehene ordered drinks for his guests. When they had all settled down to a party I begged Nana's leave to go and rest in 'my house'. This was granted, but before I reached the house with Ankomah, I was accosted by a messenger from the priest and asked to come and see the new house for the god. As I was anxious to see it, Ankomah and I followed the messenger across the road to the sanctuary.

The house proved to be an uncommonly large and well-built hut with a conical thatched roof which almost reached to the ground—the ancient way of building a sanctuary. The hut inside was whitewashed and clean. The only furniture so far was an iron rack on which lay a large assortment of daggers, knives, spears and *nkotoba*. In a corner, on the floor, was a large lion skin, covered with a leopard skin and a fine python skin. It was the bed of the priest, who had to sleep on these skins because it was believed that they helped him to get hold of the spirit of the god. A number of empty gin bottles stood forlornly in groups; gin helped the priest to remain in a state of trance.

After I had expressed my pleasure at the fine building, the spokesman of the priest told me proudly that the hut and the maintenance of the priest had so far cost £300. This made me angry, for I had thought that the hut had been built by the voluntary work of the villagers. I asked Ankomah why this large sum of money had not been spent on a school or a dispensary instead of a god, of which Tekyiman had more than enough. Ankomah gently replied: 'Do you not see, the village will get all that and more through the god, if he proves to be powerful? For he will heal the sick and punish the witches and his fame will travel, and many people from all over the Gold Coast will come to be treated by the priest and will spend their money here. And then a school or a dispensary can be built and many fine houses all round.' (As it happened Ankomah was right;

99

within six months the god proved to have been a first-class investment.)

Outside the hut I met the priest, whom I did not recognize at first as he had divested himself of his elaborate head-dress. He stood there, his right hand on his hip, ill at ease and grinning sheepishly. He looked so obviously a case for the psychiatrist; there was no humility about him, no true religious feeling. He was out for power and money to compensate an inferiority complex which was very evident. However, I gave him my hand and wished him luck. He eagerly told me that he would try again soon and that when I heard three shots, I should come at once, for then the time for the birth had come and he showed me the 'magic' circle in which the spirit of the god would be caught (Pl. 23). I promised him that I would not fail him and once more wished him luck and success.

I then walked back with Ankomah to 'my house'. It was large and roomy, and I sat down in the courtyard where I found some chairs. I was about to take out my thermos flask of water when one of Nana's attendants appeared with a bottle of rubywine, beer and cigarettes. They were very welcome. Shortly afterwards Kwei dropped in with a glass of gin in his hand and a bottle of beer under his arm, also gifts from Nana. I asked him to sit down and join me and Ankomah; later a N.A. constable arrived and also one of the Tano priests, so we had quite a party.

The last two were ex-servicemen who like Kwei had served in Burma where they had fought with an anti-tank regiment and a trench mortar unit. His war experiences had made the Tano priest crazy, but he talked sanely enough about the towns he had seen—Cape Town, Durban, Bombay, Calcutta and Rangoon. The constable told of tiger hunts, and how the regiment lost fifteen Nigerians who thought that tigers were not more dangerous than leopards, and were eaten by them. Both had been shocked by the behaviour of some of their British officers who had slept with Burmese women. Africans, in general, tabu sexual intercourse during war, and only after elaborate purification ceremonies after the war are they allowed again to come near women. The women of the enemy were therefore in the past safe from rape, but not from torture, the outlet for the frustrated sex urge. The various Akan peoples who fought the Ashanti still tell with horror what the Ashanti warriors had done to their womenfolk in the last century before the British occupation.

While we were sitting we suddenly heard three shots ring out—the birth of the god. We rushed out across the road but we only found the priest in his full outfit dancing in the open space before the sanctuary, while the women sang and accompanied themselves on their rattles. After a while the villagers, who wished to induce the god's spirit to leave the sky, formed themselves into a circle and danced. After an hour or so I had enough —and besides it was lunch-time. I asked the priest, who sat resting before his hut, whether I could go back to 'my house' without missing anything, whereupon he grandly replied that he would postpone the calling down of the god until my return. So I went with Ankomah and Kwei to the house to eat the pigeon which the chief of the Songo had given me the day before and which Santos had cooked for me.

When we returned after lunch nothing had changed. The people were still dancing; I remained only a short time because Ankomah was called away on a police case to the neighbouring Aworowa and, bored, I went back with Kwei to the house. Ankomah to my relief came an hour later, accompanied by one of his N.A. constables and a prisoner. We all sat down to finish the rubywine and smoked; except the prisoner, who stood in a corner and watched us mournfully. I was sorry for him and wanted to give him a drink and a cigarette, but Ankomah was of the opinion that he should calm down first and if he behaved well I could do so later. After five minutes I could bear the prisoner's longing eyes no longer and so Ankomah gave him a drink and a cigarette which cheered him greatly. When we had all finished Ankomah called him for interrogation. His crime had been making love to a married woman. The prisoner, a young Ashanti trader, was passing through Aworowa when a pretty woman made advances to him. He had no idea that she was married, and the husband, who had been warned by a friend, had caught them in the act. Then the enraged husband and half a dozen of his friends gave him a beating, and the police were called and took the young man into custody.

To Ankomah this was a familiar story, for the only type of crime Tekyiman was permitted to deal with was adultery. All other criminal offences went to Wenkyi and were judged by the District Commissioner. Tekyiman gaol was only a room in the old office of the palace and adulterers remained there till they had paid a fine, and the unfaithful wife a pacification fee to her husband.

When Ankomah had finished with the prisoner I asked whether I could ask the culprit a question. Ankomah agreed, and turning to the unfortunate man I inquired: 'Did you not know that there is a war between Tekyiman and Ashanti?' The prisoner, of course, had never heard of the cold war between the two states, and he now understood why the beating he received had been so enthusiastically performed by the husband and his friends. As he now showed fear Ankomah told him that he would enjoy police protection until he was safely on a lorry bound for Kumasi.

The N.A. constable then took the man away to Tekyiman gaol, while Ankomah, Kwei and I went back again to the dancing people and their priest to see whether anything had been achieved during our absence. But nothing had happened. The priest, his face now whitened with clay, danced rather forlornly before a crowd without his cumbersome outfit of skin, knives and *nkotoba*. He was a poor dancer, there was no life in him; perhaps he was exhausted from weeks of fasting and trances.

When I sat down on a chair the high priest of Taa Kese arrived, accompanied by his retinue, his drummers, and the priest of Kuntunso. Nana Kofi Mosi was in high spirits and full of his characteristic swashbuckling gracefulness. He looked more handsome than ever, and handled his long flowing robes with great elegance. He sat down; but seeing the pitiful efforts of the dancing priest he got up again and did a few dance steps as if to show him how it ought to be done. The manner in which he did it showed plainly how much he despised the priest, who in his eyes was an upstart, whereas he, the High-priest, was of the ancient Fante royal lineage and successor to a long line of successful high-priests. He and the priest of Kuntunso then took the priest between them and escorted him to his hut almost as if he were a prisoner.

Meanwhile the women decided to do some dancing but did so only half-heartedly. The priestess who had so violently hurled herself at me in the Gyaasehene's house was among them and, when she saw me, left the women and ran towards me. She embraced me passionately and then seated herself on my lap. Unfortunately she behaved most amorously; quite openly making love to me; this outraged the people and some men literally tore her away from me. They would never have dared to do so had she been in a trance. I was glad when Nana Kofi Mosi returned and sat down two chairs away from me. The priest, who had followed him, was now dressed again in all his paraphernalia and had a lion skin wrapped round his body. He started to dance again but in the same lifeless manner as before.

After a while everybody got bored. There was no sign that the god would be born, and people openly began to show that they were wearied. The drummers, taking the cue, now changed the rhythm, and the drums were beating out 'I am tired, I am tired'. As everybody understood drum language, there was much laughter: the only villagers who remained silent were financially interested in the birth of their god. Taa Kese's High-priest, who could not allow fun to be made of the priesthood, got up to leave and with him the priest of Kuntunso and their followers. For a moment Nana Kofi Mosi stopped. A plane crossed the sky high above. Everybody looked up as if this silvery bird could be a sign from heaven, but there was no message, nothing fell from the sky, everybody was disappointed.

When the High-priest had left, nobody quite knew what to do next. The drummers had ceased to play and the priest stood where he had been left. Then suddenly new life sprang up. A priest from Krobo became possessed by his god and flung himself into the open space to dance. First he stamped the ground and snorted like a horse. Then inhuman cries came from his throat. Slowly he started to gyrate, then he turned faster and faster, and finally he spun round with terrifying speed like an elemental force. He described a wide circle with great strides, fantastic leaps into the air, and gyrations. The drummers, captivated, accompanied him with vehemence, everybody was spellbound, all eyes followed him. He was like a comet in the night sky. It was the grandest dance I had ever seen; only religious fervour could have produced it.

Gradually the priest's movements became slower, then suddenly he reeled and with outstretched arms fell on the thatched roof of an unused hut near by. People ran towards him to support him under the arms. The agony in his face when he slowly came round was horrible to watch. He had burnt himself out. What was left was the wreck of a human being, haggard, hollow-eyed, the face a ghastly colour. He was too weak to walk unaided and was dragged away almost lifeless, his arms still stiffly outstretched.

Ankomah, Kwei and I silently returned to 'my house'. Just as we reached it, one of Nana's important chiefs, accompanied by his retinue, came from the other side and, obviously delighted to see me, stopped me to have a chat. In the course of the conversation he told me that he loved me and wished to marry me. If I would only say 'yes' he would go at once to Nana and give him a hundred pounds to act as my father and give me away. I declined the offer and told him that I had been married once and I never wished to marry again. But he would not take 'no' for an answer and insisted that I needed to be married, to have somebody to look after me and he could do all this so well. He would take great care of me and build a fine house for me. I shook my head and said that I loved my independence and got all the care I needed from my cook. Besides a house was no interest to me as I loved travelling. But he continued to press his case and repeated over and over again that a woman must be happy and to be happy she needed a man, and he was that man. Finally, exasperated, I turned to Ankomah and asked him 'What does a Tekyiman girl or woman say, if she does not want a man? Tell him that and then let's go.' Ankomah at once and without looking at me said something rapidly. For a moment everybody was thunderstruck, then the chief howled with dismay and his whole retinue collapsed with laughter. They laughed and laughed. I had never seen anything like it. The sword-bearers, the umbrella-bearer, all the attendants stood upright one moment; then they bent down to slap their knees, and repeated this over and over again, laughing and laughing; looking at them reminded me of pocket-knives, open, closed, open, closed. The chief, as bewildered as I was, incredulously looked at me, and feeling sorry for him, I offered him my hand and said: 'Friends, we can be friends.' As he understood a bit of English, he accepted at once: 'Yes, friends, friends,' and then, while he kept my hand in his, looked round proudly and full of dignity. His retinue quickly adjusted itself to the new situation, and put on serious faces and stood to attention.

When the chief had left I asked Ankomah 'What did you say?' Ankomah said that he was sorry but he could not possibly translate, even if he knew the English words, which he did not. From this reply and the behaviour of the chief's retinue I had to deduce that it must have been something saucy. I scolded Ankomah, but what was the use? I had asked him to get rid of the chief. I would of course have liked to know what he had said; from the anthropological point of view, I was sure, it was most illuminating, and I regretted that this piece of knowledge was withheld from me. Incidentally, Ankomah's reply and the chief's marriage offer had unexpected results at a later date when Nana heard of it.

When evening came and the spirit of the god had still not been caught by the priest, I went to call on Nana, who still sat drinking with the village elders in the Gyaasehene's house. I wanted to know whether he expected me to stay the night, for in that case I would have to return to Tekyiman to fetch my camp-bed with the indispensable mosquito-net, my bath-tub, and Santos to cook my accustomed food. Nana, who understood very well that I did not wish to remain, gave me leave to return to Tekyiman and spend the night there, although he was sorry, as the priest had told him only five minutes before that the god would be born at midnight.

It was just as well I left, for the god was not born that night, nor the following Friday or Saturday. It took the priest many more weeks and a whole month's assistance by Taa Kese's High-priest, who daily went to Akrofrom. I never learnt what took place when the great moment arrived and Dimankoma came to earth. In the olden days a priest would catch a blinding flash of lightning in a brass pan placed under a tree round which a circle was drawn. Heavenly fire alone is life-giving and divine; the soul (*kra*) and spirit of the gods are fire. On this occasion, however, I suspect that the heavenly fire was one of Messrs. Brock's fireworks! This kind of fraud, imposed on credulous believers, is quite common nowadays; the priest, after the fire has descended from the sky and the smoke has cleared, generally finds in the brass pan a palpable object, the size of a fist, sometimes covered with gold leaf. I was put wise to their tricks by Dr. M. J. Field, the author of *Search for Security* and other books. This is placed in a little shrine or receptacle shaped like a drum which is then taken to the sanctuary. In the case of Dimankoma there were two such drum-shaped shrines, one for his male and the other for his female *kra*. The male was covered with a lion skin in recognition of his solar powers (the lion is the symbol of the sun); the female was covered with a leopard skin in recognition of her powers of giving rain so that the crops could grow (the leopard is the symbol of rain and the lighting and thunder which often accompany the heavy rains).

Dimankoma is the name of a great Akan god (Damankoma, in Ashanti Odomankoma), who created the world. It shows the megalomania of the priest of Akrofrom that he called a minor deity—a 'little god'—by that name.

Meeting the Executioners of Human Sacrifices

One afternoon the Adumfohene Kofi Fofie, the chief of the executioners of human sacrifices, and his brother the Abrafohene Kodjo Adyaye, followed by two young assistants, came to see me in the rest-house to answer questions about their profession. They had permission from Nana to do so or they would not have talked, and it would have been impossible for me to get their ideas on the subject.

The Adumfohene, to my surprise, was a mild and kindly old man with nothing bloodthirsty or ferocious about him. On the

contrary, his whole manner suggested the gentleman. I was therefore somewhat shocked, not that he had killed so many in his
lifetime, but to hear that he liked his profession. He assured me
that there was nothing horrifying about this, because people died
for their own good. After all, life in heaven was much better
than, or at least as good as, life on earth and, thanks to his great
skill, the transit between life on earth and eternal life was very
short indeed.

Among the Akan, human sacrifice was largely connected with
the life of the kings and queenmothers in the Other World. There
life was thought to be much the same as on earth, except that
there was no unpleasantness, no war, no quarrels. The dead
kings went to live in the city of the god Nyankopon on the sun,
the dead queenmothers joined their clan's goddess on the moon.
There they reigned as on earth; it was their duty to continue to
give 'life' to the people of their State. This they did on the one
hand by helping the Sun-god and the Moon-goddess to shoot the
life-giving rays of the sun and moon to earth, so that the crops
should grow on which all life depends, and on the other, by
acting as intermediaries between their people and the deities, so
that they might receive support in times of need.

A king or queenmother cannot reign without a court and personal servants; and for this reason many of the people who surrounded them on earth had to follow them into the Other World.
Apart from slaves and prisoners of war, who were sacrificed to
swell their retinue, most went of their own free will. In the case
of the king, his most beloved son and daughter, many of his wives
and his 'official friend', as well as some of his ministers and
chiefs, voluntarily suffered sacrifice. The palace personnel—
cooks, stewards, cup-bearers and so on, each gave one member of
their group so that the king might be well served in his new
abode. In the case of the queenmother her husband had to follow
her as well as her 'official friend' and those women elders who had
loved her dearly. Slaves and prisoners of war, and above all,
those criminals she had pardoned on account of their beauty,
were also sacrificed to make her happy.

I noted all these beliefs and customs with which I had been

familiar as there was no secret about them. What I really wanted to know and did not dare to ask was, when did he last kill a human victim for sacrifice? Human sacrifice had been abolished by the British Government in 1901; but the custom still persisted secretly in many regions. The Kibi murder is a case in point. It greatly excited England in 1946. I came to know of another sacrificial murder which also took place in 1946. At that time I was in Kumasi, and in bed with malaria, but in order to go on with my work I sent Kofi Antubam, who was then with me, to the house of an important Ashanti chief to make an appointment for me in the following week, meanwhile acquainting him with the nature of my work.

When Kofi came to the house of the chief he was told that the chief was dead and had been buried the previous day. All the ancient customs had been performed in secret so that the Government did not hear that human sacrifice had taken place. The next day, Kofi was assured, a slave descendant resembling the chief would take his place on the bier and await a Christian burial in the presence of Government officials who were bound to come to honour the dead. The substitute had already been killed and his body prepared to lie in state. Kofi was invited to see the corpse.

Apart from the voluntary victims who had followed the Ashanti chief (probably none in 1946) there had also been others to ensure his well-being in the beyond. These were mostly people from the north who had come to find work in Kumasi and were unaware that the custom still existed to some extent in 1946. They were waylaid at night on the roads and murdered by the executioners. Their heads were cut off, put into bags and covered with cocoa beans, and as 'cocoa' were transported on lorries to Kumasi. At a later stage the heads were buried with the chief.

After a lull in the conversation, the Adumfohene asked whether I would like to see *how* it was done. I agreed reluctantly, and the chief poured out a libation and then dipped the point of his long executioner's sword into the gin remaining in his glass. He then pounced with great suddenness on one of his young assistants and, standing behind him, forced his head down. Then he lifted the sword. Luckily he did not forget himself but, at the last moment, reduced the force of the blow so that the sword landed gently on the young man's neck. He then showed me the exact spot where the sword had to cut through to sever the head from the body.

Then the old man sat down again and was sad because he had spoken to me about these things. All the executioners would now have to fast for a day to atone for this fault. I was sorry to hear it and expressed my sympathy, but he assured me that I need not be concerned because, after all, seeing that times had changed, it was a good thing to preserve the custom at least in a book so that future generations should know the truth. Then he pointed to his brother, the Abrafohene, who would succeed him after his death. He was the chief of the *abrafo*, the masters of ceremony among the *adumfo*. They were all minstrels who sang the praises of the deceased kings. But the Abrafohene alone had the right to choose the last victim at the royal funeral ceremonies. There were also women executioners who killed women with leather thongs. These were the royal wives and daughters who wished to follow their lord. At funeral ceremonies women executioners often went into trances and, like the priestesses, their persons were sacred. Nobody was allowed to touch them, even when, with knives between their teeth, they became dangerous.

The Adumfohene also gave me detailed information on the crimes which in olden days were punished with death. Princes of the royal lineage did not die by the sword nor by the leather thong, nor were they kept to be sacrificed at royal funerals; a stick with a sharp point was rammed down their throat. The death of a lover of a royal wife was also effected by the executioners; such victims were killed, after the most terrible tortures, by being seated on a keg of gunpowder and blown up.

Ordinary criminals were executed once a year at the New Year festival in autumn to which they were invited. They were seated in two rows opposite each other, their legs fastened to logs. One half would be given poisonous food to eat without their knowing it. Then, when they were merry with food and drink, they were led away to a place in the bush where they were left to die. The others were taken back to their prisons to die when a king or queenmother, or a prince or princess in the line of succession, went to heaven.

Next morning I paid a visit to the Nifahene Yao Nwim, one of Nana's important State elders, for it was the day on which he, as Chief of the Aduana clan, propitiated his ancestors, his predecessors on the stool. The office is hereditary. People from all over the place came to greet him and many brought him gifts.

When I arrived with Ankomah he sat among his visitors drinking. But seeing that it was not the custom for women to drink in the company of men, he drew me and Ankomah aside to chat with me in a corner of his courtyard. Among other things I told him of the visit of the Adumfohene Kofi Fofie the previous afternoon and how he had shown me how victims were despatched. The Nifahene looked at me, and after a pause, said: 'In olden days you would have been among the first to go after Nana's death.' 'I,' I said taken aback, 'Why me?' 'Because everybody knows that Nana loves you; and if you did not go with him after his death and accompany him on his way to heaven, he would be worrying why you are not coming. He would look back and be unhappy, and it is not proper for a king to be unhappy when he is about to join the Royal Ancestors in heaven.'

I at once protested and said that Nana did not love me as much as this, but the Nifahene assured me that Nana's love for me was great. Ankomah also said so and, to dispel all doubts on my part, added that it was Nana's love for me that made so many men in the State tell me of their love and that they wished to marry me. (Ah, I thought, so it was not my sex appeal but Nana's love. How vain a woman can be!) Then I asked Ankomah: 'But surely the men have some liberty to love whom they please?' 'No,' said Ankomah, 'If Nana loves you in his great wisdom then we all have to follow him. Besides we can all see that he is right.'

I was surprised that Nana was still regarded by his people as a divine king, with whom the men had to identify themselves. At the same time I realized that my place in the State was really that of an *Oheneaso*, which means literally 'ear of the king'. Ankomah translated the term as 'official friend' of the king, for this he is.

November

The Ancient Egyptians, who had the same institution, called the *Oheneaso* 'Unique Friend'. In many tomb inscriptions a courtier or official of the Pharaoh prided himself on having been a 'Unique Friend' of the ruler. Possibly he died by his own hand after the death of his royal friend, for the ancient Egyptians imagined their heaven in the same way as do the Akan. The Pharaohs also went to live with their Royal Ancestors on the sun and, as sons of the Sun-god, sent the life-giving solar rays to earth.

The Akan 'Unique Friend' might be any person a king had chosen to be officially his friend. He alone had the right to criticize the king openly and reproach him for actions which he did not consider right. But after the king's death he had to go with him to the Other World.

It was not the first time that I had held this office. While I was in Kumasi in 1944 I sometimes visited the late Queenmother of Ashanti, Nana Kwadu Yiadom, who greatly helped me with my work by giving me valuable information on various matters. She must have taken a great liking to me, for one day she asked me whether I would accept the post of 'official friend'. Not knowing anything about it and thinking that she only wished to have my advice, I accepted, deeply flattered. Kofi Antubam, who had been interpreting for me, giggled after we had left her, and asked me whether I knew that I had signed my life away, seeing that the Queenmother was an old woman. For if she died I should have to go with her, otherwise I would lose face with her people. I was horrified. As it happened, the Queenmother died a year later. I was in England at the time, which was a great relief to me. But on my return to Kumasi in 1946 I took part, as the guest of the Asantehene, Nana Prempeh II, in the funeral rites performed for her on the anniversary of her death. (By that time, being much favoured by the new Queenmother, I was quite safe, I thought.)

Ankomah and I were silent when we returned, and I wondered what his views were on the subject. I knew that the old custom was dead and I would never be placed in the position of having to decide whether I would or would not go. All the same, Nana was very much loved by his people, and they would certainly like to see him happy if he had to go to the Other World. I looked at Ankomah, but refrained from asking him any questions. After all Nana was in splendid health and the question could be dealt with when the occasion arose.

The Death of a Prince

November 7th. When I came to town that morning Ankomah was anxiously waiting for me at the corner of the cross-roads. Nana's youngest brother, Prince Kwesi Duako, whom I had met several times, was seriously ill, and his family expected me to go and see him. To see the Prince meant, of course, that the family wished me to cure him, or at least to suggest a cure. I protested that I was not a doctor but Ankomah insisted. It was some kind of bellyache, I must go to please Nana. Nana dearly loved his brother, only a year younger than himself, and would be terribly disappointed if I refused to help.

So we went together to a house near the palace and found the Prince lying on pillows piled high on a mat in front of his bed. He certainly looked very ill and panted so badly that he was unable to speak, and only looked at me. His heart was racing and I wondered what his pulse was. I suspected that the heart condition was not due to his illness but to a local medicine, of which he had probably been given an overdose to 'pump life into him', for I had been put wise to this procedure only two or three weeks earlier, when the Queenmother's husband had shown the same symptoms and only had a feverish cold. I wanted the Prince therefore to recover first from the medicine. I promised his family to drop in again in the afternoon and wished the sick man a speedy recovery.

In the afternoon I went first to see Nana, whom I had not seen in the morning, to hear from him what his brother was suffering from. The description 'bellyache' was too vague and might have been anything from food poisoning to appendicitis. But Nana was wild with worry and unable to explain. He only wanted to know whether I thought it advisable to send the Prince to Sunyani Hospital. I was all for the hospital, as I could not take the responsibility of leaving him longer without medical help. But alas, unknown to me the Prince had a hernia and the forty-mile drive over a corrugated road was most unfortunate in his condition. The doctor could not do much, the Prince was given morphia. He died a few hours later in Nana's arms. As I learnt from Ankomah Nana returned with the body at three o'clock in the morning. The news that the Prince had died hit the town like a bombshell. There was no sense in calling on Nana as he wished to see nobody.

The following morning about seven o'clock Nana sent one of his spokesmen to ask me to go at once with him (in the royal car) to the Queenmother's house to take photographs of the dead prince.

Arriving in town I went first to the palace to see Nana. I was received by Ankomah who led me through the audience-court-yard, which was full of people in ochre-coloured mourning cloth, to the reception room where Nana sat alone. I was surprised to see that all the pictures and mirrors had been removed and all the unused chairs and tables covered with white cloth. Nana got up when I entered and smiled, and when I sadly assured him of my deep sympathy, he laughed. He said that I ought to be happy with him because his beloved brother was now in heaven. There was nothing sad about that; God had decreed it so, and there were always more children to replace the dead. Knowing how deeply Nana had been attached to his brother, I did not quite know what to make of his behaviour. I had noticed also that all the people in the audience-courtyard had laughed and joked when I greeted them. It only then dawned on me that it was the custom among the Akan to laugh death away and to pretend to be happy about it. I realized later that Nana's self-control was an almost superhuman achievement.

In the Queenmother's house also everybody was cheerful, al-though this cheerfulness was far more forced than among the men. The Queenmother tried to smile when I gave her my hand, but her smile disappeared again at once and she looked miserable. I was taken by the Banmuhene Kwaame Twi, the royal grave priest and custodian of the royal cemetery, to see the body. The prince was lying in state on a bed in a specially built alcove, covered with woven blankets and rugs from the Sudan; gold-hilted swords, the symbol of royalty, leant against the bed. A cola-nut, a symbol of life, closed his mouth. A woman from the Banmuhene's house sat at the head of the bed driving the flies away with a switch; a coffin stood before the bed. I stood silent for a moment and thought of the *Apo* festival at Kuntunso where the prince, only a fortnight ago, had sat next to me during the rites. He had been a modest man, courteous and charming, and a devout Christian.

Now the Queenmother was called to the alcove, and the Banmuhene poured out a libation and said a prayer. I took the photographs and when I had finished the Queenmother introduced me to the dead man's two wives, who sat with out-stretched legs in a dark corner, separated from the bed by a wall. I was asked not to give them my hand; touched by death they were unclean and shunned by all. They looked up for a moment, then they sat motionless again like statues, paying no attention to what went on around them.

I returned to the palace to report to Nana that I had taken the photographs. I found him even more cheerful than before. He begged me to come back in the afternoon for a chat. When I turned to go, he called after me '*m' akyio*', I stopped and, in order to wish him also 'good morning', went back to give him my hand. He remarked that my dress fitted the occasion perfectly since it was the right colour. Knowing that red—from orange to purple—was the colour of mourning I had put on a pale purple-coloured linen frock and shoes. I was glad that Nana also approved of my blue chiffon scarf. Since the morning was cool I had taken it hoping that it would not spoil my 'mourning clothes'.

In the afternoon I found Ankomah at home and went with him to a store to buy a bottle of aquavit. Armed with it we went to the Queenmother's house. The body of the prince had gone. On Nana's orders it had been placed in the coffin and given to the Methodist missionaries to perform Christian rites over it. The bed on which the corpse had lain was however still there; the woman from the Banmu still drove the flies away, and the wives still sat in their dark corner shunned by all.

November

The Queenmother looked dreadfully tired, though a faint smile crossed her face when her uncle, whom I met for the first time, told me that he loved me and wished to marry me. She graciously accepted the aquavit and gave me two bottles of beer in return, which I had to drink on the spot with Ankomah and friends; everybody present had to drink. From time to time a woman wailed; a minstrel standing behind the Queenmother sang songs praising the Royal Ancestors, the dead kings, whom, it was believed, the prince was on his way to join. The Akyeamehene Kwabena Adyaye, Nana's chief spokesman, who stood next to me, remarked that if Nana should hear these songs 'one would not know what might happen. In olden days this was the moment when heads would roll'. I looked round for the Adumfohene, the executioner of human sacrifices, but he was not among the Queenmother's visitors.

When the minstrel had finished his songs and recitations, a white sheep, tethered to a pole in the courtyard, was dragged by two stool-bearers to the front of the bed on which the prince had lain in state. The stool-bearers held the animal by its feet, while their chief said a prayer and poured out a libation to the soul of the deceased. A third stool-bearer then cut the throat of the sheep from ear to ear and bent its head back; in a few seconds the sheep was dead. Its blood was collected in two calabashes; one was given to a woman to boil on a hearth erected for the purpose in the courtyard, so that a blood sausage (*bonsua*) could be prepared from it. (Boiled blood tastes sweet and is regarded as a delicacy.) The blood from the other calabash was later sprinkled over the offerings for the dead prince, which consisted of raw and cooked meat and the blood sausage from the sacrificed sheep.

The following day started with a thunderstorm and a downpour. When the sun came out again I went to town on foot, as Kwei was unwell, to visit the Queenmother and to thank her for the previous day's invitation. She was not alone when I arrived accompanied by Ankomah. Nana sat next to her on a wooden bench in the middle of the courtyard, a few people stood around in groups. Nana was bright and cheerful and, after he had greeted me, explained that it was his duty 'to advise' and 'admonish' the Queenmother, who insisted on grieving and being unhappy. I too should not mourn. One had to accept with a good heart what God decreed. Then he asked me to go to his palace and wait for him in his reception room as he would stay with the Queenmother for a little while. I went obediently, and on my way out noticed that the bed on which the prince had lain was still there. The unfortunate wives still sat in their corner with knees drawn up to their chins, entirely wrapped in dark brown mourning cloth. No sound came from them, nor did they move; they reminded me of the *ushabti* statuettes of Ancient Egypt.

Nana's reception room was still bare. Attendants brought me the customary two bottles of beer; one gave me a booklet to read—on tropical hygiene. After a quarter of an hour or so Nana came in, immediately continuing to 'admonish' me. The gist of his speech was always that one must not be sad; a death is God's will. And in this particular case there were three children, so there was nothing to complain of.

He took pains to explain to me that a king was just like a dictionary. All the time he has to display knowledge and know better than anybody else, and it was therefore his duty to advise and admonish all who were in need of it. I above all must not be sad, it grieved him to see me so. He said he knew that I had a very soft heart and that all unfortunate things concerning the State affected me deeply. But I must not be sad.

After a pause he changed the subject and invited me to a concert that night in the palace; he would invite only a few people. When I thanked him for the invitation and promised to come, he nodded absent-mindedly. All of a sudden the mask of cheerfulness that till now he had so carefully presented had gone. He looked dreadfully worn out and tired. I got up unnoticed by him, leaving him sitting with his head in his hands bent over so low that his head nearly touched his knees. But before I had reached the door he was beside me and, with a cheerful smile, lifted the bead curtain for me to pass into the audience-courtyard.

In the evening when I arrived at the palace its doors were locked and no guard was on duty. I asked Kwei to knock hard at the doors and, after some time, an attendant appeared with a lamp in his hand and let me in. He showed me through the pitch-dark forecourt and audience-courtyard.

The reception room, still bare, was brightly lit by a petromax lamp on a stand. All the guests were present, some twenty people, mostly members of the State Council. They sat on chairs along the wall, Nana in their midst on an easy chair. He greeted me warmly with a hoarse voice; his gestures were feverish. He asked me to sit down next to him on his left, the traditional place of the Queenmother. No women were present.

To make conversation he drew my attention to the white cloth which he was wearing toga-fashion—white is the colour symbolizing joy and happiness. Thus he wanted to convey to me that he rejoiced because his brother had now joined the immortal Royal Ancestors in heaven. He then abruptly left the room and shortly after returned wearing a long purple velvet coat. A pair of birds facing each other were embroidered in silver over his shoulders and chest. Under one was written 'Do it' and under the other 'Do not do it'. Nana pointed to the bird with the maxim 'Do it' and said proudly, 'I have done it, I have defied the Government and cut myself loose from Ashanti.' He then told me what it had cost him to make this decision, but it had to be done. He was not a slave but a king on the stool of his Royal Ancestors, the Kings of Bono.

When Kwei appeared to tell me that he had been unable to find Ankomah, Nana asked him to sit down and join the party. 'We are all happy here,' he said cheerfully. He ordered drinks for all, but when the attendants brought me a bottle of whisky and soda water, he would not let me have it, but handed both to Kwei to take home for me. He explained to me that he did this because he wished me to drink with him and as he (as a Moslem) was not allowed to drink spirits I must drink beer. So two bottles of beer were brought.

While Kwei was opening a bottle for me Ankomah came in. He had gone to a friend's house to get some sleep, for he had been continuously on duty since the death of the prince. He had felt that he could not continue any more. Nana was angry, but I pleaded for Ankomah, as I knew he was not very strong.

November

By and by the elders got up to clink glasses with me and, when it was the Banmuhene's turn, Nana said to me: 'He also is tired, you know the work he has done.' As a grave priest it had been his duty to prepare the prince's body for the lying-in-state, to have the grave made, and to supervise the burial. I had lately got in touch with him in his village Hansua and had interviewed him on the subject of burial and funeral customs as performed for the kings and queenmothers. Nana, knowing this, said: 'Ask him any questions you like. We have no secrets from you'; and then added, 'You are one of us now.' But I declined, since this would have violated a tabu. A king is not supposed to hear about rites connected with death. He is not allowed to be present at a burial nor is he allowed to enter a cemetery. Nana, perhaps remembering this, abruptly left the room, but even so I asked no questions as I became aware that the Banmuhene had other things in mind. He had called Ankomah to him and whispered something into his ear, and after further whisperings between them and the chief of Forikrom, the Banmuhene's neighbour, Ankomah came to me with the request that I should advise and admonish Nana on his return. I was horrified and refused point-blank. Ankomah reasoned with me—I had only to say the same things which Nana had told the Queenmother and perhaps add something about the war, how bravely the English had behaved when members of their families had been killed by bombs. I shook my head, I felt that I could not do it, but all the elders present insisted: 'It would please Nana, please do it.'

While we were still arguing Nana entered the room and, sitting down next to me, told me that the musicians could not come because their leader was ill. He had, however, arranged for the band to come to the rest-house when the chief musician was better to give me there the concert he had promised me. Then he put his hand gently on my arm and said softly that I was his mother, sister, and wife all in one, that since his beloved brother had gone he now had only me: how difficult, how impossible, it was for a king to make new friendships, how alone he was.

Ankomah looked fixedly at me: this was the cue, and with a heavy heart I got up to admonish Nana. I stood before him as

Ankomah told me to do, while Nana sat with his head in his hands bent so low that the nape of his neck was bare. Hesitatingly I started: 'Nana, you said just now that you regard me as your mother, so listen to me. Do not grieve because God has called your brother to him. We all know that people in heaven are happy.' Then I repeated some of the words Nana had said to me in the morning when he had admonished me. But I could not go on, I did not feel that paradise was a consolation, and I had no use for pretence. What could I tell Nana to give a new angle on the subject? I got confused; I could not think quickly enough and looked to Ankomah for help. Ankomah, without losing a moment, continued my speech where I had left off. He spoke at great length and, I was sure, very well. From time to time I said, 'yes, that is it,' or words to that effect.

When Ankomah had finished there was a long silence: Nana did not stir. After a while he looked up with tired eyes and, without referring in any way to my admonishment, started to make a speech.

In it he referred to Tekyiman's war effort, which had never been acknowledged by the British Government. Many kings and paramount chiefs had received distinctions, but what Tekyiman had done, with much greater sacrifices and under far greater difficulties, had been taken for granted. One day he would show me the papers in his office relating to all this so that I could record it; it must not be forgotten. He for his part was glad that soon there would be self-government, for never again would Tekyiman help England in her need. England altogether had proved to be a bad mother to Tekyiman and he referred to the nine villages he had lost and was not allowed to regain. Then he spoke of my position in Tekyiman.

He had learnt from the women in Tekyiman that they could not believe that I was a stranger. They realized, of course, that I was a European, but all the same they maintained that I was of the blood of Tekyiman. He himself was of the opinion that this was true, for no stranger could have done so much for a foreign people. He thanked me again for all I had done for the State, just as if I had returned the villages to him. At the end he remarked:

November

'This part of my speech ought to come at a later date, but to-morrow I may be dead, so you had better have it now.'

Nana's speech was beautifully translated to me by Kwei as Nana had asked him to interpret, ignoring Ankomah. As I smiled unhappily, he added: 'Whenever you are sad or ill in England, let me know. I shall at once despatch by plane one of my elders to cheer you up.' I was delighted of course, and then we talked about flying, and he told me that he once flew to Dakar during the war. I asked him what he was doing there but received no reply. All of a sudden he seemed far away, and looked round the room in a bewildered manner. To get him back to the conversation I told him that I too had been in Dakar during the war two weeks after the liberation of the town in 1943, and asked him whether he also saw what the port looked like at that time, a cemetery of ships. But Nana did not listen; he got up and went hurriedly to the door. There he stopped for a second and with unseeing eyes looked back while his right hand, with a gesture expressing all his despair, slid down the bead curtain. Attendants from the courtyard rushed to him with lamps in their hands and crowded round him; a moment later he was gone. There was a long silence.

Finally Ankomah asked me: 'Why do not you ask the Banmu-hene how he liked your speech?' I said that I could not after I had proved to be such a failure. But Ankomah, disregarding my reply, asked the question, to which the Banmuhene courteously answered that I had done well and that he was glad that I had come. Ankomah was much relieved and looked triumphantly at me; Nana's snub must have worried him greatly. Again there was silence. The light gradually started to fail, but nobody gave the order to pump up the petromax. The attendant who should have seen to it looked questioningly around; but, as nobody moved or paid attention to him, did nothing. Instead he went to the table in the centre of the room, laid down his head in the hollow of his arm and a moment later was deeply asleep. Everybody seemed to be weary and tired. As it was not likely that Nana would return, I got up to leave after a short consultation with Ankomah. Kwei went out to see to the car. I stood for a moment not knowing how to say good-bye and, as Ankomah was not helpful, decided on the ceremonial way. I started with the elders on the left wing of the half circle and made my way to the right giving each of them my hand. I realized at once the stupidity of it; this type of greeting was out of place here and not in keeping with my standing as an honorary Queenmother. But the elders reassured me. Each held my hand a fraction longer than was necessary, looked into my eyes affectionately and said kind words.

When I had passed the Banmuhene, one of the last on the right wing, I stopped for a moment in amazement. In front of me stood one of the attendants with his back pressed against the wall sound asleep. I wondered how one could sleep in this position; but he like the others had been continuously on duty for the last three days, ever since the prince died. Looking at him I thought of Sleeping Beauty and her sleeping court in the haunted castle. Passing the petromax lamp I turned round to look at the now almost dark room with its silent people, but Ankomah lifted the bead curtain and light streamed into the room. Attendants with lamps rushed in to show me the steps down into the audience-courtyard and the way out.

Outside the gates the lights of my car almost blinded me but the engine purred gently and I ran towards it, as to a big friendly animal. Ankomah opened the door for me. I thanked him once more for his speech, his beautiful speech, and he smiled. He said softly: 'Good night, Madame. Sleep well, Madame.'

Next morning I went to the palace to greet Nana, but he was still in his rooms and wished to see nobody. I went to see the Queenmother. She looked happier; and her husband, the Nifa-hene, and the Tanosohene who were with her remarked that this was due to Nana's admonishment. Palm wine was passed round and we all sat down. While we talked animatedly, a messenger from the palace brought me Nana's greetings and would I please call again at two o'clock.

When I returned at two o'clock however the N.A. police corporal on duty who had gone to announce my arrival to Nana, came back with a worried mien. He said: 'Nana, he booze, he sleep.' I was terribly upset. Not because I could not see him, but because he had made himself drunk in order to sleep. Only the other day I had offered him a choice of some of my sleeping-pills, but he shook his head. He looked at the little pills in my hand, while I wondered how big a dose I could give to the old herald who stood behind Nana, to demonstrate their quick results and that they had no disastrous after-effects. But Nana refused. He most probably feared to be found deep asleep should the Government police once more come to arrest him at night.

While I was still speaking to the corporal, Ankomah came asking me to go with him to the Nifahene's house opposite the palace. The Nifahene wished to see me on an urgent matter. We went over at once and found him waiting with two bottles of beer for me. He went straight to the point. The elders were worried about Nana, and I should go and admonish him again the moment he woke up. Taken aback, I refused. The Nifahene then pleaded with me: 'The whole State is worried about Nana, he must not grieve so much. Tell him that if he goes on showing so much grief, you will go away.' I shook my head. The Nifahene insisted: 'Nana loves you, that is why you can say this. You must show that you care for him, and we too must care. That is why we approach you. One cannot leave a man like this uncared for. We all love you dearly, because he loves you. You must go.' I agreed in the end with a heavy heart and returned to the palace. Nana was awake now but refused even to see me.

On the following day Nana still refused to see people. But in the afternoon the Queenmother's spokesman carrying the silver staff came to see me in the rest-house, bringing a letter from Nana with the following contents:

Nana Akumfi Ameyaw III, Tekyimanhene, regrets to announce the death of his beloved brother Prince Kwesi Duako, which sad event took place on November the eighth. Nana further requests the pleasure of Mrs. Meyerowitz to attend the funeral obsequies which are scheduled to take place on Tuesday, November the fifteenth.

R.S.V.P. to Korontihene

Next morning before going to Tanoboase and Tuobodom I

called on Nana, whom I found seated in the audience-courtyard. He was his old self again and discussed my pending visit and the political situation of the villages which had been lost to him. When I said good-bye he paid me a compliment, which Ankomah, preoccupied with other things, translated literally: 'Your flesh looks very fresh, you look fine.' This made me smile.

The Funeral

At half past nine in the morning of November 15th I was fetched by Ayerttey and a sword-bearer, who conveyed to me Nana's request to drive in the royal car to the place where the funeral custom for his late brother was to be performed. Nana himself was to be carried on the shoulders of his palanquin-bearers under the large double state-umbrella at the end of a procession of the male members of his family. As it happened Nana and I arrived almost simultaneously at our destination—the large grass-covered grounds near the Roman Catholic Mission.

I was given a place at a table at the end of the left wing of the traditional half-circle that was formed. My group included Ankomah, Nana's private secretary Mr. Afwireng, and the treasury clerk Mr. Ampomah. Nana sat in the centre under his umbrella but was invisible, as royal sons formed a dense ring round him.

By and by the elders, the great chiefs of the State and the village chiefs arrived, all under their umbrellas, the sign of their rank, and accompanied by their retinues. They took up their positions as defined by custom after they had greeted those present. One of the last to arrive was the Queenmother with her ladies. Nursemaids carried the children Kwabena and Afua. At last the Queenmother was allowed to weep; tears streamed down her face when she greeted me. Her mother and some of her women wailed.

When all were assembled it looked much like a garden party— the colourful umbrellas on the lawn, the groups of people greeting each other, and in the background the green hills of Tekyiman. It was a peaceful scene; I was glad that to avoid accidents

Nana had forbidden the firing of guns, the chief feature of Akan funerals.[1]

I did not notice my friend the chief of the executioners, but heard that he was with Nana as well as the Abrafohene, whose office it was to sing and recite the glorious deeds of the Royal Ancestors. But the young executioners, men and women, were very noticeable. The men wore leopard-skin caps and had swords in their hands. Some had their faces blackened. The executioner women wailed and lamented, one fell into a trance and rushed about with a knife between her teeth. Overcome with grief she tried to cut her own throat. A young man ran to her assistance, to save her, but when he took her knife she fell amorously round his neck, behaviour which shocked all the people who saw it. She was taken away struggling, but soon after reappeared and threw her knife viciously into the crowd. Luckily she missed. Four strong young men then took hold of her and carried her out. She escaped once more, but was caught again by one of the young men who, finally exasperated, slapped her face to bring her to her senses. The remedy worked. She came out of her trance, but the young man had committed a crime in laying hands on her. Ankomah had the unpleasant task of arresting him. Meanwhile the other executioner women also went into trances and had to be calmed down. It was some time before order was restored among them.

As people came in, the amounts of their funeral donation were announced by the heralds and the money was placed in a big bowl on my table. Mr. Afwireng, Mr. Ampomah, and Ankomah, each had a book and wrote down the name of the donor and the amount given, to prevent mistakes. Ankomah, however, was constantly called away on police duties while I was busy greeting people who came to see me. The brass bands played dance tunes, since they did not know European funeral marches. But now and then the drums took over, beating out the

---

[1] Owing to the death tabu for the king (see p. 118), the Prince had been buried already by the Banmuhene in secret; only the Korontihene and the Gyaasehene being present to witness the burial for the State.

age-old rhythms which stirred everybody and brought back a sombre mood and an atmosphere of grief.

As the funeral ceremony lasted the whole day I slipped away at lunch-time to have a meal and an hour's rest. When I returned the scene was much the same. The great chiefs and elders who had received visits now returned them. Nana also came out from under his umbrella and made the rounds (Pl. 24). Periodically he performed short ceremonial dances. When he had returned to his umbrella Ankomah took me to greet the chiefs. For some reason or other I was not allowed to greet Nana nor had he come to greet me, but I had to go to the Queenmother, who had never stopped weeping since early morning and sat like a statue of grief personified. Her women wailed, their faces unrecognizable from excess of emotion.

While I was away pupils from the Roman Catholic Mission had lined up on higher ground behind the chiefs. They were dressed in blue and white and looked like angels in a medieval picture.

At last the rites had been performed, consisting mostly, as far as I could see, of the pouring of libations to the spirit of the deceased. Shortly before sunset a signal was given and the people left slowly in a long procession. Nana, carried again on the shoulders of his men, was the last to leave the scene. The state drums followed him and behind them Ankomah who, as Inspector of Police, had to see that everybody left the grounds.

Next morning I went straight to the palace to greet Nana and to thank him for having permitted me to take part in the funeral rites for his late brother. He in turn thanked me for having come. Then I went to call on the Queenmother. She was still very upset and tears started to run down her face when I shook her hand. Her mother, with little Afua in her arms, stood waiting before the empty bed on which the prince had lain in state. Afua cried heart-breakingly and stretched out her little arms towards her mother. Kwabena was out with his father, and shortly after they came in, the boy ran towards me, as if towards a refuge from the frightening mourning, and remained close to me until I left. The prince's bed was removed the following day and things resumed their normal appearance.

November

The Sacred Rock at Tanoboase

I very much wanted to go to Tanoboase to see again the 'Rock', the great double cave in which Taa Kora, one of the Tano gods, is worshipped. I saw the caves in 1944 but when I described them in *The Sacred State of the Akan*[1] I had done so from memory, as unfortunately I had, by mistake, destroyed the notes and drawings I had made at the time. Knowing from bitter experience how faulty one's memory can be, I felt that I had to see the caves once more.

The village of Tanoboase was founded by Takyi, a prince of the Fante royal lineage, whose great-uncle, the general Amoasanka, accompanied by a few hundred refugees, had come to the Bono Kingdom (about 1550) from a Fante State which seemed to have been part of the ancient Mali Kingdom. After 1590 more Fante refugees arrived and Prince Takyi, in order to unite the Fante, got permission from the Bonohene Nana Yeboa Ananta (1595–1609) to gather them round him and found a town of his own. The town he built was Tekyiman, or Takyi-man, meaning 'Town [which is implied] of Takyi's State'. The national god of the Fante was Tano, whose shrine the refugees had brought with them. The deity's priestess at the time was Afua Ankomaa, Takyi's sister. One day, before Tekyiman was built, she fell into a trance in which Tano told her that he wished to be worshipped at the 'Rock', the great double cave, which was situated between Bono-Mansu, the capital of Bono, and Tekyiman.

Takyi thereupon built for his sister the village of Kyiase not far from the Rock and installed her as high priestess. But after a while Afua Ankomaa found that the walk to the Rock was too long and she asked Takyi to build another village for her nearer to it. Takyi thereupon sent one of his female slaves who was a blacksmith with her grown-up children of both sexes, also blacksmiths, to build it one and a half miles nearer. This village was subsequently called Tanoboase: 'Under the Rock of Tano'.

The famous Rock of Tano was seen in 1920 by Capt. Rattray,[2]

[1] pp. 128 ff.
[2] In *Ashanti*, 1923, pp. 188–94.

the author of *Ashanti, Religion and Art in Ashanti* and other books. He was the first European to be allowed to visit the caves, one of the most sacred places of the Akan. I was the second, and this great honour I owed entirely to the Tanoboasehemmaa Amaa Ntoa. It happened as follows:

When I came to Tanoboase in 1944 I was shown Taa Kora's small temple in the village situated on the main road from Tekyiman. Accompanied by the Tanoboasehene Kwabena Dwumoh, the priest-chief of the village and successor of Afua Ankomaa, the Tanoboasehemmaa and some of their elders, I was shown through the door which led into the courtyard of the temple. On the left, next to the sacred tree of Taa Kora, was the entrance to the actual sanctuary, which consisted of an ante-room and a shrine room.

In the shrine room stood a dome-shaped cone about four feet high, the top of which is said to be of gold; it is always covered with precious cloth. On it usually stands the shrine, the brass basin which contains objects representing the power of the god and some water from the Tano River. During the *Apo*, the Spring festival, it is carried on the head of the *okomfo* priest[1] of Taa Kora, like the shrine of Buruma and other gods. On some occasions gold ornaments, given to Taa Kora by various kings, and the gold-hilted swords of the god decorate the cone. The room was otherwise bare except for some old and beautifully decorated black earthenware vessels and the black stools of the priest-chief's predecessors in office. When we left the room the Tanoboasehene asked me to go out first, but seeing that the Tanoboasehemmaa was an old woman, I motioned her to go before me. This little act of courtesy earned me her friendship and support. At first the Tanoboasehene and his elders had refused to let me see the Rock. It was the Tanoboasehemmaa who, after we had left the temple, insisted that I should see it.

The Rock, which may perhaps be more accurately termed a sandstone range, contains a double cave. The two would be

---

[1] The *okomfo* is a priest who is able to fall into trances. The Tanoboasehene, although the High-priest of the god, was unable to do so and an *okomfo* had to take his place in the rites.

better described as rock shelters. The first is referred to as Ameyaw's Cave, called thus after Ameyaw, the heir-apparent and co-regent of Ameyaw Kwaakye, the last King of Bono, who rested here on his way to Kumasi and captivity after the war with Ashanti. The remains of the earthenware cups and vessels from which he drank and ate still lie where he left them in 1740 at the foot of a large stone boulder. To this cave the shrine of Taa Kora is brought on the god's birthday and during the *Apo* festival.

At the far end and to the right of the cave is a ledge to which one must climb, and here a low archway leads to the second cave. The passage is so low in some places that one has to crawl along it on one's belly; which I did, preceded by the village elders who had come with the priest-chief. The Tanoboasehemmaa meanwhile waited for my return in Ameyaw's cave.

The second cave is called the Ahenfie, which means 'King's House' or palace, because in this cave the Ashanti King Osei Bonsu Panyin camped one night when he came, at the outbreak of the Ashanti–Gyaman war in 1818, to consult the oracle of Taa Kora about his future campaign. Here too he watched the forging of the magical golden bullet which was despatched from the Rock in his presence; legend has it that it was later found buried in the body of the defeated Gyaman King Adinkra.

Before the Ahenfie a great wall of rock rises like a tower for about sixty feet. This is called the 'Eating Place of all the Gods of Ashanti', for it is believed that when the gods come to visit Taa Kora, they find their food on top of this rock. Between this rock and the Ahenfie cave is a stretch of open ground surrounded by a low stone wall. From here one has a most beautiful view. Below, as far as the eye can see, stretches the tropical forest. Somewhere in this mass of green lies the dried up Lake Bosomtwe which only fills, like so many African lakes, when the rains are heavy.

We returned to Ameyaw's cave, not on our bellies but walking upright through another passage. The elders may have thought that I would shirk crawling on the ground full of ants and other insects and would turn back, but they had been mistaken. The Tanoboasehemmaa received me warmly and, seeing my filthy dress and hands, reproached the elders: 'Look what you have

1. Nana Akumfi Ameyaw III, King of Bono-Tekyiman

2. Wenkyi Road with signpost in Tekyiman

3. Houses in the native style in Tekyiman

4. The Queenmother's husband Nana Kodjo Korey with Afua on his arm

5. The Queenmother Nana Afua Abrefi washing Kwabena

7 Little Eva on the lap of a young nurse

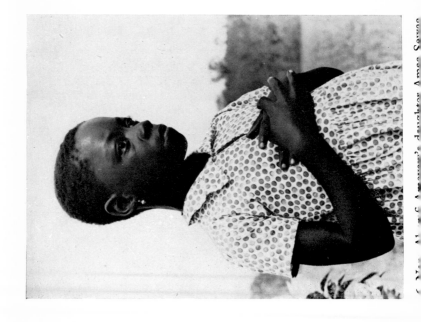

6 Nurse Abena Afuwaw's daughter Amoa Serwaa

9. N.A. Corporal Kusi standing in front of the Palace

8. The Tanosohene Nana Yaw Mensa

11. N.A. Inspector Mr. J. K. Ankomah

10. Mr. D. K. Owusu, 'Grandson of the Tekyiman Stool'

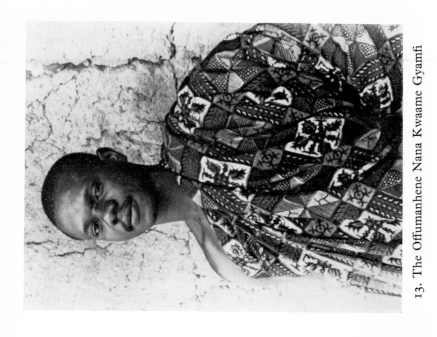

13. The Offumanhene Nana Kwaame Gyamfi

12. The Tuobodomhene Nana Kwaame Frimpon

15. Okyeame Pong's wife and daughter Eva

14. Okyeame Pong, Senior Spokesman of Nana
Akumfi Ameyaw

16. The High priest of Taa Kese Nana Kofi Mosi and his mother

17. The priest of Buruma at Bonkwae

18. The Forikuromhene Nana Kwaku Agyepon with one of his sons

19. The Nifahene Nana Yaw Nwinim

20. Priestesses

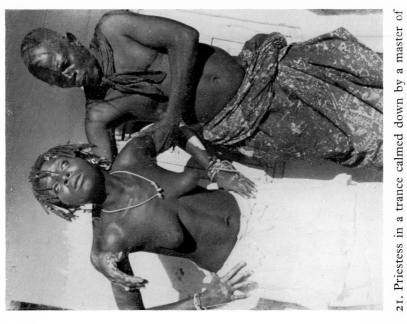

21. Priestess in a trance calmed down by a master of ceremony

23. Women dancing in a circle round magic objects and the priest of Akrofrom

22. The priest at Akrofrom

24. Nana Akumfi Ameyaw III concealed under the double state umbrella at his brother's funeral ceremony

25. The Asantehene Nana Sir Osei Agyeman Prempeh II

26. The main road at Twimea

27. The Oheneba Nana Kwabena Esi and some of his brothers and sons

28. Nana Adinkra, Regent of Gyaman

29. The author on the second trip (1945–6) with Kofi Antubam (left),
cook steward Gilbert Fenakedorh and Musha, the driver

done to the poor child!' 'Child,' replied one of the elders angrily, 'she is just as tough as Rattray.'

On my second visit to Tanoboase in 1946 I was not allowed to see the caves again. Shortly before, the Governor and the Chief Commissioner of Ashanti, who had heard from me about the Rock, had also been refused when they specially came to see the caves. It is a sacred place and not for sightseers. I cannot say whether any other Europeans, apart from Rattray and myself, have been allowed since then to visit the Rock.

However, in 1946 I was granted an interview in order to take down the history of Tanoboase. This took place in a house opposite the Tanoboasehemmaa's house and was a gathering of perhaps ten people: the priest-chief, the Tanoboasehemmaa, a few elders, Kofi Antubam, who then acted as my interpreter, and myself. There were two things about which I especially wanted information. These were: the circumstances which led to Tanoboase being abandoned at the end of the seventeenth century; and, secondly, why the predecessor of the Tanoboasehene in 1935 left the Tekyiman State at the time when the Ashanti Confederacy was established.

I got no reply on the first point, but was able to draw some conclusions. Taa Kora, the god of the Rock, had a meteoric career, for he at once became a favourite with the kings and queenmothers of Bono and was made State god. But after the reign of Taa Kora's fourth high priestess something happened and the god lost all his power and fell into disgrace. The Tanoboase people left the country but returned some hundred and fifty years later after the Ashanti–Gonja war (1810) because 'Taa Kora demanded it'. Tanoboase was rebuilt and, when the people were ready to move in, great rejoicings took place. In the evening, however, Taa Kora's priestess, Afua Amaa Nyame, refused to stay in the place on account of the wild dogs and deserted the god by going to nearby Tuobodom. Taa Kora killed her the same night for her crime, and her son—not her daughter—succeeded her because Taa Kora had made it quite clear to his people that he had had enough of priestesses. This suggests that Taa Kora owed his downfall about 1660 to his priestess.

November

Less than ten years after the rebuilding of Tanoboase the Asantehene Osei Bonsu Panyin came to Tekyiman to force all the priests of powerful gods to accompany him, with the shrines of their gods, in his campaign against the Gyaman king Adinkra. The priest-chiefs were not enthusiastic about the prospect, since Ashanti at that time was regarded as the oppressor of Tekyiman, but the Tanoboasehene saw his opportunity. He invited the Ashanti King to the Rock and forged for him the golden bullet which was to kill Adinkra. Taa Kora, after the victorious war, was richly rewarded by Osei Bonsu Panyin, and the Tanoboasehene was given the title Tanohene (King of all the Tano gods) and received the paraphernalia of a paramount chief. Taa Kora, once the State god of Bono, now became the State god of Ashanti and as such supported Ashanti in all its wars including the Tekyiman–Ashanti war of 1877–96. He lost his position after the defeat of Ashanti by the British and once more became merely one of the many gods of the Tekyiman State, whose State god was Taa Kese, Tano the Great.

In 1935, when the Ashanti Confederacy came into being, the predecessor of the Tanoboasehene Kwabena Dwumoh saw a chance of restoring the status of his god. After the Tekyimanhene Yao Ameyaw had been destooled for not joining the Confederacy, the Government made the Tanoboasehene acting chief of Tekyiman. As such he incurred the displeasure of the Tekyiman people, who finally chased him out of town and threatened to kill him if he returned. The Tanoboasehene thereupon went to the Asantehene Nana Prempeh II and declared openly that he and his people wished to serve Ashanti again. Taa Kora was once more richly rewarded by an Ashanti king. But times had changed and Taa Kora was no longer venerated by the Ashanti. No doubt they held him responsible for their defeat by the British in 1896 and 1901.

It was not easy to get all this information as I had to sort out many confused and contradictory statements and, indeed, it took me five and a half hours to get everything straight. The room was unbearably hot as we sat directly under a corrugated iron roof. Cigarettes gave out after the first hour. By and by the elders fell asleep; only the Tanoboasehemmaa remained wide awake, following my questions with anxiety. When the priest-chief also became drowsy I closed the meeting.

Only when I got up and staggered did I realize how exhausted I was, and worse, I suddenly felt crazed with thirst. I was unable to find my flask of water or any bananas in the car, and could not ask for water as unboiled water was unsafe to drink. While I was standing in the street not knowing what to do, Kofi Antubam saw an orange tree at the corner of the road. We rushed towards it to pick up some oranges but they were shrivelled from the heat and as dry as dust. We then shook some from the tree which were a little better, and I tore them to pieces with my teeth like a wild animal. I felt ashamed of behaving like this but could not help myself.

When I returned in 1949 to Tanoboase I asked the Tanoboase to see the caves again, but he said that it was Sunday, a day of rest for the god. However, he asked me to come again, and, to show me that there was no ill feeling on his side—he knew of course of my help to Tekyiman in its fight against Ashanti—he made me the present of a duck. This was most welcome as a change from the eternal chicken. As it happened I was not able to return to Tanoboase and to my great regret I never saw the Rock again.

The Sacred Source of the Tano River

From Tanoboase I went to Tuobodom and stopped with some uneasiness before the chief's house. In 1946 my good friend the priest-chief Nana Kwaame Frimpon, with whom I had danced at the N.A. police ball at Tekyiman, was still living there, but he had been exiled from his village in 1948. The new chief Nana Kwaame Asare was the former Korontihene, governor or administrator of Tuobodom, an ambitious man and a strong personality, who saw a chance of gaining power when Tekyiman opposed Ashanti and the Government. By openly declaring himself and his clanspeople for Ashanti—he suddenly remembered that his ancestors came from there—he managed to secure the chieftaincy.

November

I was not sure how he would receive me, seeing that we were 'enemies', supporting opposite sides. I would gladly have avoided this visit if my work had not made it necessary for me to see him. I need not have worried, however, for when he heard that I was there he quickly changed into his regalia and welcomed me in the most friendly way. Immediately he granted my request to ask a few questions and had the elders called together. Till they arrived we had a talk to see where we stood, and without much ado he declared that he wanted me as a friend. He was sorry that in the past (1946) he had been against me but 'now I know better, now I realize only too well how powerful you are and the good use you make of history', meaning that I had used the history of the nine villages in dispute as a weapon to help Nana in his fight.

I did not at first remember having met him before and he was most hurt about it. Then it all came back to me. In 1946 he had nearly made it impossible for me to see the source of the Tano River, which is held to be as sacred as the Rock of Tanoboase and which no European, not even Rattray, had ever seen.

And now I remembered it all. We—that is to say, the Tuobodomhene Kwaame Frimpon, the Tuobodomhemmaa, a few elders, Kofi Antubam and I—were just ready to go down the steep slope to the Tano River, when the present chief stopped us, demanding that I should give a sheep for sacrifice, otherwise he would not permit my visit to the source. A sheep at that time cost twenty-five shillings—more money than I had with me—and I discussed in whispers with Kofi what to do about it. Nana Kwaame Frimpon, who was standing next to me, saved the situation by going into a trance and declaring that the spirit of Tano which had seized him did not want a sheep. Then he rushed to the edge of the slope and hurled himself down with outstretched arms, his face lifted ecstatically to the sky, his flowing white robes spreading out like wings—surely this was an angel flying! For a moment I looked after him fascinated. When he had disappeared from view I was the first to follow him, carefully watching my steps on the narrow and uneven path which led downwards, closed in by bush. When we had all reached the water we waded up the narrowing river for fifty or sixty yards; the trees that rose from either bank met over our heads forming a tunnel. Then the river widened suddenly into the Pool, which in former days was called the Golden Pool because so much gold dust was thrown into it to please the god. The pool was shallow, for there is little water at the end of the dry season; in the middle was a mound built of clay and mud and reinforced with twigs and grass. Near the left-hand bank water bubbled up from hidden springs. The source was hidden behind a palisade of tree-trunks in which there was an opening covered by a snow-white cloth. A high semi-circular ridge covered with bush and palm trees bounded the pool on three sides.

When we reached the pool Nana Kwaame Frimpon was calm again. He said a long prayer, in which he explained to the god why he had brought me with him, and poured a libation with the white wine I had given for the ceremony. Then the spirit of Tano seized him again and the Tuobodomhemmaa did her best to soothe him. Finally she gave him an egg, which he took eagerly; he played with it for a long time, tried to bite it, even to swallow it, and then suddenly, and with great force, threw this symbol of life into the pool so that it broke. Slowly he came to himself again. He said another prayer and poured another libation into the pool. The wine left in the glass was passed round for all to sip.

Still standing in the water, he then explained to me that the source was hidden behind the curtain. When I asked him about the mound he again went into a trance and I had to abandon the inquiry. The Tuobodomhemmaa, to quieten him, took him through the door to the source, while we waited, still standing knee-deep in the pool. When he came back he said quietly that I might come and see the source. We stepped through the opening, while somebody held the cloth, and then climbed for a short distance up the ridge, carefully following a trickle of water. At length we came to the spot where the water rose from the ground. There a plain basin (which has taken the place of the golden one which the Bonohene Nana Ameyaw Kurompe [1618–33] had given to Tano) caught the first spray. One after the other the elders stepped forward to catch some of the holy water, drink it, and wet their faces with it. The Tuobodomhemmaa took off her top cloth and moistened her body to give it strength and holiness. Then we returned slowly. Beyond the pool we stopped for a second at a little bay, where every year the priests and priestesses of Tano gather to cleanse and purify the shrines of their Tano gods. At this spot, as at the pool, water bubbles up from hidden springs. When we left the bay I looked back to the source enclosed by the ridge. Nana Kwaame Frimpon, following my gaze, told me that at the time of the Bono Kingdom huge crescent-shaped elephant tusks covered with gold sheet were fixed to the rocks above the source. Tano, called Twumpuduo at Tuobodom, is a bi-sexual Moon-god, the crescent moon is his/her special symbol.

It was no good asking the new chief of Tuobodom to let me see the source again. He was not a priest of Tano and since he took office the rites for the deity had no longer been performed. The sheep for Tano which he had demanded from me in 1946 was obtained for the god after all. When misfortune fell on Tuobodom he blamed Nana Kwaame Frimpon for having omitted to sacrifice a sheep when he took me to see the source, with the result that it was sacrificed a few months later. Nana Kwaame Frimpon paid for it, as he told me in a letter.

When the elders were all assembled we went into the courtyard and while the new chief seated himself, very much the great chief, on a chair on the raised platform of the *pato*, I was given a seat among the elders. After I had greeted them I was given two bottles of beer and the chief asked me to drink one. I agreed as I was thirsty and then, realizing that the libation which usually went with it had been omitted, I asked for one. The chief thereupon called his spokesman to him who then, instead of a short prayer, launched out into a long speech, blessing me over and over again and wishing me a long life and, particularly, that all my enemies might be destroyed. When two elders tittered behind me I suddenly realized that I had made a *faux pas*. To ask in 'enemy country' for a blessing—for a libation before a drink is nothing else—was obviously tactless. And the spokesman must have been a bold man to show so openly that he was on my side, that is to

say, on the side of Nana Kwaame Frimpon and Tekyiman, otherwise he would not have wished for the death of my enemies. But
not a muscle moved in the chief's face, though he must have been
well aware of the situation.

When the libation was over the chief graciously asked me why
I had come to Tuobodom. I explained that I needed the text of
a certain song which alluded to a priest Apaaso, who was the
brother of the high priestess Takyiwaa, the sister or daughter of
Afua Ankomaa, who had founded the worship of Taa Kora at the
Rock. Takyiwaa was said to have discovered the source of the
Tano River and her brother is said to have been the first priest
to carry a shrine of Tano. There are some discrepancies in the
early history of Tanoboase and Tuobodom, and I thought that
the song might clear them up. The Chief at once sent for the
woman who alone had the right to sing the song at the *Apo*
festival at Tuobodom, and to do this, she must have been a
descendant of Takyiwaa. To my great delight she came, but
refused to sing it in the present circumstances, as first she had to
fast; neither would she reply now to my questions. The *Apo*
festival would start, however, in ten days' time and she would
then be willing to tell me what she knew of the ancient traditions
and would also sing the song specially for me, so that I could
write it down. There was nothing to do but to accept her offer
with thanks after the Chief had invited me to the *Apo*. For some
reason it pleased the Chief that I was willing to come to the
festival, and he expressed the wish that I should take part in the
play, which celebrates the rebirth of the god, and dance. When
I was surprised, he added, 'Everybody knows that you dance
beautifully. I would be very happy if I could see you dance.'

On my return to Tekyiman I went to see Nana and told him
of my visit to Tanoboase and Tuobodom and of the invitation
which I had received from the new Tuobodomhene. I told Nana
that I was quite prepared not to go if he thought it wrong from
the political point of view. But he waved my suggestion aside and
said in a tired voice, 'We are all one'—all one people, never mind
the quarrels.

Alas, I was never to see the usurper again. A few weeks later

November

Nana Kwaame Asare was dead. He suddenly developed a throat complaint and was treated for a few days in Sunyani Hospital; after his return to Tuobodom he died. 'Tano has killed him', the people said.

A Political Incident

Nana was most anxious to see me and sent for me; news had come to him of the Asantehene's anger about the Tanoso affair, 'the great battle', of which he had learnt, according to Nana's spies, through the much exaggerated reports in the newspapers. Reprisals on the part of the Asantehene might be expected, but it was impossible to say what action the Government would take. Nana believed that he might be exiled again for a period to Accra or to another place farther away; or possibly destooled and, as in Tuobodom, a chief might be chosen to succeed him who was more amenable to the Asantehene and the Government. In any case he thought it wise that I should know all about the royal clan and its ten lineages, of which only the princes and princesses descended from Nana Abrefi (she was a princess and lived about 1800) had the right to the stools; I could then oppose the choice of the Government candidate, if I thought it right to do so. He therefore dictated to me at great length the history of the various lineages and gave me the reason why their members were barred from the succession. He also mentioned certain ambitious princes, who might take advantage of the situation. When he had finished he said, 'Now you know all; I leave the succession in your hands, in case the Government exiles me to a far-away place and I am powerless.'

Nana then told me how terribly worried he was lest little Eva might die too. I said that I saw no reason to worry about her, since she was a strong and healthy child, but he shook his head and called for his eldest daughter, now nine years old, who was born before he became a king. The child appeared in a few minutes and stood before him, sweet and shy, while he talked to her, speaking very fast. Suddenly he turned to me and said: 'She is yours too, you can take her'; and there and then named her Eva too. I thought it untimely to give me a substitute when little Eva was still alive, but as this feeling was difficult to put into words, I just accepted her gratefully, for the child was lovely and I took to her at once. Two 'Evas', though, were confusing and I therefore drew Nana's attention to my second name 'Leonie' and suggested that she should be called Eva Leonie to distinguish her from little Eva. Leonie, however, proved to be a difficult name to remember and Nana asked me in some irritation what the name meant. I said, '*Gyattaba*—lion cub.' Now the name pleased him; 'It is a royal name,' he remarked, for among the Akan the lion symbolizes the king, and Nana's throne chair was decorated with two crouching lions. The little girl Amaa Sewaa *Gyattaba* said nothing; she just looked at me with her antelope eyes (Pl. 6) and remained standing before her father, who continued talking to me, saying that he did not wish the child to be an expense to me and he would pay every penny for her education. Later she should join me in England to help me with my work. For the present she was at school in Tekyiman. I called Gyattaba over to me, delighted with the child, but she was so shy that she did not even look at me. Two days later I met her in the street and she came up to the car to greet me. She smiled: we had become friends.

In the afternoon was a council meeting and Nana begged me to take part in it. The meeting was postponed till the next day, however, when in the afternoon unexpected visitors arrived. Nana, who thought it important for me to meet them, sent for me. To my surprise I was led into the office and not into the reception room; nobody had told me that the visitors had come secretly and the office was a better place to avoid causing talk in town.

When I entered the room Nana introduced me to two men, whom I judged to be in their thirties, emissaries of Dr. Nkrumah, who at that time was fighting the Gold Coast Government for 'Self-Government Now'. Nana then proceeded to give me the gist of his conversation with them, interpreted by his secretary Mr. Afwireng, to the great surprise of the two men who were both violently anti-British and anti-white in general. They did not like it at all that I, a European, was let into the secret of their visit and were much taken aback when Nana told them about my position in Tekyiman. They had come to get political support for Dr. Nkrumah and his party, then still in its infancy; in return Dr. Nkrumah promised to help Tekyiman in her struggle to regain the nine villages. Then there was the question of party funds and Nana told me how much he had subscribed. Finally I sat down with the two men, the younger of whom, when independence was achieved, became first a member of Parliament and then an ambassador, while the older obtained a succession of high positions which made him world-famous.

Nana soon left us as we talked rapidly in English; our conversation turned mainly on the future of the Gold Coast. We discussed how best to put an end to corruption in the hospitals, and I was just going to say, 'And what about the corruption of the police, extorting money from the market women?' when loud shouts were heard outside. One of the N.A. corporals came rushing into the room looking for Nana. He told us that a white police officer with three African constables had arrived in Tekyiman to arrest Nana. Then a N.A. sergeant came with the news that it had all been a mistake; the white police officer was on his way to Wenkyi, but seeing a traffic policeman on duty at the cross-roads grandly waving him on stopped to inquire whether any high official was in town. People then gathered round his car because they believed that the police officer had come to take Nana away. They had not forgotten the night in February when Nana was arrested and kidnapped, and had disappeared for a week, and the Government had not let them know that the king was in prison. The misunderstanding would never have arisen if Corporal Kusi had not had the bright idea of posting himself as a traffic policeman at the cross-roads to honour the two foreign visitors. This gave him the chance to tell everybody who came to inquire the great news of the arrival of the two Nkrumah men. It was impossible to keep secrets in Tekyiman.

The news that Nana was to be arrested had spread like wildfire and more and more people gathered round the police officer's car; nothing could convince the people that this was not so.

Many went to their houses and fetched guns, sticks, and knives to fight for their king. When Nkrumah's two men, Mr. Afwireng and I went outside the office to see what was happening, the situation had worsened and threatened to become very ugly indeed. Shots were fired into the air and the old war drums had been taken out and were being beaten furiously. It looked dangerously like bloodshed; the Tekyiman people were in a lynching mood. The two Nkrumah men, so violently anti-European, and Mr. Afwireng were horrified at the idea that the white police officer might be killed. One of them said with deep regret, 'There is no more confidence in the Government now'; which sounded strange from the lips of a person who was fighting that same Government by every means. The other remarked anxiously, 'There may be traitors among the people to provoke them so'; thinking possibly of Dr. Nkrumah's policy of non-violence. Both were unaware of the people's almost insane fear that their beloved king might be taken from them again, and that they might be left leaderless. After a few minutes the two Nkrumah men could not stand it any longer and both rushed to the scene to prevent a disaster, followed by the equally upset and distressed Mr. Afwireng.

I was left behind alone, thinking 'It should have been I who went to help the only other European present'. But I felt tired and apathetic; all I could think was that one more death was added to millions. Besides, without speaking the people's language fluently, I felt intervention to be a hopeless task. I took out a cigarette and looked at the ant-heap, harangued by the two Nkrumah men who, strangers in the place, were risking their lives for the hated enemy; for there was no doubt now that the people were quite beside themselves and it only needed one man to lay hands on the officer and all would be over. Awake now to the danger, I realized that Nana was the only man who had a chance of succeeding with his people. I was just about to go into the palace and fetch him when he came out, and with long strides walked towards the crowd; soon he was swallowed up by it.

Time passed. I took another cigarette. I kept looking at my watch. Shots were still being fired, the suspense was agonizing.

November

I worked out the political repercussions if this murder should be committed. It occurred to me also that I would have to report the incident to the Chief Commissioner of Ashanti. It was almost half past five now; if I left at six I could be at the Residency by half past eight. And to prevent a battle I would have to return at once to be back before the police or troops occupied Tekyiman. For the people, unarmed as they were (the old fashioned Dane guns would be hopeless against machine-gun fire) would fight nevertheless, even if they had to pay for it with death.

Time passed, five minutes, ten. I walked up and down, then fixed my attention on a lonely drummer who had stationed himself opposite me at the other end of the square, away from the crowd. He drummed and drummed. I happened to know this piece of drum language: 'Hit back at him who hits you.' He was completely absorbed in his task; then a man joined him and performed a war dance, deep in a trance. Slowly the sun went down behind Taa Kese's temple.

Suddenly three men left the crowd and came running towards me; they jumped on Nana's three-step dais before the palace. Their arms round each other they performed a war dance, while the lonely drummer drummed more furiously than ever.

At last Nana left the scene, accompanied by Mr. Afwireng and Ankomah and came towards me. With one imperious gesture he chased the dancers from the dais, and they disappeared in the alleys behind the Queenmother's house. I went into the office to wait for him there, and he entered it a minute later. He sat down, however, without taking any notice of me; Mr. Afwireng went to his desk while Ankomah posted himself before the window. Nobody said a word; attendants came in silently to shut the windows and brought lamps—by now it was dark. I looked from one to the other when the attendants had left but all avoided my eyes and nobody spoke. Deeply alarmed by now, I fixed my eyes on Mr. Afwireng who after a while looked up and gave me one of his angelic smiles. I smiled back at him somewhat relieved, then turned to Nana to say something. But Nana had already fixed his gaze on me; I was shocked to see his burning eyes and his ashen, haggard face. With a hoarse almost inaudible voice he said: 'It would have been bad for my State if my people had killed that man.' I nodded, then he added, 'It was hard to convince my people.' Then there was a pause; after a while he said, 'I am tired, I cannot talk any more, please return tomorrow morning.' But he did not get up, and when I rose he made me sit down again and then started to talk about the shocking things that had happened when he was arrested at the beginning of the year. He begged me to understand the excitement of his people and to forgive them their behaviour. I nodded; but what will the police officer do, I thought, who has just escaped death? What will he report in Wenkyi and Kumasi? What will be the repercussions of this affair? When I finally gave Nana my hand and wished him a good night he was gloomy and worried. Things did not look well. What was going to happen?

Everything was normal in town the following morning and I left for Wenkyi to do some work there. Early next morning Ankomah appeared with an urgent message from Nana that he had heard from his spies in Kumasi that the Asantehene had succeeded in getting the Chief Commissioner of Ashanti to endorse a warrant for his arrest next Monday. Would I please come in the afternoon for the meeting of the State council. I told Ankomah that I could not possibly return to Tekyiman, but seeing that I was going to Accra in a few days' time it might not be a bad idea if Nana and the State elders could prepare a document addressed to the Governor saying that I had full authority to act on Tekyiman's behalf in the matter of the arrest if this came into effect. Without this paper it was not likely that the Governor would grant me an interview to discuss Tekyiman's affairs with him.

Three days later I returned to Tekyiman for a few hours only. I had to fly to Nigeria to speak at a conference and still had to spend a few days in Kumasi and Accra. I had a long talk with Nana lasting over two hours about what best to do in a case of emergency. It was not easy to say good-bye to him and the State elders, for the future looked dark and almost hopeless.

CHAPTER IV

December

Once more on the Road to Tekyiman

On December 11th I left for Ibadan in southern Nigeria
with Dr. K. Busia, then the head of the department of
Anthropology at the University College of the Gold
Coast at Achimota (he was to become known to the world as the
leader of the Opposition to the Nkrumah Government of Ghana
after 1957). We had been chosen to represent the Gold Coast
Government at the International West African Conference. After
we had read our papers we returned to Achimota just before
Christmas. I arranged to leave for Tekyiman immediately but,
apart from my own indisposition—I suffered from the after
effects of food poisoning following the grand dinner given to the
delegates at which I had taken only native dishes—Santos went
down with a bad bout of malaria which meant a delay of seven
days.

Because of Santos's illness I lost Kwei who had been lent to me
by the transport office of the College. He had to take a party of
professors to the Northern Territories of the Gold Coast, and I
now had to wait for the return of another driver, Corporal
Kweyte. I was not happy at the exchange because I had learnt to
appreciate Kwei who was a first-rate person; I knew that Kweyte,
who had fetched me from Takoradi on arrival in the country, did
not compare with him, although he was a nice enough fellow.
Kweyte was also an ex-serviceman and had been in the same unit
as Kwei and Ayerttey, Nana's driver, during the war in Burma.

On the 29th we were at last ready to go, and we left Achimota
for Apam on the coast, where we intended to spend two nights

so as to make the travelling less strenuous for Santos, who was still very weak. Unfortunately Kweyte became feverish the first night in Apam and was not fit to drive when the time came to leave. We remained there for another day and a night and then went to Saltpond, some 120 miles away on the coast, for a further rest.

The Saltpond rest-house was cooler than Apam and altogether a healthy place at which to recuperate. We arrived about lunch-time, and then we all had a long sleep. We would have rested the following day also, and the day after, if Kweyte had not been enterprising enough to go to town in the afternoon.

He came back from his outing in a state of excitement and with the most disturbing news; a general strike had been declared demanding 'Self-Government Now'. All offices and shops were closed already and the lorry-drivers were out on strike. Kweyte asked me whether he also had to go on strike as the people had told him not to drive a European. I said, 'Yes, of course, you cannot let your brothers down; besides you told me just now that you are all for Self-Government and Independence from the British.' He thought for a moment, then said, puzzled: 'And who will drive Madame?' I shrugged my shoulders. He was silent for a while, then surprised me by saying, 'Please, Madame, let's go to Kumasi, it is on the way; more will be going on there than here.' I thought for a moment; it would be mad to reject his offer; after all, I wanted to go to Tekyiman, the strike might last for a long time and I had enough of delays. But before I agreed to the plan I made it quite clear to Kweyte that he was a strike-breaker and to drive a European in this unsettled time was asking for trouble. Stones had been thrown at European cars and, as he had just told me, Europeans had been injured. There might be stones for him too. I myself was prepared to take the risk but did not wish to be responsible for him. Kweyte, however, brushed everything aside and said firmly: 'I drive Madame', and so I arranged with him to leave as early as possible the following morning.

It was a lovely morning when we left, misty as it is in the tropics with a soft light—there is never a hard bright sun—and already hot. Saltpond was still asleep; there were few people about and no traffic in the streets. Out of town Kweyte raced joyfully along the deserted road. We soon passed Anamabu and its castle and reached the junction where we had to turn north into the tropical forest.

Seen from the road the forest is dull; in the dry season its green overlaid with dust from the laterite road. One never seems to see colourful birds or flowers, and the wild animals that have survived have long ago withdrawn into the denser and more lonely parts of the forest. Joseph Dupuis, author of the *Journal of a Residence in Ashantee* published in 1824, describing the forest along the same road as we travelled, wrote: '. . . the opacity of the forest communicated to the atmosphere and the surrounding scenery a semblance of twilight, no ray of sunshine penetrated the cheerless gloom and we were in idea entombed in foliage.' The road is wide enough today to let in plenty of light since the old tall trees near the road have been felled, but in many spots one can still see the scenery as Dupuis saw it, when he referred to the forest as 'magnificent as it was dense and intricate. Numerous plants and creepers of all dimensions, chained from tree to tree and branch to branch, clustering the whole in entanglement.'

Three months before when I travelled along the same route with Kwei it rained incessantly and then we ran into a thunderstorm. Not far from Fomena we had skidded on the flooded road and the car mounted a bank and came to a halt on its two back wheels while the front wheels were deeply embedded in soft soil. We had to get help, which was awkward since already at that time anti-European feeling ran high and I loathed having to stop a lorry and get men to put the car back on the road. However, the first lorry which came towards us stopped, for the people wanted to see the damage, and when I asked for help more than enough men stripped to the waist to lift the car. It was hard work and the rain ran down their naked backs, but they laughed excitedly. They felt proud when the car was at last standing normally again and before they left they told me that they felt sorry for me that I, a woman, had to travel alone through a thunderstorm. I laughed and gave them a 'dash' for drinks in the next town, which they accepted with cheers. They waved to me until they had disappeared from view.

At ten o'clock we arrived at Bekwai and shortly after in Kumasi where I installed myself once more in the rest-house. I left Santos to unpack and, in order to see how the strike had hit the town, drove with Kweyte through the streets. We went first to the Post Office which was guarded by troops. Then I wanted to visit a Syrian friend of mine to get the news of the town but could not find his shop in Kingsway. I got out of the car and wandered down the deserted street. I was just about to turn back when I was accosted by a young man who had watched me for some time. Realizing that I was looking for something or somebody he offered me his help, to my great surprise, and when I told him that I was looking for Mr. X, he went with me to a house some minutes' walk away. I asked how it was that he was not afraid to be seen with me; after all, there was a war on—or something of the kind. Much taken aback he replied: 'But not with women and children, we only fight the Government.'

My Syrian friend, a trader and pawnbroker, was at home and very pleased to see me again. Our friendship dated from 1946 when I came to him to buy Ashanti gold ornaments for the future museums of Accra and Kumasi—necklaces, bracelets, armlets, charms, sandal ornaments, finger- and toe-rings and so on, for which the Gold Coast Government had granted £500. I had to promise him though that the sale would remain secret, and as he did not wish me to select the ornaments on his premises, he handed over to me an old cement-bag three-quarters full of gold ornaments without making a list of the contents as I requested him to do. I took the bag to the Chief Commissioner, who made a curious face when he saw me with the gold, estimated by Mr. X to be worth about £4,000. He much disliked Mr. X's un-businesslike attitude, nor was he happy about Mr. X's demand for secrecy. However, I finally selected the finest pieces—little works of art—in his office together with the two goldsmiths of the Asantehene.[1]

[1] The Government paid Mr. X for scrap gold far below the true value of the ornaments, with the result that I had spent only under £400; which

December

From Mr. X's house Kweyte turned back into Kingsway, and drove to the market; from there to the 'rich woman', the owner or 'queenmother' of the market. To my delight she was at home and greeted me cheerfully. I sat down in one of her beautifully made modern chairs—the whole room was furnished in the latest European fashion—and told her of my experience at the market, how her women had nearly lynched me. She laughed good-naturedly, she was not surprised; all her women were solidly for 'Self-Government Now' and supported the cause with such fervour that they refused to cook for husbands and sons, and even turned them out of their houses if they failed to join the strike. Nor did the women sell their market produce to Europeans; the cooks and stewards working for Europeans were easily recognizable, as most of them were Nigerians. And what she told me was true, for on the following day Santos returned empty-handed from the market and I had to send the rest-house-keeper to get me what I needed.

In the morning of my second day in Kumasi I went to see the acting Chief Commissioner of Ashanti whom I happened to know from former times. I tried my best to persuade him that the Tekyiman were not simply a rebellious and obstinate people, but failed.

From the Chief Commissioner's office Kweyte drove me to the palace of the Asantehene, as I wished to call on Otumfor (His Majesty) Sir Osei Agyeman Prempeh II, Nana's enemy. When we came to the traffic stop, the last one before the palace, the lights were against us and we had to wait. I looked idly at a letter-writer who had his table in front of a house and was busy writing a letter for two young men. Becoming aware of my gaze he looked up and I smiled as I was accustomed to do in Tekyiman. This had a most unexpected result, for the man jumped up and, accompanied by his two clients ran with raised arm towards me shouting something. Just then the lights changed, and when Kweyte had turned the corner I asked him, 'What did the men

was a pity, because there were many more gold ornaments which I would have liked to buy. The selected pieces can be seen now in the museum at Kumasi.

shout? Insults? Am I a dirty imperialist or a filthy exploiter or what?' Kweyte said, 'No, Madame, the letter-writer said, "You are a fine European and I want to make love to you", and the others they agreed for that.'

Luckily for me Nana Prempeh was at home. We knew each other since 1936 and whenever I came to Kumasi I went to see him. As he was busy he invited me to come back in the evening so that we could have a talk undisturbed.

In the evening I returned as promised. His palace, which is built in the style of a European villa, was in darkness, but when I knocked at the door, it was immediately opened by his secretary, the late Mr. Boateng. Nana Prempeh was awaiting me in his reception room which was hung with photographs of well-known personalities. He greeted me pleasantly and then showed me to a sofa while he sat down on my right in an easy chair. Mr. Boateng took a chair opposite me. I was offered some drink and then we settled down to our talk, which ranged from general politics to things in England and my work.

Nana Prempeh was most gracious, which bothered me greatly, for it was on my mind all the time that I was engaged in fighting against him on behalf of Tekyiman. At last I felt I could not accept his friendship and hospitality while at the same time working to detach nine villages from his kingdom. So I decided to tell him the truth. I explained to him how I came to 'betray' him, and he listened attentively. When I had finished he said with a sigh, 'We are all one people, all one people', the same phrase Nana had used when I had told him about my visit to the usurper at Tuobodom, and Nana Prempeh smiled when he saw my distress. He must of course have known something of my activities, but so far had pretended to ignore them. Suddenly he asked me: 'I hear that the Tekyimanhene has submitted a Petition to the King of England, to get my villages back; is this so?' I looked at him in astonishment because I knew that he had in his possession a copy of the same Petition—it was in fact my own spare copy, which Dr. Danquah had asked for so that the Asantehene might study it.

Then the conversation turned on other things. I left about ten o'clock and promised to visit him again on my return to Kumasi. However, to my great regret, this was not to be. Nana Prempeh is an interesting personality with great charm and I valued his friendship, but this I had forfeited by my confession. An African would, no doubt, have been less clumsy and less bluntly honest than I was, and might have managed to maintain the old relationship as long as this was possible.

The following morning I went to call on the Queenmother of Ashanti, the Asantehemmaa Nana Amaa Seiwaa Nyaku. I was shown into the reception room, furnished in European style. I waited a moment; when she appeared I hardly recognized her, she had changed so much. This was no longer the easy-going princess, happy to have been elected queenmother and full of laughter, but a woman very conscious of power and authority. However, she was pleased to see me again and at once inquired whether I still lived an unnatural life. When I had to own that I did, she 'admonished' me—I was a woman and should be surrounded by a loving husband and children who cared for me. She still thought the Government cruel that it forced me to do a job which deprived me of a home, and worse, forced me to travel only accompanied by men. She, as a Queenmother, knew from the cases that came to her court how wicked men can be. I assured her that on this trip also I was in good hands, that my interpreter, cook-steward and driver only thought of my safety and comfort and that I could absolutely rely on them. Moreover, I had again found the men of her people courteous, eager to protect me, helpful in every way and anxious to please me. The Queenmother shook her head unbelievingly. Then she inquired, but did I not feel dreadful alone among men, with no woman to console me when I was sad and on whose shoulders I could weep when I was unhappy? Three years earlier when she had put this question to me, she was so full of pity for me that tears came to her eyes. Now she only remarked that Europeans were hard and inhuman; she had given up trying to understand them.

As there was no hurry to return to Tekyiman—so long as the strike lasted Tekyiman was safe—I decided to stay another three or four days, partly to visit Ashanti friends, partly to pick up some information which I needed for my work. The last day I spent buying provisions and a case of drinks—rum, Dutch gin and Schnapps for libations; sherry and Vermouth for myself and Algerian red wine for my meals to avoid drinking the tasteless boiled water.

Kweyte and I were in high spirits; the first time since my return from Nigeria I felt really well. Alas, it was a false well-being, the false well-being before an attack of malaria. While making purchases in a grocery shop I suddenly felt faint. I just had time to see a bag of potatoes next to me, and sank down on it. For a moment everything went black before my eyes; by the time the astonished African came back from behind the counter to see where I had vanished to, I was up again and made my way to a chair. After a while I recovered and told the much disappointed Kweyte to drive back to the rest-house. I was ten days laid up; the strike had petered out by the time we were on the road again to Tekyiman.

CHAPTER V

January

Back in Tekyiman

I returned unannounced to Tekyiman on January 17th to avoid a grand welcome and celebrations. To my delight Nana was free and could see me at once and we withdrew to the reception room to exchange the latest news. There was nothing much that I could let him know; he, however, had to tell me something which shocked me deeply—the High-priest of Taa Kese Kofi Mosi had been destooled because he had endangered the State. I just could not believe it; how was this possible? The attractive, talented, and elegant young man, so much loved by the people, who carried out the duties of his position so well—he surely could not have done anything irresponsible. But he had, Nana assured me, and then told me the incredible story.

Nana Kofi Mosi had fallen passionately in love with an Ashanti princess, and she had been only too willing to sleep with him. So one evening the High-priest left Tekyiman in disguise on a lorry to meet her on the other side of the border. Unfortunately for him his disguise was not effective enough, and a man recognized him and being suspicious followed him to his destination. The man then returned to Tekyiman and informed Nana. When the High-priest arrived back in town at daybreak he was arrested by Ankomah and taken into custody. Then there was a trial and Nana Kofi Mosi was destooled and exiled from Tekyiman-town.

This seemed to me harsh punishment, but Nana explained to me that it was feared that the princess was an agent of the Asantehene and had been told to use her charms to seduce the High-priest, and then to persuade him to prophesy at the *Apo* festival at Tekyiman, which was due at the beginning of next month, that evil would befall the State in the coming year if Tekyiman persisted in its opposition to Ashanti and the Gold Coast Government. Although everybody in the State was sure that the High-priest would not betray Tekyiman, there was nevertheless a danger that, when in trance, being under the influence of his passion, he might say the wrong things. The risk could not be taken and therefore Nana Kofi Mosi had to be destooled. An old man of his lineage, decrepit enough not to fall a victim to dangerous women, was enstooled in his stead.

I shook my head; I was sorry for the High-priest and would certainly miss his colourful personality at the festivals. Nana also regretted his destoolment, but then reminded me that the first step leading to the ruin of the Bono Kingdom had been due to an Ashanti woman. Only in that case the woman, also a princess, was placed in the path of the heir-apparent and co-ruler of the king. It is worthwhile telling this story here as it explains the fears of the Tekyiman people.

In 1740 the High-priest of Taa Kese at Tekyiman, when consulting the god's oracle one morning, received the 'intelligence' that a most beautiful woman with evil designs on the kingdom was on her way to Bono-Mansu. He immediately sent a message to the heir-apparent warning him of this beautiful, light-coloured and charming stranger, and stated that if she succeeded in seducing him a battle would result which would be very serious for the Bono Kingdom. If, however, she could be taken prisoner and deep incisions made in her insteps, no harm would come to the State. When the message arrived in the capital, Boyemprisi, the King's favourite son, made fun of the oracle and said that Bono was so powerful that no nation on earth could conquer it. Shortly afterwards the High-priest of Taa Kese sent another warning to the heir-apparent, begging him to be specially careful on a certain day, for by this time the High-priest had learnt the day on which the woman would arrive. He again advised the heir-apparent to get hold of her straight away and make the cuts in her feet.

The day came and the beautiful woman—she was in fact the

new Queenmother of Nkoranza, not yet presented at court, and sister of Baafo Pim the traitor (pp. 18 & 83)—sat in the market-place, where she was duly discovered by some servants whose duty it was to bring any pretty woman they saw to the palace. When they arrived, the councillors, remembering the warning of the High-priest, wanted to seize her and make the cuts in her feet but the heir-apparent, at once enamoured, said that he could not allow so beautiful a woman to be hurt or disfigured. The councillors were angry, but when Boyemprisi supported the heir-apparent, the latter was strengthened in his resolve to have his own way. He seduced her the same night. Next morning the strange woman had disappeared, and when this news spread a sense of gloom prevailed in the city; everyone thought that she had taken the spirit of Bono with her and that the oracle's prophecy would come true. When the High-priest of Taa Kese received the news, he told the heir-apparent that Bono was now faced with war and that the Kingdom would fall in forty days; furthermore, the royal house of Bono-Mansu would come to Tekyiman. Boyemprisi consoled the heir-apparent, saying that it was all a fairy tale and that no harm would come to him.

Alas, what the High-priest of Taa Kese had prophesied came true; Bono was conquered by the Ashanti and the dynasty of Bono came to rule in Tekyiman.

Deep in thought I went from the palace to Taa Kese's temple to greet the Tanohemmaa, the mother of Nana Kofi Mosi. She was naturally very unhappy about the fate of her son, but cheered up a little when I told her that I had brought her a long-sleeved sweater to keep her warm during the harmattan season which had just started. The harmattan is a dry wind which blows particles of sand from the Sahara over the whole country and it can be very cold at night.

In the afternoon I made the rounds and visited the elders in town. During the following two days I went to chiefs and people in the villages surrounding Tekyiman to make appointments for further work. I also went to see the Queenmother at Nsuta, a newly founded village, some eight miles from Tekyiman, where she had gone for a holiday. I was sorry to see her without the children for I had brought them toys and a sailor suit for Kwabena. On the way back from Nsuta I stopped for a moment at Bonkwae to greet Okyeame Pong and to see little Eva II and to give her a rattle.

Back in Tekyiman from this excursion I found an excited crowd before the palace, among them musicians with brass instruments. Curious to know what was happening I stopped, and when Corporal Kusi saw me he took me into the palace where I found Nana surrounded by people in the audience-courtyard. He hailed me and shouted that he had something important to tell me. When I managed to get near him he informed me that there would be a dance that night; he had just arranged with the leader of the new Krobo brass band to play in the Sannahene's house. This dance was to be in my honour to celebrate my return to Tekyiman. Nana then introduced me to the leader and the more important members of the band. I was delighted, of course, and promised to come. I only wished that I had known about it earlier. It was half past five and I was dead tired after long hours on the road since early morning on a particularly hot day. I had two and a half hours to take a bath, eat, and rest; not very much as I was expected, of course, to dance through the night.

My Election as Queenmother

At eight o'clock punctually, wearing an evening dress and the bead necklace the Queenmother had given me, I appeared in the Sannahene's[1] house. This time I had made sure, by asking Nana direct, when I was expected to arrive, in order that I should avoid the mistakes I had made on other occasions. I knew the Sannahene's house, for I had visited the chief, Nana Kodjo Kyireme, several times during the past months. It was situated near the cross-roads and in the same street as the rest-house.

When I entered the courtyard where the dance was to take place I saw that many of the people were already assembled. The Tekyiman brass band played 'God save the King' to announce my arrival. I had hardly sat down when Nana walked in preceded

[1] The Sannaahene was in the past the chief treasurer of the State.

by the Krobo dance band. He was dressed all in white, in a robe that vaguely reminded me of a monk's habit. He was in a happy mood and eagerly sat down next to me while the Tekyiman band once more played the first bars of 'God save the King'. The Krobo band then took over and played a Highlife with great gusto.

The ball was opened when Nana jumped up and gave a solo dance in the old traditional style to the tunes of the Highlife, the brass band being reinforced by the old-fashioned drums to hot things up. Young men joined him and by and by formed a circle around him; Nana went on dancing alone round and round the petromax lamp which lit up the courtyard.

Suddenly Nana broke through the circle and grabbed me by the arm. Together we danced the Highlife while the young men, one after the other, each took a girl and danced around us. It was a long dance; by the time Nana stopped I felt exhausted and faint. Twice on the way back to my seat everything went black before my eyes. Luckily there was a pause—the band was also tired—in which Nana ordered drinks for me; I was glad of the respite. I hoped to recover but knew already that the malaria had returned. Barely recovered from the last attack I had done too much in the three days after my return; I should have taken things more easily. This was not a fresh bout but low fever (tertiary malaria) which I knew from past experience. However, I could not go to bed now.

Nana, luckily for me, was busy seeing people and I could drink my beer and rest. Ankomah, also busy, left me in the care of a young girl when he realized that I was not well. She looked after me charmingly but refused the beer and cigarettes I offered her. Meanwhile more and more people kept coming in till the place was thronged and there was hardly room to dance.

Suddenly heralds called for silence; Nana was to make a speech. He took up a position in the centre of the yard; young men of the aristocracy surrounded him. Then Ankomah came, took me by the arm, and steered me through the crowds till I stood before Nana. There was silence.

Nana opened his speech by telling the people that this dance was given in my honour, to celebrate my return to Tekyiman. He and the whole of Tekyiman were happy to have me back, for I was the *kra*, the life-giving soul of Tekyiman. Tekyiman he knew was my proper home and I had promised him always to return there from my wanderings. He then referred again to the help I had given to the State, all through the years since I first came to Tekyiman six years before. On account of this he and his elders had decided to make me an Honorary Queenmother. My name should be that of the first Queenmother of his lineage, Ameyaa, who had given life to the Bono Kingdom (*c.* 1295). He then thanked the Sannaahene for having allowed his courtyard to be used for the dance, and the two bands for having come.

The people then dispersed and formed a circle round the edge of the courtyard. Nana took me by the arm and said that now he was going to introduce me to 'my' people. There might be some who still had not met me. And so I went with Nana, very much the proud father and I the beloved daughter, right round the circle, smiling and shaking hands. Almost everybody seemed to be there, except for the rightful Queenmother who, as I knew, was happy to be allowed to stay at home with her husband and children.

After the greetings and acclamations Nana brought me back to my seat. But I had to get up again at once to make a speech, for which I was completely unprepared; I had never thought of this possibility. Ankomah took me to the centre of the courtyard and again I stood before Nana, surrounded by young men. I addressed the assembly and then thanked Nana and the elders for the great honour that had been bestowed on me and expressed the hope that at all times I should be worthy of it. I was happy to be regarded as the soul of Tekyiman and hoped to be for ever Tekyiman's good spirit. But a good spirit could only do its work if it had the support of the people surrounding it. I stressed once more, as in all other speeches which I gave, that unity is strength and that the people of Tekyiman should remain united behind their great leader and King, in their fight for freedom and justice. Then feeling that my speech was too short for African taste and unable to think of anything more to say, I turned to Ankomah for help. I asked him in a low voice if I had forgotten anything I should have said and, if so, would he kindly say it for me. Ankomah thereupon embarked on a fairly long speech, which first puzzled and then alarmed me. I had only envisaged a few more words of thanks, not this torrent of words delivered in a passionate voice. However, the people seemed satisfied with it. When he brought me back to my seat I asked what he had said with so many words. Ankomah replied with just one word: 'Admonishment.' I nearly fainted. 'Well,' he said hotly, 'you are a Queenmother now and it is the Queenmother's duty after her election to admonish the King and her people.' I felt unreasonably bitter; if I hated anything it was a display of superiority, seeming to know better than others and letting them feel it. But alas, customs differ, and the Queenmother, essentially the mother, is expected to chide her son, the king, and her children, the people.

The next dance was again a Highlife and again I danced it with Nana. But soon he handed me over to one of the princes. By this time everybody was in high spirits. When the next dance started Nana came to my seat and took me by the hand. It was not to dance, for we made our way through the dancing couples across the courtyard. On the other side Nana stopped for a moment in front of a door which was unlocked. Together we entered a small room in which there seemed to be nothing except a bed and a paraffin-lamp on a table nearby. I dimly wondered what this was all about but before I had time to think, attendants appeared with drinks on another little table. They were followed by the Tuobodomhene, and we all three sat down on the bed. Since Nana Kwaame Frimpon still spoke better French than English at the time—he had been a trader in the French Ivory Coast before he became a chief—he translated Nana's words into French and I replied in French. I soon knew, as Nana immediately spoke of it, why he had called me to this room, namely to have a talk with me about my new duties as head of State. He made it quite clear that he wished me to be treated by his people as their true Queenmother, that it was more than merely a title that he and his elders had conferred on me. And he had given me the name

Ameyaa, because she had been a great Queenmother, a great woman and life-giver—besides it pleased him that her name and his, Ameyaw, were the same and that thus we were linked together. Then we drank and I told him that I was happy because it was a great day for me and that it meant much to me to be a queenmother. Nana then gave orders for Kweyte to appear and when he came all hot from the dance and the beer, he told him that I was now more than ever a precious person. I must be looked after very well and if anybody—which God forbid—should do me harm, then he (Kweyte) must let him know at once, so that this person could be punished. Then we all left the room and joined the dancers.

I was glad when I could sit down again because, for the second time, I had suffered a blackout. I felt so faint and had such heart palpitations that I called for Ankomah to come. He brought me some lukewarm soda water to drink and, since Nana was busy, I was able to sit through the next three dances. I was just recovering when I got Nana's request to come at once to the little room. I protested to Ankomah and begged for a further rest of half an hour, but Nana's request was an order and it was unthinkable for Ankomah not to obey. Leaning heavily on his arm we literally fought our way through the crowds.

By the time we arrived on the other side of the courtyard I was feeling faint again. Ankomah left me standing at the open door while he went to look for the Tuobodomhene, who had to act as interpreter again. I slowly went into the badly lit room and then stood leaning against the wall near the door with eyes closed. After a while, feeling a bit better, I opened them and then saw Nana opposite me sitting on the bed holding his head in his hands. He was so absorbed in thought that he seemed to be unaware of my arrival. Anyhow he made no sign that he knew that I was there. I wondered what it could be that took all his attention; it looked like trouble—had the Ashanti invaded the State, or did the Government wish to arrest him again? I had no clue and was too tired to think. I closed my eyes again and remained leaning against the wall. Time passed. The room was stiflingly hot. All the same I felt better after a while and decided to risk the walk across the room and sit down next to Nana. But I remained standing and looked at Nana and did not move. In the end I pulled myself together and sat down on the bed. Nana still gave no sign that he was aware of my presence. We both sat motionless, I could not say now for how long.

At last the Tuobodomhene arrived and sat down next to me. He addressed Nana, who then looked up and spoke rapidly. Nana Kwaame Frimpon translated into French. There was trouble, but not of a political nature; what was distressing Nana was something I never expected—the offer of marriage from the chief who, at Akrofrom, had told me that if I agreed to marry him he would give Nana £100 to act as my father. I was surprised that such a small matter could have such an effect on Nana. I had been amused at the chief's proposal at the time, it never occurred to me to regard it as an insult, as Nana apparently did. For he apologized over and over again for the chief and begged me to forget what had happened. In the end I gathered that it was not so much the chief's proposal that had upset him as Ankomah's reply, the vulgar words that he had put into my mouth and which had made the chief's retinue collapse with laughter. I begged Nana not to worry about so small a matter, which indeed I had already forgotten. But Nana was deeply worried. For a moment I could not understand it but then it came to me; Nana always emphasized, and had done so again in his speech that night, that I was the *kra*, or soul, of Tekyiman. The *kra* is pure, it is divine, for it is a particle of the life-giving force of the Supreme Deity, and in order that it may give life it must never be defiled. Nana obviously felt that the chief's marriage offer and Ankomah's vulgar reply had defiled my *kra* and that by this act they had endangered the State, for now I might no longer be able or willing to inject life into Tekyiman. I assured Nana that there was nothing to fear; no insult had been received as none had been intended, either by the chief or Ankomah, and I begged him not to punish them.

It had been a difficult conversation which had left me utterly exhausted. I begged the Tuobodomhene, when there was nothing more to say, to ask Nana, as gently as he could, to allow me to leave as I was not feeling well. I knew that this would annul all my words and upset Nana afresh when he had just been quietening down, but I was desperate; I just could not bear any more. The Tuobodomhene, who realized that I was really ill, did his best to convince Nana of the truth and that I had to have a rest. But Nana would not hear of my leaving; if I was desperate he was no less so. What was he to say to his people? Finally, when he saw that I really meant to go, he asked the Tuobodomhene to call Ankomah and Kweyte. In the few minutes I was alone with Nana I told him with feverish words—putting all my feelings into my voice—how sorry I was to leave early on such a night, to have to disappoint him, to spoil his evening, hoping that he would understand my feeling and that only illness made me act as I did. When Kweyte entered I begged him also to tell Nana once more that only illness was to blame for my behaviour.

Outside the room hell was let loose; the crowd was like a wall and it was impossible to get through. Luckily Ankomah was soon at my side and made a way for me. Outside the compound I promptly collapsed. Ankomah had just time to catch me and prop me up against the house till I felt better. The cool night air, such a complete contrast to the stifling heat in the little room and the no less stifling heat in the courtyard, made worse by hundreds of sweating bodies, soon refreshed me. After a while I could walk to where my car was parked, but Kweyte was nowhere to be seen; it was only when Ankomah opened the door that we saw him in the darkness, his arm round the waist of a girl; both sat motionless like trapped animals as we looked at them. The girl was the one who had looked after me when I felt faint for the first time that night. She struck me again as beautiful, with her large eyes, the eyes of a gazelle, and her slim and graceful body. Ankomah next to me giggled; 'She is my sister,' he said. 'Not possible,' I replied, seeing that they were so unlike each other. 'Same father, same mother, or father different, mother different?' I inquired, 'Or maybe mother's sister's child, or clan sister, or what?' For I knew how widely the term 'sister' was applied. As it happened the two had the same father. I then inquired where his sister lived, and when I heard that her house was just across the road,

January

I turned to Kweyte and told him to take the young lady home 'one time', which means 'quick' in pidgin English. They both scrambled out of the car and disappeared into the night while Ankomah and I looked at each other with amusement.

From my bed in the rest-house I listened to the music right through the night; it was six o'clock in the morning when it stopped. I could not sleep, although desperately tired, so I entertained myself by reviewing my life and made the startling discovery that this night had really been the high point, and I told myself that I should be radiant and happy this night of all nights, January 20th.

Africa had been my first great love. I saw myself again ten years old in bed with an injured knee. It was my brother's birthday. I was wild with fury that I could not take part in the children's party and that neither my mother nor my governess, nor the maids, had any time for me, seeing that they were busy first with the preparations for the party and then with the visitors. Being unruly and spoilt I called every few minutes for my mother, and neither chocolates nor cakes could keep me quiet. When nobody came any longer I resigned myself to my fate and wondered what I could do to amuse myself. At last I remembered that I had brought a book home from the school library and decided to read it. It was in the desk of my room and, jumping out of bed on one leg, I managed to get it. I looked again at the title—*Stanley's Travels in Africa*, written for young people aged fourteen to sixteen. Then back in my bed I started to look at the pictures and, enthralled, began to read. When my governess came to see why suddenly all was quiet, I shouted at her: 'Out, out, I am busy, I wish to see nobody.' But when my mother came and sat down on my bed I showed her the book with its wonderful pictures of black people carrying Stanley, or walking in single file through the bush in a long procession, some armed with bows and arrows and spears, and the exciting African landscape. 'That is where I want to go,' I said, 'Africa, and I want to be like Stanley discovering unknown regions.' My mother suggested that when I was grown up I should have forgotten all about it, but I said, 'Never, never!' When I was out of bed again I pored for hours over the map of Africa, trying to see whether there was still any spot in the continent that had not been charted, and I almost wept with rage to think that, even if there was one, by the time I was grown up it would have been discovered by somebody, somebody who was not me. Fifteen years old I read Frobenius's books on African cultures and civilizations which renewed my interest in Africa.

When at last I was grown up there was no road for me that led to Africa. By and by I gave up the idea and found other things equally important to me. In the end I got engaged to be married but broke the engagement three times, feeling dimly that this was not what I really wanted. In despair my fiancé gave up and told me that he would leave Europe and go to Africa. 'Africa?' I said surprised, 'then of course I will marry you.' And so we married and went to Africa, first to South Africa and then to West Africa. We travelled a great deal all over the continent and when he died in 1945 I went to Tekyiman. The discovery I had made in West Africa was not indeed a geographical one—I did not explore unknown lands—but I did discover the unknown past—the ancient Bono Kingdom. Tonight I had been given an honoured name—the name of Bono's first Queenmother—and Africa was mine in a way that I had never imagined in my wildest dreams.

At seven o'clock Santos came into my room to lift my mosquito-net and give me my orange juice. Then I got up; I contemplated once more my extraordinary fate; how happy I ought to have been now that all my childhood dreams had come true. I also thought that Byron was right when he wrote that we owe nothing to ourselves and everything to Dame Fortune. But alas, I felt too ill to rejoice; everything seemed grey and hopeless, the burden of living weighed me down, the slightest movement was a major effort.

After breakfast I went back to bed, dressed as I was. I did not know what I should do. If I did not go to thank Nana for my 'coronation', I should have to own to being ill, which would have the result that the whole of Tekyiman would come to commiserate with me. This I wished to avoid because I knew from previous experience that my temperature would be normal again by five o'clock and I would then feel on the top of the world. On the other hand, if I went to see Nana, he would regard it as proof that my 'illness' of the night before was not genuine, but pretence. I could come to no decision; but by noon I felt better and made up my mind to go to the palace.

I first picked up Ankomah, who was still in bed when I called, but he dressed at once and came with me to see Nana. We found Nana sitting on his dais in the audience-courtyard, and he told us that he had been receiving various deputations this morning. Among these was one from the women of Tekyiman to congratulate him on the new Queenmother but at the same time expressing the wish that I should be given the name Kruwaa and not Ameyaa, the name Nana had selected for me. They felt that they no longer had any real relationship with the Queenmother Ameyaa—after all, 650 years lay between her time and this day— whereas they still remembered their former Queenmother Kruwaa. She had ruled the Tekyiman people during the whole time of their exile in Gyaman (1874–95) and had sustained them with her strength and unshaken belief in final victory, just as I had done and still did in the present crisis. Therefore the women thought that her name was a better choice.

Nana was sorry about this change of name and so was I, but he had to bow to the will of the women and so did I. The Queenmother Ameyaa was nearer to his heart as the founder of his dynasty, and also to me, though for different reasons. Kruwaa was essentially a mother to her people; Ameyaa was primarily a ruler and had built up the new kingdom on a solid foundation. Bono had been founded by refugees from a number of states whose people naturally wanted one of their own princes to succeed after the death of the first King, Ameyaa's brother. To avoid civil war, and also being ambitious for her own family, Ameyaa confiscated the royal regalia and let her people know that either her son was to succeed as king or she would rule without a king. After three years, it is said, the people gave in and elected her son Akumfi Ameyaw, after whom Nana was called.

From the palace I returned to the rest-house. My talk with Nana had somewhat revived me, but I still felt very ill. I went back to bed after an early lunch and slept deeply until five o'clock. When I awoke my temperature had risen from 96° to normal and I felt well. The relief which one experiences is quite incredible; one can hardly believe that a few degrees in one's temperature can make such a difference.

After a walk in the garden I sat down with a book when a visitor called. I was surprised, as I had made no appointments and was sure that Nana had given instructions that I was not to be disturbed. The visitor was in fact an Indian who was passing through Tekyiman, the head of the Moslem Ahmadiyya Mission in Kumasi. I had not known until then that there were Moslem Indian missionaries in the Gold Coast and was keen to meet him. We greeted each other with interest and sat down outside the bungalow in the fresh air of the late afternoon.

The Indian was a small man, he could not have been more than five feet, and of very delicate build. His most notable features were his eyes, which were enormous and dominated a thin face. He seemed to be all spirit. I felt when I looked at him that he had divested himself of all worldly ambition, even of his own personality, in order to be worthy of a mystic union with his god, to be wholly possessed by the god. The mystic union with the deity, he told me, was indeed the main aim of his sect and was achieved by communal concentration in the mosque. As the sect believed that the spirit of Jesus had descended into Mohammed, Christ was worshipped as his ancestor.

It was dark when he left; he had stayed one and a half hours.

Stolen Documents

Next morning I left, as scheduled, for Wenkyi. I had hardly arrived when I got an urgent message to return to Tekyiman for a State Council meeting. An unforeseen emergency had arisen.

After a quick lunch I left Wenkyi for Tekyiman but arrived too late for the meeting. Chiefs from all over the Tekyiman Kingdom had taken part in it, and as they had assembled an hour earlier than had been arranged, Nana did not wish them to wait for me. Many had to make long journeys on foot to their villages which some of them had left at four or five o'clock in the morning.

Nana was much relieved when he saw me and led me at once into a small locked room where the royal paraphernalia was kept —the state umbrellas, stools and so on. I noticed too that he made sure that we, including Mr. Afwireng his private secretary, entered the room unobserved by the palace personnel. Something very unusual must have happened for Nana to take such precautions. I had not long to wait before I knew.

After we had sat down, the three of us close together, Mr. Afwireng handed me a document marked 'Top Secret' and what looked to me suspiciously like a Government file; it was marked 'Tekyiman' and 'Confidential'. I first examined the document. It was a deportation order made out in Nana's name; only the signature of the Governor and the Chief Commissioner of Ashanti had to be added and the date inserted. I had no doubt that the document was genuine and told Nana so.

Then I carefully looked through the file, and I was certain that this was the same file as I had seen three weeks before, on the table of the Acting Chief Commissioner when I had talked with him in Kumasi. This file was definitely not a fake. Besides, it was not likely that any person would take the trouble to copy a thick file that had been swollen by recent letters, some several pages long, which had passed between the Secretariat in Accra and the Supreme Court to ensure that Nana's deportation without trial to a place outside the Gold Coast could not be disputed on legal grounds. This file, moreover, was kept in a safe to which, apart from the Chief Commissioner's secretary, only the African chief clerk had access.

I asked Nana how this file and the document marked 'Top Secret' came into his possession. He grinned boyishly; it had been sent to him with the compliments of the Chief Clerk of the Chief Commissioner in Kumasi. The Chief Clerk had lost his job when he went out on strike for 'Self-Government Now', and in revenge had stolen the file and the deportation order and sent it to Tekyiman, to the people whom he knew to be most vitally interested in both. His revenge was especially effective as the only other existing file on Tekyiman had also been stolen from the Secretariat in Accra during the strike by a clerk who thought that Nana Prempeh presumably might want to know what the Government was going to do in connection with the Tanoso affair. This left only the correspondence which had passed between the District Commissioners and Tekyiman, which was kept in Sunyani and Wenkyi.

I wondered what would be the repercussions of this affair seeing that the Gold Coast Government had lost many of the most important Tekyiman documents. The order for Nana's deportation could be written out again, but suppose I had questions asked in Parliament with reference to the deportation, and the Governor was unable to quote details? How far could the officials piece Tekyiman affairs together again? I thought about it for a minute or two and then decided that it would be best, after all, to have the file returned by me via the Governor. At the same time I could have a talk with His Excellency on Nana's deportation. But what would be the Governor's reaction to the theft of the documents? In the end I decided to take no risks, and finally agreed with Nana that it would be best to bury the file and the deportation order in a safe place.

Then I settled down and read through the file, starting with the Tanoso affair. There was absolutely no doubt that the Gold Coast Government meant business. Nana was to be destooled and deported together with all those elders and chiefs who openly supported him. This meant, of course, that Tekyiman would cease to exist as a State and become a province of the Kumasi State in Ashanti. Ashanti chiefs, or Tekyiman chiefs obedient to Ashanti, would take the place of the former Tekyiman chiefs and elders. With a heavy heart I asked Nana what the State Council had decided to do in the matter. Nana replied, full of pride, that all his elders and chiefs had declared their loyalty to him; that it had been agreed by all to act again as was done in 1877, namely to transfer the Tekyiman Government to Gyaman (in 1950 situated in the French Ivory Coast) and to sabotage the rule of foreigners and traitors by burning their crops and by making life insecure for them.

The evacuation, Nana continued, would take place immediately his spies let him know that the deportation was to come into effect, and could be carried out in one night. Orders had already gone out to all Tekyiman drivers and lorries belonging to Tekyiman subjects to stand ready to return to Tekyiman without delay on receipt of an agreed signal. Tekyiman was only about seventy miles from the border of Gyaman; the important people would be evacuated first, the others could come later.

As I listened to Nana's impassioned words and to Mr. Afwireng's matter-of-fact translation, my only thought was: This must not happen! I could not bear to think of the people's suffering, for it would be a catastrophe for the Tekyiman to lose their precious cocoa crop and all their personal possessions, which they would have to leave behind unguarded. And a catastrophe for the Gold Coast Government, for if an African people under British rule were to seek refuge in a French Colony because they could not get justice, it would create an uproar in the world press. No doubt too, Dr. J. B. Danquah would try to bring the case to the notice of the United Nations. No, I decided, the evacuation of Tekyiman had to be prevented at all costs. I had to get permission from Nana to act as I saw fit in this matter. Owing to the strike and its aftermath there might still be time; I reckoned that it would be two or three months before the Gold Coast Government took action with regard to Tekyiman. Nor would the Government be likely to proceed before a reply to Tekyiman's Petition to the King of England had been received.

In two and a half months I should be back in London and could see the Secretary of State for the Colonies about it. But in order to prevent Nana's deportation I would have to reveal Tekyiman's decision to leave the Gold Coast. I therefore told Nana that I must have authority to use this information, otherwise I would be unable to help him and his people. Nana looked at me for a long time and I held his gaze. I knew perfectly well that he could not give me authority to act as I wished without the agreement of his State Council, and the members of the Council had dispersed and could not be recalled. It was a frightful responsibility from him to take. He looked at me and I looked at him and, as he did not give way, I stiffened. I knew how hard it was to make a decision which might cost him his stool if things went wrong, but all the same I had to get his permission to act as I thought fit to save the people from becoming homeless refugees in a foreign country. I could have reminded Nana, of course, that only two days ago he had created me Queenmother of Tekyiman, but I did not feel inclined to do so. In the end Nana said: 'I place the State in your hands.' 'Your State is safe in my hands.' The words shot out of my mouth, then I realized how enormous these words were. I would have softened what I had said but could find nothing to say. Somehow I knew in my innermost heart that things would turn out all right. I tried to encourage Nana, who relaxed after a while, seeing that I was so sure that luck would be with me.

At six o'clock I returned to Wenkyi, for the following day I had to travel over a hundred miles to Lungero on the Black Volta River. I felt tired, it had been a hectic day and I soon went to bed. That night I had a dream which gave me great pleasure because it had such vivid colours and was composed like a picture. In the centre of the picture I saw myself driving a dilapidated black car on an asphalt road the colour of gun-metal; right and left were black waters almost engulfing the car. A turquoise-coloured sea enlivened the background and on the right, in the far distance, a lighthouse flashed brilliant red light. In the foreground a figure (which was myself) was standing high up on a balcony waving a white lace handkerchief at me driving the black car on the dangerous road far below. The figure on the balcony was elegant, wearing an early Victorian dress of white satin with a crinoline, in marked contrast to my other self in a black leather jacket driving the car below.

The heavy responsibility I had taken upon myself manifested itself in this strange and significant dream. The derelict black car I was driving on the dangerous road represented the Tekyiman State, while above on the balcony, I, as the incarnation of Queen Victoria, promised victory and a happy issue from danger and difficulty.

January

Visiting the Ruins of Bono-Mansu

The following day I went to Nkoranza and then left for Lungero near the Black Volta River, the capital of Mo, which borders on the northern regions of the Tekyiman and Nkoranza States. As soon as I could I returned to Nkoranza to pick up Ankomah in order to go to the ruins of Bono-Mansu, the former capital of the Bono Kingdom.

The ruins began at Mansu, a village that had sprung up on the fringes of the old town, seventeen miles north of Nkoranza, and it was believed that they extended southwards for about ten miles. At Mansu I called on the Mansuhene who ruled one side of the village, and on the Adiakahene, the chief of the Adiaka clan people, who ruled the other. Neither of them was at home. This was a pity, especially with regard to the Adiakahene Kwaame Kra, as I had greetings for him from Nana; although a Nkoranza subject, he was also a court official at Tekyiman. His anomalous position was due to historical factors. The Adiakahene was a descendant of the Adiaka-Mo kings, the last of whom, Adu Kodjo, with his followers came as a refugee to Bono-Mansu. He was given a post at court by the Bonohene Akumfi Ameyaw I (1328–63) which his successors retain to this day. The sceptre of the Adiaka-Mo kings was transformed into the Adiaka-*pomu*, meaning staff of the Adiaka people. It is about as long and as thick as a man's arm; it is said to be of wood, probably a branch of a sacred tree, and encased in gold. At the death of each King of Bono, and later of Tekyiman, a piece from the shroud of the dead king was tied to it, so that by now the staff is covered with about thirty pieces of cloth (if the older pieces have not rotted away). I had hoped to see it and when I heard that the Adiakahene was at Yefri, a village near by, attending a funeral, I went there. I introduced myself to him and, as he knew all about me from Nana, he was willing to give me the history of his people, there and then. The owner of the house, whose son had died, insisted that I should first drink some beer; then he was kind enough to put a room at our disposal, to which we retired: the Adiakahene and all those elders who had accompanied him to Yefri, Ankomah and I.

January

The Adiakahene Kwaame Kra gave me much interesting information but he could not show me the Adiaka-*pomu*. The staff was only taken out of its shrine on special occasions.

From Yefri I returned to Mansu and this time found the Mansuhene at home. He agreed to show me again the ancient rain-water basin of Bono-Mansu, a brass basin of unusually large size which now stands at the end of the village, surrounded by a stockade. It must have stood originally either in the Bono-Queenmother's house, for the queenmothers as rain-makers were responsible for rain in times of drought, or in the temple of Ntoa, Bono's first State god. Ntoa, the sky god, was also a weather god, a god of rain, storm, lightning and sunshine. The two-pronged spear, which was used in rain-making ceremonies, may have belonged to either the Queenmother or the god.

I then sat down to talk with the village elders, but without the chief, who had excused himself. After our talk, I asked if I might visit again that part of the ruins of the ancient city which I had been shown in 1946. I knew that there was nothing to see, as the houses, which had been built of beaten earth, had been burnt down by their inhabitants when the Ashanti came, and those that had survived the fire had been washed away by rain long ago: now dense bush had overgrown the site. But I remembered having seen shown by the Mansuhene a tree under which I had picked up some potsherds. This time I wanted to get permission to take some back with me. This tree was of medium size, not one of the giants, which had survived the disaster and had once divided the main road into two one-way streets.

I was just about to leave with the elders for the tree when I was held back by the Nkoranza rest-house-keeper, whom, much against my will, I had taken along with me. Ankomah and I suspected that he was a spy in the service of the Nkoranzahene or the Korontihene of Nkoranza, both of whom I knew distrusted me. No doubt he had been instructed to find out whether I was engaged in any political activity, and if so to prevent it at all cost. Probably it was thought that I would try to revive in the Bono people of Nkoranza an interest in their old kingdom and create in them the desire to be ruled again by a king of the old dynasty, that is, by Nana. Needless to say I had no intention of stirring up trouble in the Nkoranza State. I looked at the rest-house-keeper for a moment and noted with interest the obvious anxiety in his eyes, but I got angry when he insisted that last time I never went with the Mansuhene to the tree to be shown the potsherds. He was afraid, of course, that I might have conversations with one or the other of the elders which he was unable to overhear, and that we might be plotting something, and he would get the blame. I did not know what to do; I could, of course, disregard him, but I did not wish to get the elders into trouble. Also the tree looked a long way off and I had a bad cold, and did not much relish walking in the heat. So I gave the signal to return, to everybody's relief; they all wanted a rest and a drink. There was no look of triumph in the rest-house-keeper's eyes, which somewhat reconciled me to him.

It was four o'clock by the time I was back in Nkoranza town, faint with tiredness. I went straight to bed after I had said goodbye to Ankomah, who had to return to Tekyiman. He promised to come back the next day, but when Kweyte woke up in the morning with a high temperature—malaria—and I with low fever, I sent Ankomah a message to come when we were better.

CHAPTER VI

February

Nana's Illness

Four days later Ankomah returned to Nkoranza with the news that Nana was ill. I discussed with him whether I should visit Nana the following afternoon, but Ankomah was of the opinion that I should wait till I was requested to do so.

Next morning I was just about to leave the rest-house when a messenger from the post office brought me a note asking me to ring Tekyiman *Ahenfie* (palace) urgently. I went over to the post office at once (it was only two minutes away) taking Ankomah along as I wanted him to keep the postmaster, a brother of the Nkoranzahene, busy while I phoned, to prevent him listening in.

As it happened Mr. D. K. Owusu was on the other end of the line, the same Owusu who had acted as Nana's ambassador when I first arrived in Kumasi in October. He told me that Nana was very ill and wished me to come and see him. I replied that unfortunately I had an appointment with the Nkoranzahene that morning and had to witness the beginning of the *Apo* festival at Seseman, but I would come in the afternoon not later than five o'clock. Mr. Owusu reluctantly agreed to this, but as Nana did not wish to do anything without my advice Owusu asked me whether I thought it wise to call in Dr. R. E. G. Armattoe from Kumasi, seeing that Nana refused to see the doctor from the Sunyani Hospital, who had treated his late brother. I knew Dr. Armattoe well, an Ewe from Togoland; he was not only a good and experienced doctor—he had practised for many years in Ireland—but also the author of several books and founder of the

Lomeshie Research Centre for Anthropological Race Biology in Londonderry. I recommended him warmly. But as it was not ikely that Dr. Armattoe would arrive from Kumasi before lunchtime, I asked Owusu to see that Nana was kept quiet and given some aspirin and quinine. I would most certainly come at the earliest possible moment.

When I returned to the rest-house, however, after the visit to the Nkoranzahene, I found another message from Owusu to come immediately to Tekyiman. I left at once with Ankomah and forty minutes later was at the palace door, where Corporal Kusi was waiting for me. He took me and Ankomah without delay to Nana's bedroom, which was reached through a courtyard leading off the audience-courtyard, it was full of people. Many of Nana's wives sat listlessly about, among them the mother of little Eva with the child in her arms, while princes and elders stood silently in groups, their faces grave. I had to wait a moment while Corporal Kusi informed Nana of my arrival. Then I went in myself with a heavy heart.

Nana's bedroom, a tiny, airless, whitewashed room, more like a monk's cell than a king's apartment, was full of people. I nodded to the elders and then greeted the Queenmother and elderly princesses who sat on low stools round Nana's bed, all bent with grief; it was like a death-bed scene. Nana, prostrate on his bed, smiled faintly when I said in my best Twi: '*M' akyio* (Good morning), Nana, *Wo ho ye* (How are you)?' He thanked me warmly for coming. I took the offered chair next to his bed and proceeded to take his temperature. There was dead silence in the room; everybody followed my movements with the greatest interest.

Nana's temperature was 102°, not so bad, I thought, probably malaria. I then asked, like a good doctor, where the pain was and was much relieved to hear that he suffered only from headache and backache, all symptoms of malaria. Nana did not look to me particularly ill; the whites of his eyes were beautifully clear, not at all tinged with yellow; I somehow felt there could not be much wrong. It then occurred to me that he might, perhaps, be suffering from shock, the deportation order, the decision of his people to leave the State, the responsibility he had taken upon himself by giving me freedom of action—all this might have been too much for him.

When I was told that Dr. Armattoe had not been asked to come as the elders had decided to keep Nana's illness secret, it was left to me to treat him; a responsibility which frightened me, but for the moment I had to accept it. So again I prescribed rest and quinine and left some veganin that I had brought along for his head and backache. I was just going to leave when Mr. Owusu informed me that Nana had taken nine M and B 693 tablets, bought on the local market for the black-market price of a shilling each, to kill any infection he might have. I knew the drug, which I had taken myself once after a bout of malaria, but to take nine all at once seemed to me excessive. I thought it best therefore to treat it as an overdose, and told Mr. Owusu that it would be good for Nana to take plenty of water to get some of the drug out of his system. After that I tried to comfort Nana and the people in the room, by telling everybody that there was nothing to worry about, and that Nana would soon be well again. I left then and rushed back to Nkoranza.

The next day I returned to Tekyiman and installed myself again in the rest-house; then I went to see Nana, but heard from Corporal Kusi that he had left the town. Surprised, I went to see Owusu, who told me the latest news in whispers. There had been too many people who wanted to make sure that Nana was alive, or at least not seriously ill. The elders, worried and annoyed, then decided to hide him, as I had especially emphasized that he needed rest. The Gyaasehene had therefore transferred him the previous night to his house in Akrofrom.

Owusu then informed me that the District Commissioner, having heard that Nana was ill, had come to see him with Father B. from the Roman Catholic Mission to offer medical help. 'But', continued Owusu, 'seeing that Nana wished to be treated only by you, I told him that nothing was wrong with Nana and that he was away on duty.' I was not very happy to hear this because I was sure that Father B. knew a good deal more about medicine than I did and I would have been glad to be relieved of the responsibility for Nana's health. I consoled myself with the thought that, if Nana got worse, I could still press for a doctor, but shuddered when I remembered Nana's beloved brother, who died because a doctor saw him too late. Rather upset now, I decided to go to Akrofrom, and was glad that Owusu was free and could accompany me.

When we arrived at the house where Nana was staying we had to wait a while till somebody came to open the heavily bolted door. Then we had to wait another few minutes in the courtyard while one of the attendants announced our arrival to Nana. Finally we were led into a really bright and airy room furnished with a comfortable bed. Nana looked very tired but told me that he had had a good sleep and felt fairly well now. I took his temperature and was relieved to find it 100°. I did not wish to give him further medicines except quinine, but this shocked Owusu, who thought that I should give Nana at least some fruit laxative, to which I agreed, seeing that it was harmless; 'But please a little only, a little, a little.' I emphasized a little because on the previous day I had said that Nana should drink plenty of water; he must have been given gallons of it for Corporal Kusi had told me that 'Nana, he piss all the night'. Once more I insisted on rest and, assuming the role of a good doctor, added that this year there would be no *Nkyifie* celebrations for him. *Nkyifie*, the first day of the *Apo* festival in Tekyiman, was to be celebrated the following day, and for the king the rites were of great importance, for they renewed the power of his divine life-giving *kra* and that of his Royal Ancestors. Even so I thought it bad for him to get out of bed and told him so. Nana smiled faintly and said that he would postpone the rites for another forty days. When the Queenmother arrived with her retinue I wanted to go but Nana begged me to stay a little longer as he wished to tell me some things about *Nkyifie*. I shook my head, he had talked too much already and it was most important that he should conserve his strength. Nana saw the point and gave in. He then called one of his attendants from the small room connected with his bedroom and whispered something into his ear. A few seconds later a bottle of the finest Mangoustan Rum, '*d'origine carte grise'*, was brought in, which Nana handed over to me. 'Doctor's fee,' I thought; but no, it was a present for me to drink on *Nkyifie*.

In the late afternoon while I was working on my notes in the rest-house, Owusu, accompanied by Mr. Ampomah the treasury clerk, arrived unexpectedly in a taxi with a letter that one of Nana's messengers had brought from Accra. Owusu, addressing me by my Queenmother's name 'Nana Kruwaa', asked me to open it and read it. Reluctantly I did so and, as the contents were important, I insisted that, if Nana was not too unwell the next day, he should be informed about it. Owusu agreed, and suggested that, in that case, I should go to Akrofrom and take the Tuobodomhene with me, as the news also concerned him. He added that he would see him about it at once, which I thought a good idea.

When we arrived next morning in Akrofrom I found, to my great relief, that Nana was much better. He was lying on a bed in the courtyard enjoying the fresh morning and had no temperature. When he heard that there was something important to discuss, he gave orders to be taken back to his bedroom. While he was helped by his attendants, I talked to the Nifahene and the Tanosohene who happened to come in at that moment. Then we all went together into Nana's bedroom. It did not take long to come to the decision to refer the matter to Dr. J. B. Danquah, who acted as Nana's lawyer in political cases, to take the necessary action.

The Nkyifie *Celebrations in the Sacred Grove at Tekyiman*

In the afternoon of that day I worked on my notes in the rest-house; the large table in the living-room was strewn with papers and notebooks. About five o'clock I was disturbed, which I resented very much; Ankomah appeared unexpectedly accompanied by the treasury clerk, and asked me to come with him to the sacred grove at once; the *Nkyifie* celebrations had started already. I was much taken aback; Nana had said only yesterday that he would postpone the *Apo*, and I could not understand why he had changed his mind. Ankomah gave no explanation, he said the time was too short, nor did he allow me to change or to search for the questionnaire which I had prepared with reference to *Nkyifie*. I was bundled into the co-op car in which Ankomah and Mr. Ampomah had come, and a few minutes later arrived at the cocoa plantation near the cross-roads. We got out and walked through the plantation into the bush that had grown over the ruins of the old town of Tekyiman.

When we arrived at the entrance to the grove, a narrow opening cut through trees and bush, we met the Korontihene, followed by a large retinue. He was beleaguered by the Banmu people, who looked after the grove, demanding from him thirteen shillings for libations, which was their due. The Korontihene and his people having gone, Ankomah and I entered the large circular clearing in the grove where the people were already assembled.

In the centre of the clearing stood a small tumulus, the grave of the last king of Bono, Nana Ameyaw Kwaakyie, who is said to have committed suicide on that spot after being defeated in the war with Ashanti (1740). In the *Nkyifie* rites he is venerated as the great ancestor from whom Nana inherited his divine kingship.

Originally, the tumulus, in the form of a dome-shaped cone, was protected by a high thatched roof which rested on seven pillars, beautifully decorated with divine symbols. The same decoration had adorned the low wall which connected the pillars at the bottom to a height of about three feet only, leaving one opening which gave access to the enclosure within. Its ground-plan was rectangular and identical with the Ancient Egyptian hieroglyph for 'room' or 'house' (⬛). In 1950 the thatched roof had been replaced by corrugated iron supported on wooden poles instead of the original pillars. The low wall was also made of wood with wooden benches along it on the inside.

On these wooden benches, squeezed tightly together, were sitting the Queenmother, the Gyaasehene, who was to represent Nana in the rites, and the Banmuhene, who was in charge of the libations and offerings for Bono's last king and would have welcomed Nana in the name of the dead king. Next to him sat the chief of the stool-bearers, custodian of the Chapel of the Stools, who here represented the Royal Ancestors, and the Sannaahene, who was in charge of the *puduo*, the gold that represented the *kra* or life-giving soul of the Royal Ancestors. I was also pleased to see that Okyeame Pong, Nana's senior spokesman, was there, as well as the Akwamuhene and the Twafohene (Kwasi Wusu), two of Nana's elders, who, as heads of the various groups of the royal clan, had a right to their places.

Then I went to greet those who sat on stools in front of the 'house'—the Tuobodomhene, the Offumanhene, the Tanosohene, the Ayokohene, who represented Nana's lineage, and the Queenmother's spokesman. A little farther away sat the Nifahene under an umbrella, surrounded by his retinue; the Kyidomhene, whose ancestors were generals in the army, also under an umbrella and in the midst of his retinue; and the High-priest of Taa Kese, Kofi Mosi, encircled by a number of Tano priests. The Korontihene and his people formed a group apart.

Before I could offer my greetings to those farther away and wave to the commoners, who thronged the edge of the clearing, I was requested to return to the 'house'. Ankomah and I were given a place to sit down and I was told that the rites were now to begin. I looked round with interest; everybody sat solemnly with downcast eyes. A calabash was brought in and filled with palm-wine from an old earthenware vessel. This I was given with the request to pour out the first libation. For a moment I was numb with shock; I looked at the Queenmother, then at Ankomah, and wished that the great honour had not been bestowed on me. Finally, prompted by Ankomah, I said the prayer that was expected of me and poured out the libation to Bono's last king, Nana Ameyaw Kwaakye. Then I took a sip, and after that the Banmuhene took the calabash and filled the libation cups round the grave with some of the palm-wine. The calabash then made the rounds, everybody drinking from it while the minstrels sang the praises of the dead King and the Royal Ancestors in general.

Then it was for me to make an offering, and I produced the bottle of Dutch gin which I had brought for the purpose. Some of it was poured into the now empty calabash, and this time the

M   177

February

Banmuhene poured out the libation and prayed for long life for me and success in all my undertakings. Then he poured some of the gin into the libation cups round the grave, and again the calabash made the rounds. I took a sip from it like the others and also poured some of it on the ground for the Royal Ancestors.

After this had been done, more people, late-comers, came into the 'house' to greet those who were assembled there, among them the priest of Kuntunso and my old friend the Tanohemmaa, who was followed by five or six priestesses. The priestesses curtsied before everybody—they reminded me of butterflies, they moved so quickly from one to the other—and when they had fluttered out of the 'house', they started to dance. A minute later they were all in deep trances.

Then we had to wait for the offerings to be cooked on temporary hearths by the head woman of the Banmu and her women. Meanwhile we in the 'house' passed the time in conversation. I was asked about my experiences in Nkoranza and in turn asked various questions about the *Apo*. It was much like a party, but soon conversation became difficult for lack of subjects to talk about. I could have asked many questions relating to all sorts of things, but without my notebook I felt it to be useless.

After a little while the first offerings, ready cooked, were brought in in a large, old earthenware vessel. The Banmuhene got up, took the golden spoon of his office, dipped it into the vessel and filled four little bowls with the *eto* (mashed yams) and *fufu* (mashed yams beaten into a glutinous, doughy mass). He said a short prayer to the dead King and then placed the four bowls round the grave in such a way that they formed a cross.

Following this a snow-white ram was brought in and sacrificed over the dome-shaped cone by two stool-bearers, so that the ram's blood flowed over it and also into the libation cups and offering bowls. The carcass was then dragged out and another snow-white ram was led in and sacrificed in the same way. The carcasses were then cut up. Certain interior parts of the rams which had a special significance were handed over to the head woman of the Banmu to cook; the rest of the meat was cut up into the traditional portions and distributed to the houses of the elders, so that their families also could partake of the sacred meal.

We had to wait during the cooking of the sacred meal, which was to be shared by the living with the dead King in order to renew the bond between them. It consisted, apart from the meat of the rams, of three different kinds of beans, plantain, pawpaw, garden eggs, tomatoes and ground-nuts. I reckoned that it would take at least an hour if not more, and was somewhat alarmed at the prospect sitting there, unable to move and not knowing what to say. I looked at the sun which was near setting, and was suddenly seized with panic. The whole time I had been sitting there I had been thinking of the dead King. I had been told that a hole led from the top of the cone down into the grave so that he could listen to what was going on above. I knew that in the grave there was at best a skeleton, but the image of him, alive and listening, a wizened old man, leaning on his elbow and cupping his ear, unnerved me as time went by. I tried to overcome my mounting anxiety and if I did not manage to leave now, I would have to stay to the end, because soon it would be dark, and I could not possibly go alone in the darkness through the bush, the ruins beneath my feet. Still I hesitated; I thought of the rituals to come: the food would be brought in and the Gyaasehene, representing Nana, would say the prayer for the well-being of the State and then eat the traditional three mouthfuls. The Banmuhene would fill little bowls and offer the food to the dead King. Then the Queenmother and all those assembled in the 'house' would one after the other say the prayer for the well-being of their clan, each taking the three mouthfuls from the large bowl which, in the past, would have been made of gold. Then the earthenware vessel with the *eto* and the *fufu* would be carried outside and bits of it would be given to everyone assembled in the grove, including the commoners lined up on the fringes of the clearing, so that everyone could share in the sacred meal. While this was being done, each person in the 'house' would pour a libation to his ancestors. The Akyeamehene, chief of the royal spokesmen, would say the closing prayer. After that the Queenmother would give the signal for the rejoicings to begin, for the ancestors had accepted the offerings and there would be a good harvest and happiness in the State. Finally all the people would leave the grove in a procession.[1]

I looked at the assembled company in the 'house' and at the blood-stained grave with its libation cups and offering bowls, and still feeling unnerved turned to Ankomah; I asked him in a low voice whether it would be regarded as an insult to the dead King if I left before the end of the rites. Ankomah shrugged his shoulders and said, 'You can please yourself, you are a Queenmother'. After a moment's thought I begged Ankomah to tell the people that I wished to go. There was a moment's surprise but nobody inquired why nor begged me to stay longer. Among the Akan any woman, not only a queenmother, can leave a meeting or assembly without being questioned. I went the rounds, shook everybody's hand and left the 'house'. I also greeted those outside and was relieved when I had passed the entrance and stood once more on the ruins of the old town. But then I paused in doubt and asked Ankomah again whether I had committed an offence and ought to go back. He shrugged his shoulders; if he had said that it would be better if I returned, I would have done so. But as he said nothing I took him roughly by the arm to make him hurry, for it was getting dark.

When we were three-quarters of the way through the darkening bush we were waylaid by two young men. I did not understand what they shouted; from their gestures I thought that it might be something like 'your purse or your life', as I caught the word *sika* which means 'gold' or 'money'. I felt like knocking them down, but I controlled myself and listened with patience. When it went on too long for my liking and Ankomah would not tell me what it was all about, I simply said good-bye and went off. Then all three got excited. At last Ankomah told me that the two young men wanted to tell me that I was standing on holy earth and about the dead city under my feet, and that to this day gold could be found in the ground in little pots which the inhabitants had buried when the Ashanti attacked the town. I thanked them curtly and dragging Ankomah along, we walked as fast as we could to reach the main road.

[1] The rites are described in full in *The Divine Kingship*, pp. 146–9.

February

In the main road all was quiet; night had come. The co-op car had gone and Kweyte was in town; I had given him the afternoon off. We walked in silence. At the entrance to the rest-house compound I asked Ankomah whether he would like to come in for a drink, but he declined. I looked after him till he had disappeared in the darkness, then looked at the rest-house, behind it the shadow of the hill of the guardian god Botene. Santos was sitting on the porch, a hurricane-lamp at his feet. In this dim light he was working on a fishing-net, which he wanted to bring home to his family. Like most Ijaws of the Niger delta he was a fisherman whom fate, for a short period of his life, had transformed into a cook and steward. He had started the net in Kumasi while I was ill; since then it had grown to a monstrous size. I nodded to Santos and went into the living-room while he continued to work on his net. I sat down and had a drink, then, getting restless again, I went out into the garden. When I saw that Santos was too much engrossed in his work to watch me, I escaped, and started to walk along the road to Nkoranza unable to bear being shut up in a room.

It was a dark night, the moon came out only occasionally. The little hills along the main road on my left looked black and the bush on my right looked menacing. But the road was like a dusty white ribbon and I followed it doggedly mile after mile. I walked fast, glad of the silence around me. But then came the moment when I had to stop, too tired to go on. For a moment I longed to lie down in some hollow in the bush, but if Santos discovered my disappearance he would give the alarm and people would be sent out searching for me. So I had better turn back. Arriving at the rest-house garden I saw Santos still bent over his net. I slipped into the house and called for 'chop' (West African jargon for 'dinner'). Santos came in; although I had called for dinner unusually late he made no remark.

When N.A. Corporal Kusi arrived (my guard for the night—there were six who came in rotation) I withdrew into my bedroom, while Santos and Kweyte put up their mats in the front room; Corporal Kusi made himself comfortable in the old cane chair in front of the entrance. Evidently Santos and Kweyte were soon asleep, as one could hear the slightest noise right through the rest-house; all the windows except those in the living-room were open and the two rickety doors which separated me from them left an open space above them.

Towards morning, I was rudely awakened by an uproar. I looked out of the window and called for Santos and Kweyte; I could hear their voices, but at first they took no notice of me. Then Santos, on the way back from the garage, came rushing towards me to tell me the tale: 'a strange man' had got into my car—the garage was no more than a shed—and had tried to drive it away. Luckily Corporal Kusi had heard him and after a short fight had managed to give him a knock-out blow. He bound his hands and was now marching him to Tekyiman jail.

Ankomah later told me that the 'prisoner' was a madman from a border village on the Nkoranza side and was sometimes found wandering about. When he came into Tekyiman territory he was usually arrested, kept for two or three days in prison 'to cool him down' and then returned to his family. This time his family would be ordered to keep him locked up till I had gone. He, by the way, could not drive a car. Of course I rewarded Corporal Kusi for his watchfulness and valour. In the fight with the madman he had received such a black eye as I had never seen in a black face! He looked ghastly. But Nana also rewarded him and he suddenly found himself a hero!

Visiting Nana at Akrofrom

The following day I stayed in the rest-house; I did not feel like seeing people, not even Nana, after my flight from the sacred grove the previous afternoon. But next day I had to go to Akrofrom. As usual I went to fetch Ankomah but he was not at home. This was odd, and I grew alarmed when I was told that no one knew where he was. I would not let the matter rest until at last I found somebody who whispered in my ear that Ankomah had gone into hiding but could be found at a certain address. I went at once to the house, which was not far away, and found him lying on a mat conducting a lively conversation through a half-open bead curtain with his 'cateress', who was busy preparing some food for him. He apologized to me but refused to move. I did not know what to make of his behaviour and thought that it had something to do with my leaving the sacred grove; probably he was held responsible and had become my scapegoat. But he denied this hotly. Finally when I told him that I had to go to Akrofrom to thank Nana for the *Nkyifie* invitation, and asked what reason I was to give for his absence, he decided to come out of his lair.

At Akrofrom we were at once led into the courtyard where Nana was lying in a deck-chair covered with a rug. To my relief he had no temperature and felt comparatively well. I told him about *Nkyifie* and how much I had missed him, but did not say that I had left early, nor did he seem to know it. While we were talking a party of elders arrived, among them the Offumanhene and the Queenmother's spokesman. At Nana's request I stayed a little longer, then left to visit the priest who had given birth to the new god.

Ankomah and I found him dancing in front of the sanctuary, painted white from head to foot and holding a sword in his hand; he was deep in a trance. All the same he recognized me and came to shake hands with me, but he was trembling violently and could not quite focus his eyes. He threw a bowl of white clay over me to purify and bless me. Then he threw an egg on the ground to read some omen. He nodded with satisfaction and then announced for all to hear—a great many people had meanwhile assembled—that I had a good spirit.

On the way to my car I was followed by some women who had accompanied the priest's dance with their songs and rattles. At last they summoned up courage and asked me to dance for them as they had heard that I was a great dancer. I did not feel like dancing without music and in general was not keen to exhibit myself, but Ankomah said that they had honoured me by asking and that I could not refuse. I then took two rattles from the women to use them like castanets and started to dance something which could be vaguely described as Spanish. On the sandy ground that was the only possible choice. For the first time I understood why there is so much stamping and footwork in Spanish dances.

When I had finished an old man, who looked to me like a beggar, with his long, filthy trousers full of holes, a string instead of a belt round the middle, and a much worn shirt, loudly acclaimed me. He fished sixpence out of his pocket and gave it to me, thanking me volubly for the dance and expressing his admiration. I felt like giving him back his sixpence which must have represented a fortune to him, but I knew better. I held up the sixpence triumphantly for everybody to see, then held it for a second to my mouth as if kissing it, while I turned to the old man and slightly bowed to him. The old man was overwhelmed, tears came into his eyes and he thanked me over and over again. The women were much less enthusiastic; I had a feeling that I had shocked them. They thanked me stiffly and I then had to give them four shillings for the honour of having been asked to dance.

When I went to the car Kweyte, who had joined Ankomah while I was dancing, said shyly: 'Madame has danced beautifully.' I felt embarrassed and did not know what to reply to this. Ankomah nodded agreement and then said seriously: 'Yes, very beautifully.'

Back in Tekyiman the car was stopped by a tall, well-dressed man who started a violent argument with Ankomah. As Ankomah refused to tell me what was the matter I waved to Owusu, whom I saw talking to somebody on the other side of the road, to find out for me what was happening. Then I had the story. Ankomah had stood security for some well-known person in town who owed money to the tall man which he was unable to pay. The tall man now required Ankomah to pay the few pounds owing to him. Ankomah did not have the money, nor did he feel inclined to pay a debt which he did not owe; hence he had gone into hiding, but now he was caught. As I happened to have three pounds with me I gave them to Ankomah to prevent the tall man going to Nana, and then I chided Ankomah for not having come to me with his worry. He could have asked me for the money, particularly as he was due to receive money from me at the end of the month.

Anyhow I was glad that now I knew the reason for his odd behaviour and that it had nothing to do with me.

The Birthday of the State god Taa Kese

On the morning of Taa Kese's birthday Owusu told me that another urgent letter had arrived from Accra and that the Korontihene and the Nifahene were waiting for me in Nana's office to discuss the contents with me. We did so and after the meeting the two elders went to Akrofrom to tell Nana about it, while I went with Ankomah to Hansua where I had an appointment with the priest of Nana's *kra*, Kwasi Takyia. I needed some more details about the rites for the kingly *kra* (the concept of the *kra* is identical with that of the ancient Egyptian *ka*).[1]

In the afternoon I was working in the rest-house with an old man, Kwaame Nyame who, except for Nana, knew most about the history of the Bono Kingdom. About six o'clock I went to town to the Tano temple; I had an invitation to take part in the ceremonies for Taa Kese, Tano the Great, State god of Tekyiman, whose birthday was being celebrated.

The Queenmother and all the elders were already assembled in front of the temple and sat in the traditional half-circle round the circular three-step dais of the god. On it stood the shrine; veiled, as Taa Kese's rebirth had not yet taken place. This was to be celebrated on New Year's Day, the following Monday. After I had greeted all the elders and the Queenmother I was given a seat next to her, then the new Tano High-priest came and curtsied before me. He was a rather decrepit old man, a sad contrast to the former High-priest Kofi Mosi with his beauty and his striking personality. The High-priest then said a prayer and poured out a libation from a calabash filled with palm-wine. This was passed round for all of us to take a sip.

Townspeople came up one after the other to greet us and then stood around us. There was much coming and going. After a while priestesses danced in the dim light of the hurricane-lamp. I talked with the Queenmother and the elders; there was a happy

[1] See *The Divine Kingship*, Chapter V.

informal atmosphere, everybody seemed to enjoy spending the warm night in a social gathering. Later the High-priest danced to honour me. The whole evening he had been trying by every means to single me out, telling me about the god, making me get up to look at the shrine or telling the people that they must cherish me. At nine o'clock all was over and everybody returned home.

In town the *Apo* was celebrated daily with singing and dancing by the people. Two days after Taa Kese's birthday and one week after *Nkyifie*, on Friday, was the 'great day of abuse' which is said to have been founded in the belief that grievances and evil wishes harboured secretly by one person against another endanger, in some magic way, the process of growth. To avert this everybody was permitted to say openly what he thought of his neighbours, and could insult them without punishment; he could even insult the king and queenmother. On this day, if Nana had been well, he would have had to fight a battle in the streets with the Korontihene, both carried on the shoulders of their men and supported by their people, all clad in old historic battledress and armed with clubs and sticks. This battle was said to dispel old feelings of antagonism which arose when the aristocracy of Bono-Mansu came to rule in Tekyiman after the break-up of the Bono Kingdom, thus ousting from power the family of the Fante prince Takyi, the founder of the town and ancestor of the Korontihene. Apart from this, the battle commemorated an historical event.

Since Nana was unable to come, there was a party in the Gyaasehene's house. When I arrived the courtyard was already thronged with people standing in groups, talking and drinking. The Queenmother was accompanied by little Kwabena, and when the boy saw me he ran towards me, took my hand and stayed with me. He told everybody that I was his 'wife'. I was glad to see him recovered from yaws and strong for his three and half years. After half an hour Owusu came to tell me that a messenger sent by Nana wanted to see me and was waiting in the office. Kwabena had gone back for a moment to the Queenmother who wanted to give him a drink, and thinking that I would be back in a moment I left the party without saying good-bye to him.

February

Nana's message was to come to Akrofrom at once as another urgent letter, this time from Dr. Danquah, had arrived from Accra. Owusu had already told me about it but I had missed seeing the Korontihene, who had taken the letter to Nana. I left for Akrofrom taking Owusu along.

On my way back, stopping at the palace for Owusu to get out, I was given a message that the Queenmother urgently wished to see me. I picked up Ankomah at the office and went to her house. The Queenmother apologized for troubling me and half laughing said that she hoped I would understand; Kwabena was most distressed about my sudden disappearance from the Gyaasehene's house. He had gone from person to person inquiring, 'Have you seen my wife? My wife has gone.' He was still upset and she would be grateful if I would see him. I was touched of course, and Kwabena was called, and ran towards me crying 'My wife, my wife has come!' I apologized to him for having left without saying good-bye but he hardly listened. He kept my hand in his and I had to stay with him a little while.

The following evening the whole court, presided over by the Queenmother, sat in a semi-circle before the palace. The townspeople in a long procession came to greet her and the elders. I sat next to the Queenmother; Kwabena, who had been allowed to stay up, between us. Priestesses danced again to entertain the people. A young one 'saluted me too much' and would not leave me when she went into a trance, lying at my feet, her arms round my legs. When at last she went, the priestess who was so enamoured of me at Akrofrom when the god was to be born, came up to me to greet me in a new way. I had to stand up for the greeting. She took my right hand in hers and lifted it high up, then she gently turned round to let her head rest for a little while on my breast. I gathered that it was an old ritual greeting with a symbolic meaning, but I could not get an explanation for it.

The following day, Sunday, the last rites of the *Apo* should have been celebrated in great style in front of the palace and all along the main road. But owing to Nana's absence only a few elders were present and a few Tano priests danced forlornly among the people.

February

On Monday I went to Akrofrom to greet Nana and wish him good fortune in the New Year which started that night. He was happy to see me and told me that he had a surprise for me. He would tell me at last the names and deeds of his Royal Ancestors, the Kings, who had lived before Asaman who had founded the Bono Kingdom in 1298. I was thrilled because this was of great importance for my work. Nana had several times promised to talk about this but something had always happened to prevent it. As it was essential that nobody should hear what was said— this type of tradition is kept absolutely secret—Nana had cleared the house opposite of people. He asked me to go over with Ankomah, as he was still busy for a moment, and have my 'Breakfast' meanwhile. This was most unusual, but I did as I was asked and sat down with Ankomah at a table in an open-walled room facing the courtyard and waited. Shortly afterwards an attendant appeared with a table-cloth, two plates and a knife, and a large basin filled with pineapples, oranges, and bananas.

When we had finished and the attendant had cleared the table, Ankomah and I waited for Nana to come. An hour passed. Getting restless after some time I asked Ankomah to go over and inquire when Nana was coming; perhaps he had forgotten about me. Meanwhile I walked about in the deserted house. After ten minutes or so Ankomah returned looking worried; although he had knocked hard at the door nobody had come to open it. Really disturbed by now, we returned to Nana's house and knocked, and finally hammered at the bolted door. But nobody came. We looked at each other. Something upsetting must have happened to Nana, evidently everybody was busy with him. But what? The Gyaasehene had come to see him just when I left; what news did he bring? All the political news went through my hands; what else was there to upset Nana? Then I thought I knew what it was; the Gyaasehene had told him of my flight from the sacred grove when he heard that Nana intended to tell me about the Royal Ancestors. He must have impressed on Nana that I was not worthy of being told. Ankomah denied it, but I was sure of it. Did not the Gyaasehene have to tell Nana everything? And I thought of the dance in the Sannaahene's house the night when Nana proclaimed me Queenmother, and how he was told about the marriage offer of the chief which had spoilt everything and killed Nana's joy. It must be the Gyaasehene, I thought, and wondered whether he was against me or Nana that he should time his news at such unfortunate moments. Ankomah, of course, was horrified at what I dared to suggest. Standing in the deserted street in front of a door which would not open I felt as Adam and Eve must have felt when they were thrown out of paradise. I did not know what to do; should I go home? Ankomah shook his head and, while we argued, the door opened and an attendant appeared. Ankomah explained my situation to him; he replied that Nana had gone to bed. Then he went to inquire while we waited again. After a few minutes he brought back Nana's request to return to the house.

Ankomah and I, deep in thought, sat down again at the table where only an hour ago we had been so happy. The same attendant appeared again, this time with two bottles of beer from Nana, compensation for our waiting, and the message that Nana was not well enough to work with me today.

New Year's Night at the Tano River

In the late afternoon of New Year's Day priests of gods who were regarded as sons of Taa Kese assembled with the shrines of their gods in the temple of the State god. After a short rite had been performed the shrine of Taa Kese was carried out into the courtyard on the head of a priest. There a procession of priests was formed, most of them carrying the shrines of their gods; the priest with Taa Kese's shrine came last walking under a state umbrella, for Taa Kese was Abanmu Tano, State god of Tekyiman. The procession went up and down the main road three times, townspeople excitedly following it. Others lined up on both sides of the road to watch the procession pass.

When it became dark the Tano priests turned into the square before the palace to greet the Queenmother, the elders, and me; we were assembled already and sat in the traditional semi-circle.

February

Prayers were said by various priests and libations poured out to ensure a good New Year. Then the priest of the god Ati Kosi, a Tano god from Tanoso, went into a trance; all he said was that if the State stood firm, and if unity were maintained, all would be well. He also said that I should be trusted for I would save Tekyiman and Tekyiman would be victorious in the end. Then all the priests arranged themselves in a procession to go for a purification ceremony to the sacred grove on the banks of the Tano River, not far where the river crosses the Sunyani road. Nobody was allowed to go with them except the Queenmother who, in the rites, as the incarnation of the Moon Mother-goddess, presided over the rebirth of Taa Kese and his sons. She did not go, however, and asked me to take her place. This was really a very great honour and I accepted with delight.

The priests who carried the shrines of gods and others in the service of Tano had to go first; when they were out of sight a second procession was formed by priests of other gods of Tekyiman—they had come as visitors—Ankomah and I joined them.

It was a dark night, the moon had not come out yet. We walked along a bush path full of holes and protruding roots. A torch-bearer, his torch a burning bundle of palm-leaf stalks tied together, walked beside me, but the light was dim and I was glad that I had taken my torch from the car and could hold it in front of me. Even so I stumbled several times because we had to walk briskly to catch up with the others.

After about a quarter of an hour's walk we arrived at the entrance to the sacred grove where we were waylaid by the Abrafohene (master of ceremonies) of Taa Kese and his assistant. They were lying across the path, the Abrafohene held in his hand a flint knife, encrusted with the blood of sacrifice, his assistant held an ancient iron knife on which was stuck a piece of freshly cooked yam. A little fire was burning beside them and next to it stood the pot in which the yam had been cooked. The Abrafohene kept me back in order to explain to me why he was lying there, but I was unable to understand what it was all about. I somehow gathered that the flint knife symbolized the sacrifice,[1] and the yam

---

[1] As known from similar rites connected with the gods, such as Ntoa

the offering which in ancient times took place in the grove but which now takes place in the temple of Taa Kese.[1] Then the Abrafohene told me why this spot in the forest had become sacred. It was here that Taa Kese had revealed himself to the Fante prince Ameyaw, son of a king of Bono (c. 1660) and had told him that he wished to be worshipped in Tekyiman.

When Ankomah and I entered the small clearing of the grove along the river all the priests were already seated on the ground with the shrines of their gods before them. They formed a large U, the symbol for conception, because Taa Kese and his sons were to be born anew to the Moon mother-goddess. I was given a place in front of the U with Ankomah next to me; we also sat on the ground and, like the others, faced the priest who was conducting the rites in place of the High-priest of Taa Kese, who although elected, had not yet been enstooled.

Everything was ready for the rites to begin when I felt something biting me painfully. Alarmed, I told Ankomah about it because tropical insects can be poisonous. Ankomah without replying to me immediately informed the chief priest[2] who at once stopped the proceedings so that I could disappear and rid myself of the insect. I thanked him gratefully and went with Ankomah to the narrow mouth of the entrance to the grove. There I took off a warrior ant of considerable size. Then I saw others walking up my mosquito-boots. Poor Ankomah had to kneel in front of me and kill them off one by one, while I held the torch. When we went back and sat down again—the place brushed clear of ants—Ankomah gave a short account of what had happened. When I heard the word *n'kran*, which I knew meant 'ant' I burst out: 'A giant ant, ours in England are small and good-natured.' All the priests laughed but the chief priest cut them short and gave the signal to begin.

A priest at once got up and went to the riverside and there

for instance, the totem animal of the deity was originally sacrificed with a flint knife.

[1] The gods originally had no temple in the towns, but were worshipped exclusively in their groves.

[2] The new High-priest of Taa Kese was not yet enstooled in the temple and was not allowed therefore to preside in this important rite.

loudly said a prayer: 'The cycle of the year has come round, may the New Year be a good one.' Other priests followed him and bathed in the river to purify themselves, others only wetted their faces and hands. While this was going on a Tanokwa, an assistant Tano priest, drew water from the river in a large basin and from it filled little bowls which contained white clay and *adwera* leaves for consecration. Each of the priests took one of these little bowls and carried it back to his shrine. Then they all uncovered their shrines and scrubbed them on the outside with the mixture. When this had been done they marked each shrine with three vertical white lines and crossed these with three horizontal lines, to show that it had been freshly consecrated. Some of the priests also marked their faces with a white line from the hair to the bridge of the nose. Then the spokesman of Taa Kese took up his position by the riverside to say the main prayer for the well-being of the State and all its people, and also prayed that Tekyiman's enemies might perish. A Tanokwa then uprooted a large *summe* plant and gave it to the spokesman who dipped it in the river and sprinkled everyone with the holy water. I must have got a special blessing, for so much water was used that it ran down my face and the front of my dress. All the shrines were likewise sprinkled while each priest said a prayer to his god. Then the shrines were covered up again.

Ankomah and I were the last to leave. When we came out of the grove the Abrafohene had just lit three fires: one in honour of Taa Kese; one in honour of the State and the Queenmother, who owns the State as a mother owns a child; and one in honour of Nana. When the Abrafohene saw me he lit a fourth fire in my honour. I was deeply touched and thrilled when my fire became one with that of the god and then joined the State's and Nana's. Sparks flew all around us, the dry grass burned so easily. Ankomah tried to drag me away, but still I stood and gazed. I adore fire! Then the bush behind us started to burn and it became really dangerous for us. The Abrafohene finally gripped me by the arm and we ran along the path to safety. Then I stopped again to look back and saw 'my' fire, raging across the low bush. It was now impossible to go back; the entrance to the grove was

closed nor could we in the second procession go back the way we
had come for the fire followed on the heels of the priests. So we
made our way down to the main road to Sunyani.

It was a glorious night, the moon was out now and shone
brightly, the sky was covered with stars. It was lovely walking
through the warm night. There was no need to walk in a procession, single file, as the road was wide; we walked in groups,
the priests talking together in lively tones, one or another stopping from time to time to speak to those walking behind. Suddenly there was a burst of laughter; the priest from Krobo, Kofi
Wusu whom I knew well, told a story which must have been a
funny one. I asked Ankomah what the joke was, but he would not
tell me. But the little priest said: 'Tell her, tell her,' and so
Ankomah, embarrassed, told me: 'This morning priest Kofi
Wusu overheard two Christians saying that Nana is too old-
fashioned. He should stop all this business with the Royal Ancestors and pagan customs like the *Apo*. They are a disgrace to
the modern Gold Coast. Priest Kofi Wusu got angry and abused
them and told them that he would report them to Nana. . . .'
'Well,' I said, 'Why did everybody laugh?' 'The abuse,' Ankomah
replied, 'I cannot translate it.' Whereupon the little priest let
loose a whole string of obscene words and everybody laughed
uproariously once more. But then we heard *aferihyia pa-o* called
out in the distance, meaning 'a good New Year to you', and we
all started to hurry back to the town.

In the courtyard of the temple the Tanohemmaa and some
priestesses were waiting for us and, forming a single file, we
walked past the offerings the Tanohemmaa had prepared—large
basins full of mashed yams with and without palm-oil, *fufu*, three
kinds of beans, and other vegetables. Then we entered the main
room of the temple, a bare room in which the shrines of the gods
stood along the walls. Taa Kese's shrine was erected in the
middle of the wall to our right on a four-step altar made of mud
and resting on a five-legged stool. Blackened stools of former
High-priests stood like the shrines of Taa Kese's sons on a
slightly raised portion of the floor. All the shrines were uncovered
and made ready for the offerings. The Abrafohene then called out

the names and titles of Taa Kese, and the talking drums were beaten while the Tanokwa filled little basins with the offerings and placed them on or in front of the shrines. Prayers were said and libations poured out but no sacrifices were made. If Nana had not been ill it would have been his duty the following morning to sacrifice the rams.

After a while Ankomah and I left. We were just stepping out into the main road when I was stopped by the Nifahene and the Queenmother's spokesman, silver staff in hand, which meant that they were on an official mission. To my surprise it concerned me. It had been announced that I had been bitten by an ant and they wished to assure me in the name of the State of everybody's deep sympathy. I did not know what to say, I felt so embarrassed and ashamed; at first I thought they were making fun of me, but seeing that they were serious about it, I thanked them as graciously as I could.

Walking towards my car I said bitterly to Ankomah: 'To-morrow the whole town will know of my mishap, maybe little songs will be made about it.' Ankomah was horrified at this idea; it would be abuse; in olden days if some person did that to a Queenmother he would have been executed.

When Kweyte saw me coming he jumped out of the car and opened the door for me. 'Madame,' said Kweyte, 'I heard you were bitten by an ant; can I offer you my methylated ointment'— and he started to search for it in his pockets.

In the rest-house I wondered how I could have dealt better with the situation. But there had been only two ways open to me; either to suffer, and I shuddered when I thought of all the other ants marching up my mosquito-boots, or to do what I did. The worst of it was that this should happen when I had to represent the Queenmother!

CHAPTER VII

March

The Royal Village Twimea

I had again to go to Wenkyi and Nkoranza for a week and was happy when I was back again in Tekyiman and in the rest-house which had become a home to me. The bliss was short, however; on the following afternoon the District Commissioner sent me a message that he required the rest-house for the Bishop of Accra. I went at once to Akrofrom to tell Nana, who could not understand it as the Bishop usually stayed at the Roman Catholic Mission. Nana thought that the District Commissioner wanted me out of Tekyiman—perhaps the Government was going to punish Tekyiman now for the 'Battle of Tanoso'—and the District Commissioner, to prevent me interfering, proposed to turn me out of the rest-house. Nana decided that he should not be allowed to do so and after a moment's thought invited me to stay for the few days at Twimea in his cousin's house. I was greatly surprised; Twimea was the royal village inhabited only by members of the royal family; of course I accepted with pleasure.

Next morning all my belongings were packed up once more by Santos and Kweyte, and accompanied by Ankomah we all drove to Twimea in high spirits. First we followed the Sunyani Road for eight or nine miles, then turned into a bush path on the right which led to a village, and after another mile and a half through the bush we arrived in Twimea.

Twimea, which I did not know, looked very different from the usual African village. There could be no doubt that this was a residential area—some fifteen handsome, well-built houses lined both sides of the main road; there were no shops or stalls of any description; no children played in the road and chickens and goats seemed to be absent (Pl. 26). A little market at the end of the village took place twice weekly I was told.

I was to stay with Oheneba ('King's son') Kwabena Esi who owned the last house on the right side of the main road coming from Tekyiman. He was already expecting me and was sitting with members of his large family in the main courtyard of his house (Pl. 27). He welcomed me warmly and offered me a chair next to him. Then he called the rest of his household together to greet me. Most of these were women—his own wives and grown-up daughters and also some of his sisters; among the men there were his grown-up sons and some of his younger brothers. I caused a sensation among the children who had never seen a European before; some were frightened by my white face and began to cry, which amused everybody. When the excitement had died down and most of the women and children had left, the Oheneba told me about his great sorrow. His daughter had died at Akrofrom three days before after she had confessed to the priest that she was a witch and had committed a crime (she had probably wished for the death of a person and that person, unluckily for her, had died). The funeral was over already as witches are buried straight away; but people had come nevertheless to express their sympathy, which had made him happy. He then went on to tell me that his daughter had left behind a nine-months-old baby—the one that had cried so much when it saw me—and it was a great consolation to him that people would never tell the child about the fate of its mother; luckily no stigma would be attached to the child.

Shortly after the Oheneba took me to the house opposite, which belonged to the Queenmother's husband to greet the Odikro ('headman') Kwaku Adae, and representatives from each house and others who were eager to meet me.

At last back again, I was shown my room which delighted me. It had a barred window giving on to a lane and, in contrast to the rest-house, I could lock my door. The room had a bed, a table, a new armchair with plush cushions, and a chair for a visitor. It even had a wash-basin on a stand and a small cupboard. Framed photographs of friends of the young man who had given up his room for me, adorned the walls. Near the window were pinned up illustrations cut out from a wartime number of the *Sphere*. One showed a soldier with his arm round a white girl, a blonde in a summer dress; the face of the soldier was cut out and the face of a young African was substituted for it. A whole page from the *Sphere* with the caption 'Fraternisation in Full Swing' showed Fräulein with allied soldiers on the sandy shores of the Wannsee.

Hardly had Santos put up my camp-bed, which I preferred to the owner's bed as I could fasten a mosquito-net to it, when there was a knock at the door; the representatives of the houses had arrived to return my visit and I had to go out to chat and drink with them in the courtyard. I then went back into my room to read a bit before lunch. It was late, for there was no kitchen stove or table for Santos and the women were embarrassed by a foreign man in their midst. Finally he was given a corner and a hearth, consisting of three dome-shaped cones, where he could cook for me.

As soon as I had finished my lunch Kweyte came into my room with a worried mien. 'Madame,' he said, 'Madame had forgotten to inquire about the latrine.' Well, I had not, there had been no occasion to do so and I had hoped to be shown the place without having to ask for it. Kweyte with eyebrows up and anxious to help me 'in a matter of great importance to Madame', begged me to be allowed to take matters in hand. I gave him permission much relieved; in a few minutes he was back with Ankomah, the brother of the Oheneba and other male members of the family; I was asked to go with them, they would show me the place. Slightly uneasy, I followed them, reassured by their air of importance. We went right through the compound—the courtyard surrounded by the main rooms including my own—then another courtyard that served as kitchen, then another flanking servants' rooms, till we reached the back entrance, then through it into the adjacent forest. We walked and walked through trees over uneven ground till we finally reached a little hut, the size of a dog-kennel, made of fresh palm-leaves. It had no door but was so cunningly situated in a deep hollow that privacy was assured.

March

This was it, Kweyte announced with pride—'Your latrine, Madame'. I thanked the brother of the Oheneba for the great consideration shown to me and asked him to convey my thanks and delight to the Oheneba. Then I expressed my admiration for the structure which made everybody happy.

Back in the courtyard I met the half-crazy Tano priest, the ex-serviceman, who greeted me cheerfully: 'Hallo, Sister.' I was especially nice to him, for I gathered that it was he who had built the latrine for me, the only one who, thanks to his army training, would have known how to do it. He looked well, to my surprise; only two weeks ago I had seen him collapse while dancing in a trance. He had lain motionless on the ground with a stiff arm raised to the sky in a catatonic attitude. It remained so while he had been carried out unconscious into the compound of a house near by.

The Oheneba had asked me to treat his arm, and I had promised to do so, much against my will. A thorn from a tree had entered the palm of his left hand which had gone septic and blood poisoning had set in; his whole arm up to the shoulder was swollen. I wanted him to go to Sunyani Hospital as I regarded his condition as serious, but he would not hear of it. Now the bucket with hot water for which I had asked was ready and, surrounded by most of his family, I took off the bandage of dirty banana leaves which was fastened round his hand by an equally dirty string. For about half an hour I had his arm up to the elbow immersed in the hot water into which I had poured some Dettol, every few minutes adding more hot water in the hope that this might do the trick. Then I treated the wound with iodine and bandaged it properly. I burnt the filthy banana leaves and the string, to the great surprise of the family.

A little later a messenger from the Nifahene arrived to inquire whether I had arrived safely and was satisfied with my room and my host. The messenger had to go back at once to report to his master, who in turn had to report to Nana. Since it is important for a messenger to get everything clear, I showed him my room, pointed out to him the comfortable chair, the table on which I could do my work and then took him to the kitchen yard to introduce him to Santos, who had taken charge of the gifts which had been given to me by my host—chickens, yams, eggs, tomatoes, onions, and bananas enough to feed myself and my crew for a day. I was to receive a fresh supply daily, as the Oheneba made it clear to me that I was his guest.

When the messenger had gone I rested for an hour or so, and then decided to take Santos with me for a walk through the village. Poor Santos felt out of place in the house as I saw when he brought me my tea, his mournful eyes were even more mournful than usual. Apart from everything else, he was homesick for his wives, his children, his fishing in the Niger River, and his home town. I consoled him by assuring him that in a month's time he would be starting on his homeward journey.

I also felt that I had to console Kweyte and took him along on my next round. He was equally homesick; he had now been two months on the road with me and news from his home was not good. A week before, after he had received a most upsetting letter from his wife, he nearly went off to Accra to see her in order to beat up her would-be lover. I am sorry now that I did not keep her letter or make a copy of it, for it was written by a letter-writer in the most flowery English. In it she told in detail how the man next door had tried to make love to her and how until now she had withstood his advances, but she feared that she could not hold out much longer but would succumb to his honeyed words. Her dear husband must come soon to save her before it was too late. I did my best to calm Kweyte down; I could not spare him to go to Accra and I advised him to send a wire to his wife telling her to return at once to her parents and stay with them until he fetched her. In the prepaid wire she promised to do so, but Kweyte was still worried lest the man might follow her and there might be others paying her attentions. I said that I was sure, since she had written to him for help, that she would be true to him and would wait patiently another month.

When I saw Ankomah walking towards us I sent Kweyte to look after the car which was parked in front of the house, and was surrounded by children, some of whom were crawling over it. Also I wanted to take Ankomah for a walk. First we visited various houses and chatted with the people, then we went by the empty market-place and got into a conversation which was most interesting to me. I told Ankomah about Kweyte and his wife and that I was afraid he might suddenly leave me, whereupon Anko-mah, in great indignation, blurted out an account of Kweyte's misbehaviour in Tekyiman. His last love affair had nearly caused a scandal. With the greatest difficulty he had avoided a court case and had begged the people to forget about it so as not to worry me or upset Nana. What was it? The usual thing—seduction of a married woman; luckily Kweyte had not known that she was married, and the woman's husband was absent from Tekyiman. Compared with Kweyte, Ankomah said, Santos was an angel: he never looked at a woman. And, he added, Kwei and Gilbert Fenakedorh, who had been with me on my first and second trip, had also behaved well. They each took a temporary wife and led a decent life; everybody in the town spoke highly of them. Gilbert's temporary wife had been a daughter of the destooled Queenmother and I now understood why the princess, when she saw me, always inquired after Gilbert and asked me to greet him from her. Then there was Musha, my driver on the second trip. He had been almost as bad as Kweyte, according to Ankomah, but more discreet. Thinking of Musha, I could not help remark-ing to Ankomah that I saw nothing wrong with enterprise in love, which shocked him. That I, of all people, who led such an irreproachable life, could defend immorality! I then told him of Musha's adventures in Dagombaland, to see what Ankomah's reaction would be. It was in Yende, I said, Musha had just come back from the market and was telling Gilbert something exciting in the kitchen. I clearly heard their voices and I wanted to know what it was as I had caught the words 'King's wives', and thought that it might be something of anthropological interest. And so it was; Musha had strayed into the beer-garden at the market—he would—and had met there several young wives of the eighty-year-old king of the Dagomba, who were offering local beer—and themselves—for sale. I told Musha that I must meet these wives, and off we drove to the market. There they were, a merry crowd; Musha pointed out his special friend and introduced me to her.

March

(I wondered what the late king, who in 1936 had so proudly shown me his harem, would have said to this state of affairs!) Ankomah, of course, was duly shocked; the idea of a king's wives acting as prostitutes was abhorrent to him. Among the Akan in the past the lover of a king's wife was killed with the most terrible tortures. Every limb of the wretched man's body was cut off, his back was flayed and the skin displayed before his eyes, after which he was placed on a keg of gunpowder and blown up.

Of course, continued Ankomah, there were prostitutes in Tekyiman but they were all foreign women, four Yoruba and one Ewe, and they lived in a brothel. Only strangers visited them, no Tekyiman would think of going there. When I heard that there was an Ewe woman among the prostitutes I suggested to Ankomah that I should go and see her, because I was interested in the fate of the Ewe prostitutes who, generally at twelve years old, were sold to the brothels in Accra. When they returned to their homes in Togoland they were waylaid by the priests who took most of their earnings. The Ewe prostitutes, as in ancient Phoenicia, served the goddess, and hence the priests thought themselves entitled to their money. Ankomah unfortunately was shocked that I wanted to 'honour with my visit' a brothel woman, and I had to abandon the inquiries in this field.[1]

In the evening after supper we all sat outside in front of the entrance, which had a small roofed porch—my host, his brother, a few young men, and children, as well as Ankomah, Kweyte and Santos. Down the road in front of the other houses old men were sitting in chairs while younger people and children sat at their feet. In some houses women were singing. By ten o'clock most people had gone in, but I continued to sit with my party a little longer, the night was so lovely and I was not tired.

[1] Prostitution was not introduced from Europe. William Bosman in *A New and Accurate Description of the Coast of Guinea*, published in 1705, says for instance (pp. 211–16) that all the small towns on the Gold Coast had two or three prostitutes, slaves, who had been bought by the elders for the town when they were young and beautiful. But as the prostitutes were obliged for the remainder of their life to refuse no man, not excepting little boys and the old and sick, they were soon worn out and suffered from venereal disease. Once ill they were deserted and 'thus these unhappy creatures come to a miserable end'.

March

When the whole village was asleep I felt that we also should retire, and I said good night to them and went to my room to fetch my torch. I came out again, nodded to them, as they were still there, and disappeared in the direction of the forest. When Kweyte saw this, he lost his head: 'Madame, I come with you, you cannot go alone. You might lose your way and there are leopards.' I shook my head and said that I was able to look after myself, but when Kweyte persisted Santos got angry with him for his improper behaviour. In the end I ordered Ankomah to hold Kweyte till I was back. I understood very well what prompted Kweyte's outbreak of anxiety about my safety. He once told me his dilemma: 'If you serve an important black man and he dies, then they seize you to be his human sacrifice; if you serve an important white man (worse, of course, a white woman) and he dies, then the police will take you and hang you in prison.'

Next morning while I was having breakfast and was just pouring some rum into my tea, Kweyte stormed into my room: 'Madame, Madame, come quick, a woman is dying.' Slightly bewildered—after all what could I do about it?—I got up at once and hastened with him across the road to the Queenmother's husband's house. The courtyard was full of people, and in the middle of them, lying on the ground was the 'dying woman', writhing in agony and crying out with pain. Nobody knew what to do with her, and the Queenmother's husband was absent. I knelt down beside her to find out what was wrong, and after much questioning of those around me was finally told that this was not the first time that she has behaved thus: about a year ago she was treated for her sickness in Sunyani Hospital. I asked to see the hospital card, but all I could gather from it was that she had been an out-patient and was seen by the doctor once. I deduced from this that her trouble, whatever it was, was not serious, and that the complaint was probably of a hysterical nature. I asked Kweyte to get me the French medicine that I had bought at the Nkoranza-Seseman fair, a glass of water and a spoon.

When Kweyte came back I poured some of the *Alcool de Menthe 'Etoile'* into the water and gave it to the woman to drink. After that she was quiet for a moment then she started to throw herself about again, sobbing and moaning. I knelt down next to her again, stroking her bare back, saying all the time in a sing-song voice, 'All will be well, well, all will be fine, all will be well, well, all will be fine,' till she calmed down and was lying still. Then I went on stroking her back and saying over and over again, 'Sleepy, sleepy, drowsy, drowsy, sleepy, sleepy, drowsy, drowsy, drowsy,' till she closed her eyes and lay completely relaxed. Stopping for a moment to rest my hand, I noticed with horror that I had used my left, the bad hand, the tabued hand, the hand used in black magic. I looked round alarmed to see whether anybody else had noticed it. But people stood or sat motionless like idols, staring with vacant eyes into the distance. Then I looked down at the woman at my feet, who sighed contently and then moved a bit to make herself more comfortable. I bent down and saw that she was asleep. I looked round and then, unable to bear the sightless people, I asked Kweyte to tell them when I had gone that the woman was all right, and left hurriedly. A few minutes later Kweyte came rushing into my room telling me that the people had carried the woman in and had put her to bed. She had awakened for a second and smiled happily, now she was asleep. I had hardly finished my breakfast when a deputation arrived from the Queenmother's husband's house to thank me for the miraculous cure.

I had to visit Nana for news and Nana Yaa Amaa, one of the woman elders of the Queenmother, to get some more information on funeral rites. At four o'clock I returned to Twimea and I was just going to eat my lunch when I was told that a woman wished to see me. I went out to the entrance door and was greeted there by a very pretty young woman who shyly offered me a basket of eggs. As I could not make out what she said, I called Kweyte, who excitedly explained that this was the 'dying woman' whose life I had saved and that she had come to thank me. I looked at her in surprise, unable to recognize her; the face I had seen was swollen from crying and contorted with pain. I then found out, that she was the first wife of the Queenmother's husband, and that she had three children by him and three weeks ago had given birth to a fourth. Owing to the possessiveness of the Queenmother, who never let her husband leave her side, his first wife felt neglected: which, of course, she resented very much. Her 'sickness' as I now realized, was nothing else but a violent protest at the state of affairs. I promised that I would talk to her husband; he was due to arrive the next day as he had been informed already of the events of this morning. Meanwhile I gave her my bottle with the *Alcool de Menthe 'Etoile'* to prevent a relapse.[1]

When she had left me the Oheneba wanted his hand treated. The hot water was ready. To my surprise the arm was normal, the swelling had completely gone and the wound was almost healed. If something was miraculous it was surely this. All the same I gave him a new bandage and told him that from the next day onwards a plaster might be necessary for a day or two to protect the new skin that was growing.

The following day was Sunday. I woke early because somebody walking along the street was singing a most melancholy, haunting song. The verses ended: *'Kwae, kwae'* (remember, remember). Other people, coming out of the houses joined him and when the people had reached the little Methodist Chapel for Sunday service, one could hear their voices no longer.

At nine o'clock I went to Tekyiman and was met by Owusu who informed me that he had some important letters from Kumasi which he wanted me to see. We then drove together to Akrofrom to hand them over to Nana and discuss their contents with him. It was four o'clock before I had my lunch in Twimea.

Next morning I left the royal village not to return. I had to go to Nkoranza to witness the last day of the *Apo* at Seseman. When I passed the rest-house I saw that it was empty. I knew already from Nana that the Bishop had stayed exactly one night in the Mission with the Fathers: presumably he had changed his plans.

[1] *Alcool de Menthe 'Etoile'* was strongly recommended as an unfailing preventive against cholera, influenza and other troubles 'resulting from unhealthy weather'. Moreover 'a few drops will promptly restore the equilibrium of the nervous system shaken by intense fright, a fall, or a violent blow'. . . . It was also recommended for sea-sickness, dizziness, weakness and spasms. The glass bottle was in a wooden container that could be unscrewed in the middle below a red ribbon and it was this that made me buy the medicine, which was apparently invented a century ago.

March

My Return to Tekyiman

Back in Tekyiman once more, I went first to the Post Office to see whether there were any letters for me; but before I could ask the postmaster, a man pulled timidly at my sleeve and, when I turned round to him, said: 'You are Jesus Christ, my brother sick, you help him.' I protested that he had mistaken my identity, but the man took no notice. Exasperated I asked him at last where his brother was. He pointed to a youth leaning half-fainting against the wall of the post office. Seeing that I had to do something I asked to be allowed to feel his brother's forehead. It was hot, the youth obviously had fever, but whether it was malaria or pneumonia, I could not tell. I then asked the man whether his brother had ever taken quinine, and when the reply was in the negative I turned to the postmaster to get some from him; quinine could be got from any post office in the country free of charge. The postmaster had unfortunately run out of quinine, but remembering a 'chemist' a few houses farther down the road, I asked the man to come with me. Luckily for me the 'chemist' was open and had forty grains of quinine left, that is to say post office quinine which he had got for nothing and offered to sell to me for a shilling. I was angry and refused to pay it; in the end we agreed on sixpence. When I got out my money and saw that I had tenpence I gave it to him—after all, he had shown some enterprise in getting the quinine. Furthermore, I had looked round the shop, there was one shelf with a few patent medicines and another with soap, talcum powder and pomades. It did not seem likely that this chemist made much money, and my guess was right, for he could not thank me enough. The man, with his sick brother behind him, had followed our conversation and haggling with great anxiety; his English being limited he probably did not understand much of it, or if he did, he had no money. I gave him the quinine as a gift and he cheered up; I then turned to the chemist and asked him to tell the man in his own language that his brother had to take three (five-grain) pills each day and not more, in three separate doses, in the morning, at midday, and in the evening. A few days before, when Okyeame

Pong, Eva II's father, had malaria I had given him a tube of post office quinine containing the full amount and had impressed on him and his family that he was to take three pills a day and no more. But when I had gone each member of his family remembered something different, with the result that the old man swallowed the whole sixty grains in one dose. I nearly fainted when I heard it. For two days, Okyeame Pong said, he was dizzy and deaf, his heart racing, but he survived the overdose, and the malaria 'she was gone'.

Returning to the post office to get my letters and newspapers, I was held up a second time. A man brushed against me, dressed in a poor cotton cloth, one end of which was pulled over his head in such a way that it made a hood, concealing most of his face. When I looked at him, he threw back his 'hood' and to my astonishment I recognized the exiled High-priest of Taa Kese, Kofi Mosi. I greeted him warmly, being genuinely pleased to see him, and this immediately transformed him, and restored some of his self-assurance and swaggering elegance. He had come secretly to Tekyiman to visit his old mother and to see once more the temple of his god which was his life. I was again struck by his beauty which, however, was not always apparent; at times he could look downright ugly, and I often wondered what kind of a person he really was. He gave no sign of being deeply religious like other high-priests I knew. One might perhaps describe him as a prince of the church, proud of his ancestry, his gift of oratory, and conscious of his personal attractiveness. When he left me I looked after him, as he walked away into exile, his head held high, a lonely figure in a wide and empty road.

From the post office I went over to Nana's office to get the latest news. Owusu was glad to see me and introduced me to a messenger who had just arrived from Accra with a bag full of letters, all copies from confidential Government files made by a clerk who was, I suspected, in Nana's pay. I looked through them with interest; the Government still had not made up its mind whether to deport Nana and, if so, when. I decided to go to Akrofrom to let Nana have them and was glad that Owusu had time to go with me.

March

When we arrived we found Nana in the front room of the house and in the middle of a speech in which he was urging the members of his State Council not to let themselves be provoked by the pro-Ashanti party at Tuobodom where political feelings were running high following the death of the usurper. Nana asked me to wait for him in the courtyard till he had finished as he still had to discuss some local matters with the Council. Owusu remained with Nana.

Out in the courtyard an attendant brought me a chair and, as he could not find a cushion for it, simply went into Nana's bedroom and brought me his pillow to sit on. I objected, but the attendant, Anto by name, assured me that it was all right. Anto, a young man, seventeen years old, was the nephew of the Boyemhene, chief of one of the nine villages which, following a quarrel with the then Tekyimanhene Kwasi Twi, had gone over to Ashanti in 1935. When I came to Boyem in 1946 the people were regretting their rash action and asked me to let Nana know that they intended to return to Tekyiman if an occasion should present itself. Such an occasion had not yet arisen. Meanwhile Anto, who was regarded as a successor to the stool, had come to Tekyiman and openly declared his allegiance to Nana. Nana had taken the young man into his service and made a friend of him, keeping him constantly in attendance by day and causing him to sleep in the ante-room at night. Anto served Nana with almost passionate devotion, but the elders disapproved because they suspected him of being a spy. Whereas Nana was illiterate, Anto could read and write and had many opportunities of reading confidential correspondence, about which Nana was inclined to be careless. It seemed to me, however, that the question of Anto being a spy was not important. It was impossible to keep anything secret in Tekyiman, everybody knew what was going on. The important thing was that Nana had found somebody who really cared for him and surrounded him with love.

When Anto had gone, leaving me with a Government publication to read (the only literature about the place), I lit a cigarette. Watching Anto in the distance, talking to some of Nana's wives, I must have forgotten to extinguish the match properly. Anyhow in a minute the pillow was ablaze, but I managed to beat out the fire before the flame had caught my dress. But alas there was a gaping hole in Nana's pillow! I showed the hole to Owusu, when he came to tell me that the elders had gone and that Nana was now free to see me, and asked him to tell Nana that I would bring him a new pillow-case. The idea that I would buy a pillow-case for the royal household amused Nana greatly.

In the afternoon of the next day I went with Owusu to the village of Bamiri two miles from Tekyiman, which I had never visited before. I had been invited by the Odikro Kwasi Asare the founder and chief of Bamiri, as far back as November, but had never found the time to go there. I was welcomed by the people with cheers and when the excitement had died down a little the Odikro made a speech in which he thanked me first for having come and then, at great length, for what I had done for Tekyiman, dwelling particularly on how I had sustained the State in all its trouble with Ashanti and the Gold Coast Government, and expressing the belief, which was also that of his people, that I was a reincarnation of their old Queenmother Nana Kruwaa. I had done what she had done in the terrible war against Ashanti in the last century. It was therefore right that I should be given her name. He then begged me to acknowledge the people of Bamiri as *my* people and redeem them and save them from destruction. After that the elders got up one after the other and, filing past me, each gave me his hand, with tears in his eyes imploring me to continue helping Tekyiman; they on their part would pray for the success of my work. It was a most moving scene, and I promised them solemnly that I would do everything in my power to help them when I was back in England. They knew already that I was leaving Tekyiman in two days' time not to return except for an hour's stay on my way back from Gyaman.

The next day at Bisedan I had a similar experience. On all previous occasions I had been the anthropologist doing her work; this afternoon for the first time I was addressed by the chief and his elders as Nana Kruwaa, and acknowledged as 'the mother of the Tekyimanhene': that is to say, as their Queenmother. Again the people implored me to help and save them from extinction.

March

By that time the whole population of the Tekyiman State knew of the Government's intention to deport Nana and depose those elders who remained faithful to him. For the village people it meant the end, and they felt that I alone was able to prevent a disaster of such magnitude.

The following morning I went to Hansua, the Banmuhene's village, and then to Kuntunso and Bonkwae. I said good-bye to all my friends and then went on to Twimea to make my farewells there also. In the afternoon, accompanied by Owusu, as Ankomah was busy, I said good-byes in Asueyi, Krobo and Akrofrom.

At Akrofrom I had my last talk with Nana, whose health by then was fully restored. He remained 'hidden' at Akrofrom to avoid having to see the District Commissioner or having to visit him at Wenkyi. At the end of the conversation I mentioned casually that I could not obtain petrol in Tekyiman and it was likely therefore that I should not be able after all to leave on the following day. I told him that I meant to send Kweyte to Wenkyi where I could get petrol from a Syrian trader, but unfortunately Kweyte was not feeling very well and I wanted him to rest when we got home.[1] I was slightly upset about it because I like to adhere to my schedule. Nana was surprised what difference could it make to me whether I left the next day or the day after, such a small thing! But when he saw that it mattered to me he promised to see that petrol was there for me. After all he was a king and could command people, and, if necessary, he would order every man, woman and child to line the road from the border of the Wenkyi State to Tekyiman eighteen miles away and pass from hand to hand the four-gallon tin I required. That was how things were done in ancient times. I looked at Nana; I knew he was thinking of the golden basin filled with sacred water for the king's purification ceremony on New Year's Day, which was passed from hand to hand by the chiefs of the Bono Kingdom, all on

[1] Kweyte had an attack of nerves. Driving while he was feverish, often unable to focus his eyes properly, had produced anxiety in him and he dreaded having to go to Wenkyi. I did not force him as I, having had the same experience, but had to drive during the war when I had to finish an urgent piece of work, am now unable to 'touch' a car. I gave him luminal and aspirins and he drove me to Gyaman, and back to Accra, without further complaints.

horseback, from the source of the Tano River to the king in his palace. I found Nana's idea of equating the tin of petrol with the golden basin of sacred water delightful; it appealed to me immensely. We both looked dreamily before us but after a while I wondered dimly what Nana's subjects would have to say. Timidly I suggested that the lorry which went to Wenkyi in the late afternoon could take my empty tin along and that somebody from Tekyiman could bring it back to me on the lorry leaving Wenkyi for Tekyiman early next morning. But Nana, otherwise so passionately progressive, would not hear of it. I could see how much he wanted to present me with the petrol in the grand manner—it would have been something to be remembered in the history of Tekyiman. However, in the evening the petrol-lorry from Kumasi arrived, which settled the problem.

Nana allowed Ankomah to go with me to Gyaman, for which I was grateful. Our first stop was Kyiraa, a small town on the Sunyani road where we went to see Nana Kofi Adomah, an uncle of Nana's and a charming old gentleman whom I had met several times in Tekyiman. I brought him Nana's greetings. He introduced me to the Kyiraahene and some of his elders who gave me valuable information on the town's history. Our second stop was Sunyani, the largest place in the region, and a town in the European sense of the word. It was the seat of the Senior District Commissioner for the Brong-Ahafo region to which Tekyiman belonged. I knew the Senior District Commissioner as he had visited me in Tekyiman and was glad to find him in as I wanted to have a talk with him. Lately the Tekyiman N.A. police force had been disbanded by order of the Government and I wanted to know from him what was behind this move and what the Government expected to achieve by leaving the Tekyiman State without police. The Senior District Commissioner, sympathetic to Tekyiman and its many troubles, deplored the action as much as I did, but said that he could do nothing about it, as a legal point was involved which was not of the Government's making. He blamed Dr. Danquah for having created a precedent in Pamu, the capital of Domaa, and patiently explained to me the ins and outs of the case (I have forgotten now what it was all about). Anyhow Ankomah, the Inspector of the force, Corporal Kusi and the others who had guarded me during the night, all lost their jobs, which was a blow; especially to Ankomah, who felt that he had lost not only financial security but also status. Unless he left Tekyiman, which he was not prepared to do, he would be unable to get work.

Bondugu

I was excited to be back again in Bondugu, the capital of Gyaman, for it is a most picturesque town, many of the houses built in the old heavy Sudanese style, with flat roofs, their windowless walls lining the narrow alleys. One can wander around and think oneself back into medieval times, so untouched by European influence is the heart of Bondugu. Moslems seemed to dominate the streets and the market, although the ruling caste are the Domaa. They conquered Gyaman and its capital towards the end of the seventeenth century, after they had been driven out of Asantemanso situated south of Kumasi, the town they had founded three generations earlier on land that had been given to them by a king of Bono. The Domaa of Gyaman still regard themselves as Bono (Brong) and its rulers never forgot the old relationship. In 1877, when the Ashanti–Tekyiman war broke out, the Gyaman kings welcomed the Tekyimanhene Nana Kwabena Kofi and his people when he transferred his government to Bondugu for the duration of the war. And again in 1950 Gyaman had declared itself willing to receive Nana and his people in case the Gold Coast Government followed up its intention of deporting Nana and his elders.

When I had arrived for the first time in Bondugu, in 1946, there was no French official in the town; they had all gone to Abidjan to attend a conference. When the Regent, Nana Adinkra, heard of my arrival at the rest-house, he immediately sent a sword-bearer with a message to come and greet him, while the talking drums in front of the palace announced my arrival to the people.

I found the Regent seated in his pavilion, surrounded by elders with whom he had been sitting in council. Nana Adinkra was a handsome young man, charming but arrogant at times, elegantly dressed in plush cloth; he spoke fluent French. He asked me what 'my mission' was and when he heard that I wanted information especially on Asantemanso, he promised me all the help he could give. We liked each other immediately and I was happy that he was so friendly and interested in my work. I noticed that while we talked he took a light-skinned infant on his lap which he fondled and made much of. Seeing that I looked surprised, he handed it over to me to play with. He explained that it was the child of his niece. She had been married to a cousin but when she did not produce the desired prince or princess was beaten by her husband and finally divorced. Then she had an affair with a Greek trader and to the surprise of all got this light-skinned bonny baby. The Domaa being matrilineally organized a child had the rank and status of its mother, so that the child, if it was a boy, could succeed to the throne, and if a girl, to the queen-mother's stool. For this reason Nana Adinkra honoured the child and its mother by playing with it.

The following day I happened to meet the child's father. He was a Greek communist who was unable to return to his country; he had no money. He poured out all his homesickness and his loneliness among this foreign people, who made much of him but could not give him what he was longing for—his own people. The princess, whom he had saved from disgrace by giving her the child, loved him passionately, she was a wonderful wife, she had even learnt to cook Greek dishes which he had taught her, but she was not his own kind. He had no hope of ever seeing the brilliant sunshine and the blue sky of Greece again; he was condemned for ever to live in Africa's steaming heat under a hazy sky without people who thought and felt as he did. I tried my best to console him; I myself was in some sense uprooted as he was; I understood him and showed my sympathy, wishing that he could see his home again although I feared that a return might not prove to be the blessing he imagined.

I had three days alone with Nana Adinkra and his elders before the French officials came back. The news of their return was given me by the Senegalese corporal, who should by rights have been mounting guard at the Commandant's house, but who had constituted himself my guard in the hope of getting a good tip. The news soon became reality for me when a French lieutenant came to see me in the rest-house to find out who I was and what business had I, a white woman accompanied by three Africans, in this part of the world. Unfortunately my passport gave him cause to distrust me, for it stated that I was a South African, born in Germany, resident in London and, what was worse, it had been issued at Accra. He could not understand why I had a Gold Coast passport seeing that I was a South African, or an English one seeing that I lived in London, and my explanations made no sense to him. To cut matters short I produced a paper which I had received from the Crown Agents in London before I left, stating that I was an officer of the Gold Coast Government and had to be treated accordingly. This, as I could have foreseen, made matters worse. An officer, a woman, and wearing no uniform—funny people these English, he must have thought, judging from the way he looked me up and down. Of course I could only be a spy, or was conspiring to get Gyaman to join the Gold Coast; in fact Nana Adinkra, in rebellion against the French in 1940, had fled to the Gold Coast where he had remained until the war was over. For the moment the lieutenant said nothing more but this was not the end of it.

The same afternoon Nana Adinkra and some of his elders came to the rest-house to give me information on various things I wanted to know about their history and religion. We were sitting happily together, drinking and talking, when a French officer appeared and requested me to come with him at once; Monsieur le Commandant wished to make my acquaintance. I pointed out that I had visitors, as he could see, but would be ready in an hour's time. The officer glared at me and then barked out: 'Monsieur le Commandant comes first here; will you kindly follow me.' I would have refused, but Nana Adinkra, suave and diplomatic, came to my rescue. 'Yes, of course, Madame, Monsieur le Commandant comes first in my town, I shall wait for you here until your return.'

For a moment I was speechless, not on account of what he had said, but because for the first time he had addressed me with 'vous'; until then it had always been 'tu'. 'As-tu bien dormi, Madame?' he would ask me in the morning, or 'As-tu fini le perrier? Tu sais ce n'est pas bon ici de boire l'eau' and so I had also used the 'tu'—'As-tu bien dormi, Monsieur le Roi?' or 'Tu sais, ta ville est vraiment pittoresque, c'est l'Afrique ancienne'; 'Tu penses, Madame? Mais si sale, il n'y a pas de canalisation ici.' It only then occurred to me that Nana Adinkra had used the 'tu' because the French were in the habit of addressing their African kings and chiefs with 'tu', a relic of the eighteenth century. They, the kings and chiefs together with their subjects, had to use the 'vous' of course. Nana Adinkra, always diplomatic, had probably foreseen that I might address him with 'vous' in front of the officials and he did not wish to be corrected by them in my presence.

I left reluctantly with the French officer, and outside the rest-house on the road I was introduced to Monsieur le Commandant, his wife and three French officers. I was made to enter one of the two cars in which they had come and noticed with alarm that we were not driving to the Commandant's house but right out of town. I was furious because I realized that I would be unable to return at the earliest possible moment. I was also taken aback that nobody told me where we were going and did not ask, as I presumed that I was being kidnapped.

About four miles from Bondugu we stopped in front of a bungalow, the home of a French mechanic who had a garage there. We sat down in a miserable-looking garden and drinks were served. Suddenly everybody was pleasant and I was made to feel that I was a welcome guest. I was given a tumbler full of Vermouth, undiluted, at which I protested, knowing from experience that in the heat a quarter of this liquid would be enough to make me drowsy. Monsieur le Commandant just laughed. When I saw the others, including the wife of the Commandant drank the same amount and that plenty of ice was added I calmed down. In fact I remained unaffected by the drink and wide awake during the four hours, from six o'clock till ten, that we were there. I had nothing to complain of, everybody was most charming to me and I replied to the endless questions, none of which touched on my reasons for being in Bondugu. What the French wanted to know was: 'How does one make love in South Africa? Are the South Africans like the English and keen on virgins, or do they, like us French, prefer the experienced woman? Women, I should know, are like wine, it's the vintage that matters. A woman is at her best at the age of forty. We French are connoisseurs in this field. Did I agree?' Then becoming more personal, did I prefer English or South Africans to French lovers? I was so imprudent as to reply that so far I had not had a French lover and therefore was unable to give an opinion on the subject, whereupon Monsieur le Commandant gallantly said that this could be remedied. I said, yes, of course in Paris, where I intend going when I have finished my work in West Africa. But not in Bondugu. Here I was too well guarded, for my boys were sleeping on their mats outside my door and would not let anybody enter my room. Eyebrows went up—in front of my door? It was the custom for travelling French officers and officials to have their boys sleeping with them in the rest-house room at the foot of their beds—something which horrified their English counterparts. Needless to mention, the Bondugu rest-house had no special rooms for boys.

And so the time passed. When at last we were in the car again, I hoped to be driven back to the rest-house but it was not to be. I had to have dinner in the Commandant's house—the whole party was invited—and by the time we sat down to it, it was almost eleven o'clock. I sat next to Monsieur le Commandant; on my other side, two places farther down, was the young lieutenant who had been so upset about my passport. He had only joined us now.

It was well after twelve o'clock before I was allowed to go back to the rest-house. The garage mechanic brought me home and when I got out of his car in the darkness I almost fell over Gilbert Fenakedorh who was sitting before the entrance of the rest-house compound. I later learnt from Kofi Antubam that he had been stationed there ever since it got dark and, to Kofi's amusement, had never stopped looking in the direction in which

I had disappeared. But Kofi himself had not gone home but had waited for me. Only Musha had gone to sleep, the only one who had not been anxious about me. 'Madame, big white master', 'Madame much power'—no reason to fear.

Kofi then gave me an account of what had happened after I left. Nana Adinkra and the elders continued to drink and answered the questions put to them. Suddenly Nana Adinkra noticed a Frenchman standing in the shadow below the veranda railing, obviously trying to overhear the conversation. He called out to him, 'Lieutenant, Madame is out, come and join us and drink some of her excellent whisky.' The lieutenant came up and sat down and asked Nana Adinkra what work he was doing with my interpreter. Kofi calmly informed him that I was interested in the Moslem population of Gyaman, their religion and customs, which unfortunately was contrary to what I had said to the lieutenant when he questioned me in the morning. In the end when I had not returned by seven o'clock they all left. The lieutenant by the way never mentioned to me his visit to the rest-house, although he had ample opportunity to refer to it in the Commandant's house.

This was in 1946, now in 1950 the Commandant was a Gaullist, who had been in London during the war with de Gaulle as chief of the Fleet Air Arm. He was no less suspicious of my activities in Bondugu than his predecessors had been. I could have avoided misunderstandings if I had written to M. Monod or M. Mauny of the Institut Français d'Afrique Noire at Dakar and asked them for introductions. I knew them and they were acquainted with my work. But being casual about such things I had omitted to do so in 1946 as well as in 1950. In order to know more about me the new Commandant invited me to dinner one night. Although we were alone there was no talk of love and no personal questions were asked. He spoke with longing of London, and how much he admired the English. He gave me his card and asked to be allowed to visit me there one day. He was a man extremely conscious of his power—he ruled an area which was bigger than Belgium, as he said with pride. It was clear from his conversation that in his case also 'M. le Commandant came first'.

March

I stayed a few days in Bondugu waiting for Nana Adinkra's return from Abijan where he had been decorated by the French for his anti-Vichy activities during the war. Most of the time I wandered about town with Ankomah, collecting bits of information and making friends here and there. What surprised me again was to see naughty children. Among the Akan, away from the coast, naughty children do not seem to exist, they are invariably well behaved and obey without fuss. This is the result of loving patience on the part of their elders, and is also due to their respect for the child who, it is believed, becomes an ancestor in heaven and as such might have power over his parents. Also the Akan woman is not frustrated but has rights safeguarded by the Queenmother who rules all women, unlike the veiled Moslem women who are apt to vent their grievances on their children. So one sometimes sees them in the streets dragging their unwilling children with them, shouting at them when they are not quick enough, and hitting them when they go into tantrums.

One morning I went with Ankomah to visit the house in which Capt. Binger had stayed which is now decorated with a memorial tablet 'Ici logea Binger'. Capt. Binger wrote the brilliant book which has now become a classic *Du Niger au Golfe de Guinée*, which was published in 1892. At the head of a French contingent he fought Samory, who had conquered large territories in the western Sudan, but he still found time to interest himself in the history, religion and customs of the people with whom he came in contact. Having travelled in much the same regions which he traversed I have always found his observations and judgments correct and the material he collected reliable. I have a great admiration for him and was glad that he was honoured by a memorial tablet and that the room in the house in which he stayed in Bondugu had been turned into a museum by the descendants of his host. Alas, there was said to be only his helmet and sword which he had left behind and the Koran which he had studied in order the better to understand the Moslems. I could not see the objects as the owner of the house, the Alimani Ali Trinité, was absent. Ankomah, of course, had no idea who Binger was and I told him about his book and what it must have meant at the time for a white man to be alone in an unknown hostile country. I quite forgot that Binger had been far from alone. Somehow confused, I really tried to convey to Ankomah Mungo Park's experiences who, in 1799, really quite alone, explored the western Sudan, never knowing whether he would return alive. I must have told my tale very well for when I had finished Ankomah had tears in his eyes, pitying the white man who had such a terrible fate. I then became aware of my mistake but did not correct it.

When we came back to the car we found Kweyte most upset. He was in tears and could hardly speak. While he was waiting for us some of Nana Adinkra's elders had brought an old man whom they had convicted of theft to undergo public punishment. He was first flogged and then made to go on his knees all around the square. Soon the old man's knees were bleeding and he was in a pitiable state. I was surprised, because I knew that in 1947 the French had abolished the old barbaric punishments meted out by the chiefs and had replaced them, as in British Colonies, by fines. It must have been a disgusting sight, and I was much relieved to have missed the scene as it would have been difficult for me to let a thing like this pass without comment or protest.

I finally left Bondugu without seeing Nana Adinkra, which I regretted very much as I would have liked another conversation with M. le Roi. But I had to catch a plane leaving Accra on April 5th and I still had to spend some time in Kumasi and Accra. On the way back to Tekyiman we stopped at Nsawkaw where I wanted to photograph some ancient brass objects which I had not been able to get good pictures of on my former visit in 1946.

Good-bye to Tekyiman

I left Nsawkaw about one o'clock and was in Tekyiman about three. Nana, his health fully restored, had returned to his capital that morning. He was sitting in a State Council meeting when I arrived and, after he had welcomed me affectionately, promised to see me at five. But at five he was still being greeted by people expressing their joy that he was back. He then decided to visit me in the evening in the rest-house and say good-bye to me there. Outside the palace I met Ayerttey who, to my surprise, was wearing a long moslem coat and I could not help remarking on it. He explained to me full of pride that Nana had converted him to Islam. For a second, thinking of the hours Nana must have spent with him, I was almost jealous of Ayerttey!

In the evening I waited for Nana from eight o'clock onwards. By nine he had still not come; at half past nine Ankomah appeared with the Nkwankwahene Yao Frempon and the spokesman, Kwasi Timpuduoh. We drank and waited; at half past ten a bearer brought Nana's message—he was unable to come tonight but would visit me at six in the morning.

After a short whispered colloquy with the Nkwankwahene Ankomah got up to make a speech, Nana's speech. Once more I was told how much Tekyiman owed me for the support I had given over the years in the fight for freedom and the nine villages. Every little item was repeated again. I looked at Ankomah; I had never seen him so serious, but now he stood here for his King and the State and was fully conscious of the responsibility which rested on his shoulders. After half an hour or so I could not stand it any longer and begged leave to go to my bedroom for a moment. I was desperately tired, and if Nana came at six it meant that I should have to be up at five. I sat down on my bed, drenching my forehead with eau-de-Cologne, trying to pull myself together. Then I picked up my blue chiffon scarf, which Santos had washed and ironed and which was lying neatly folded on my table. I had promised to give it to Ankomah when I left as he was keen to have it 'to remember me by'. When I returned to the room Ankomah was still standing ready to continue Nana's speech. He took the scarf without a word and put it over his head, tying the ends under his chin, so that he looked like a girl. Then he spoke, it must have been for another half hour. At the end of his speech the Nkwankwahene handed over to me Nana's good-bye present, a large thick envelope containing pound notes. I refused to accept money. Nana and I had made a pact in which I had promised to help the Tekyiman State politically and, in return, would be given all the secret traditions which I needed for my work. The State and Nana as its head had honoured its part of the bargain and I mine, as was made clear to me by Nana's speech. Money had no place in this transaction.

The Nkwankwahene quietly replied that Nana knew my views on the subject as I had often expressed them, but I had given him a present when I arrived in Tekyiman and it is right for a king to be generous to a beloved friend. I must not insult Nana by refusing to accept his gift. In fact Nana had foreseen that I would behave thus and for this reason had sent him instead of one of the State elders, whose persons were sacred. Since he was an elected chief of the young men, I might with impunity insult him as much as I liked, if I wished to do so, by refusing a king's gift. In any case he had orders from Nana not to leave till I had done as he wished. This clinched the matter, for by then it was almost twelve o'clock. I took the envelope and asked the Nkwankwahene to thank Nana in my name for his speech and his most generous gift. But I could not help adding that I would like to hand this precious present over one day to little Eva.

When the Nkwankwahene and the spokesman had gone Anko-mah said good-bye to me. His last words, spoken in a toneless voice, were: 'I feel as if my own mother is dead.'

I went to bed but could not sleep. I did not dare to take sleeping-pills as I had to be up so early. Nana, however, did not come at six but well after seven. He was accompanied by Okyeame Pong, the father of Eva II, and Ankomah, who had to interpret. I thanked Nana once more for his speech and his gift while he avoided my eyes. Then we talked politics, which made us both feel happier, while I had to drink some of the wine which Nana had brought with him for me. In the middle of it Owusu arrived to say good-bye and to bring me his present—chickens and eggs for the journey. A little later we were joined by the Offumanhene and two of his elders, who had to tell of a new disaster which had befallen his village. The Asantehene had now taxed his stool's cocoa-trees: this additional tax was quite unjustified seeing that Offuman already paid tax on the cocoa crop into the Ashanti treasury.

March

When everybody had gone Santos and Kweyte packed up the car. An hour later I was in town. I said good-bye once more to Nana and all those elders who had assembled in the audience-courtyard. Then I went round to see the Queenmother. I was glad to hear that Kwabena was out with his father which saved the child the painful moment of saying good-bye to me. At last I was ready to leave—my heart was heavy.

On April 5th I flew to England.

Epilogue

My Activities from London

When I was in Bondugu I posted to Mr. A. L. Bryden, Solicitor and Privy Council Appeal Agent, a copy of Tekyiman's Petition to H.M. the King, a letter from Nana and one of mine, in which I requested him to hold up H.M's reply to the Petition, if it had been already prepared, as I was shortly returning from Tekyiman with new evidence in the matter of the disputed villages. Mr. Bryden, when he had seen me in his London office and I had given him my material, then suggested that a Memorandum should be attached to the Petition which had just reached the Colonial Office. I myself wrote a short summary of the Tekyiman–Ashanti dispute and sent it to the Secretary of State for the Colonies, the Right Hon. A. Creech-Jones, at the same time informing him in a letter that the Gold Coast Government intended to deport the Tekyimanhene and his most important elders to a place outside the territory and that the Tekyiman people intended to emigrate to the French Ivory Coast, the moment they heard that the order had been made. Mr. Creech-Jones, sympathetic and interested in the case, promised to look into the matter and did. Nana, eager that I should be well informed, through his contacts got me copies of the cables that had passed between the Colonial Office and the Gold Coast Government.

I decided to make use now of a letter which I had found in the Public Record Office in London when I searched for Tekyiman's Treaty with Queen Victoria. This letter was written in April 1897 by a Mr. Hull, Travelling Commissioner of the Colonial Secretary, and describes his visit to Tekyiman. The most important part is paragraph 2, in which he states that 'Ngwasi (Agwase),

Epilogue

Inchara (Nkyraa), and Fuman (Offuman) all acknowledge the sway of Tekyiman, which extends along the Bontuku (Bondugu) road as far south as Tanoso'. And again, in paragraph 23, that the Chiefs of Ngwasi, Inchara and Fuman regard themselves as being 'under Tekyiman'. This means that, of the nine villages, Agwase, Nkyraa, Offuman (I and II) and Tanoso certainly belonged to Tekyiman at the time and Boyem, Tuobodom and Subinso as well, since they are situated on the above mentioned Bondugu road. So far the Asantehene and the Government had claimed that these villages had served Ashanti up to 1901 when, after their final defeat by the British, the Ashanti Kingdom was broken up. I wrote to Nana about Mr. Hull's letter and what this discovery could mean for his case. The excitement in Tekyiman was great. Owusu described it to me in a letter:

The letter was received on the 19th [April] which was Munukuo[1] day. The villagers who came to celebrate the Munukuo as well as the people in town who always ask of you, when they heard that you had written a letter to your son, ran to the ahenfie [Palace] and asked Nana (your son) to tell them contents of it. It was very terrible scene. The letter was read to them, but I could not express joy and praise given to you. In the night about 9 p.m. all aged women gathered in front of the palace to play Adabo or Ngyinabaa[2] throughout the whole night to praise your wonderful discovery. No pen can describe your praise in ancient town Tekyiman and you deserve to be called Ohemmaa [Queenmother] Kruwa.

Nana, there is nothing strange in your State. Your son sent me to Accra on the 25th with a copy of your letter to Dr. Danquah. Dr. Danquah was very pleased and did not know what to say. I am returning to Tekyiman today and I hope to take special time to write you.

> With many greetings to you, Nana,
>
> Yours grandson,[3]   D. K. Owusu

[1] On *Munukuo*, every sixth Wednesday, Nana's Royal Ancestors were propitiated.

[2] *Adabo*, or *Ngyinabaa* (meaning meeting of women) consists of dancing and singing songs in praise of the Queenmothers.

[3] Owusu was a 'grandson of the Tekyiman Stool' (see p. 46); by signing himself thus he acknowledged me as Queenmother.

Epilogue

Although Mr. Bryden made use of Mr. Hull's letter in the Memorandum, Dr. Danquah thought it important enough to exploit it from the legal angle and wrote a six-page Supplementary Petition, signed by Nana and the State elders, to be added to the first Petition to H.M. the King, dated 29th June 1949.

The rest of 1950 was far from happy for the Tekyiman people, as a series of annoying incidents occurred. It is not the place here to go into detail, as except for one they did not affect the main issue: the Government, about to introduce District and Local Councils as a first step to Self-Government, still treated Tekyiman as part of Ashanti (Tekyiman's secession from Ashanti had so far not been acknowledged by the Gold Coast Government). Nana and his elders sent a telegram to the Governor in Accra, followed by a lengthy document in which they pointed out that Tekyiman had not been consulted and could not be expected to join the Asanteman (Ashanti Confederacy) in local government. Tekyiman demanded a separate local administration and first of all a copy of the report by the Three Select Committee (see below).

In December things came to a head when the young Nana Agyeman Badu of Domaa, another Brong[1] (Bono) king in the Ashanti Confederacy, opposed the Asantehene in a meeting to discuss the Report of the Three Select Committee on Local Government in Ashanti. The incident was reported to me by Nana in a letter dated December 29th:

. . . Nana Domaahene and the whole Domaa Division [i.e. State] has gone out of the Ashanti Confederacy. Domaahene is now my brother with one determination towards the welfare of Brong. If God wishes, some of the Brong chiefs will join Tekyiman and Domaa.

The matter with Nana Domaahene came as follows: About the 28th of November 1950 there was a meeting of the Ashanti Confederacy Council (now Asanteman Council) at Kumasi to discuss the Report of the Three Select Committee on Local Government in Ashanti.

[1] The ancestors of the Domaahene ruled up to the middle of the seventeenth century in Asantemanso near Kumasi which at that time belonged to the Bono Kingdom.

Epilogue

During the meeting the Chiefs were called one by one to accept the Report. Nana Domaahene was called also to say his views. Nana Domaahene made a motion that since the Report on Local Government in Ashanti reached the Chiefs only about two or three weeks before the Meeting of the Council, he was not able to study the Report with his State and therefore the Council should adjourn the Meeting to enable the Chiefs to study with their States before they would be able to accept the Report. Nana Domaahene's motion was rejected and he was still asked to say his views. Nana Domaahene further stated that the Three Select Committee took nine months to formulate their views according to the Report and it would be highly impossible for a Chief and his people to study the Report within two or three weeks. Domaahene added that he was warned by his State or Division not to participate in the discussion on the Report since they had not studied.

Nana Domaahene therefore walked out of the Council Hall, took his car and went to Domaa. The day was on the 28th November 1950. On the next day the Domaa State Council met and a resolution was passed to discontinue the Domaahene's membership of the Ashanti Confederacy on certain grounds stated in the Resolution.

The Asanteman Council met and appointed a Five men Committee to meet Domaahene and to settle up the differences. Nana Domaahene was advised by his Elders and people to meet me at Tekyiman for talks to re-affirm the relationship between Domaa and Tekyiman. The visit of Domaahene was reported in the papers. Since then the Five Men Committee has not been able to meet Nana Domaahene to say anything about the settlement of the differences. The Ashanti Confederacy Council was warned that Domaa would be another Tekyiman if the matter was not properly handled.

But the Domaa State Council and the people are even more determined than when I started the Tekyiman case, and strongly united, more than anything I can express, to be one only with Tekyiman. The Domaa Division is larger and more populated than any of the Brong Divisions and has also more grievances since the restoration of the Ashanti Confederacy.

Nana Domaahene spent four days with me before he returned to Domaa to hold meetings with his State Council. He spoke with me

Epilogue

on the telephone today and told me that he will soon return to Tekyiman and hoped to spend a fortnight here. I will write you more next.

As far as this letter is concerned I can only say that Nana Domaahene had shown admirable courage. One has to know something about the atmosphere in the Ashanti Confederacy Council to appreciate his action fully.

After this incident things moved quickly. One morning a few weeks later I received the following telegram in London dated 12th February 1951:

Tekyimanhene, Domaahene, Drobohene, Abeasehene assembled Tekyiman this 9th February—send greetings and pledge their unflinching loyalty—Nananom decided breaking off from Asanteman Council—Brong-Kyempem Federation inaugurated today among Brong Chiefs —God save Brong Chiefs long live Brong Federation—(signed) Owusu Assistant State Secretary Tekyiman.

This means that the Kings of Tekyiman, Domaa, Drobo, and Abease, assembled in Tekyiman on February 9th and send greetings to me. They had sworn an oath in which they pledged their unflinching loyalty to each other. The Kings decided to break from the Ashanti Confederacy and inaugurated the Brong-Kyempem Federation, i.e. the Federation of the 'Thousand Brong' or Bono people.[1]

This victory telegram was soon followed by more informing me that Atebubu, Suma and other Brong States had also joined the new Federation. Then I received all the details of the meetings, declarations, copies of documents, memoranda and so forth to keep me informed about 'my subjects' movements' as Owusu so nicely put it.

I was delighted, of course; I had never believed that anything like this could happen. I thought back to the day when Nana and I sat alone (Owusu interpreting) in the audience-courtyard and he was in a black mood, fearing the worst for his State. I should have cheered him up and consoled him. Instead I said with some

[1] Bono-Kyempem was a title of the ancient Bono kings.

Epilogue

annoyance: 'Why do you not get allies in your fight among the Brong chiefs, who all have grievances against Ashanti. Why do you not raise again the old Bono Kingdom by uniting them and rob Ashanti of half its territories. I do not like the word defeat, it is not in my vocabulary.' Then I reproached myself for having spoken thus; to tell a man who his fighting with his back to the wall, with a pistol at his chest, so to say, to go over to the offensive, was an insult. It was also unfair and silly. Embarrassed I looked at Nana—he said nothing, just sat there with downcast eyes and I wondered what I could say to annul my words. I did not know at the time that with my rough words I had planted a seed, a seed which now had become a little tree, difficult to uproot.

On February 28th, about a fortnight after the first victory telegram, I received my first communication from the Brong-Kyempem Federation, signed by five of the Brong Chiefs. 'As you, Mrs. Eva Meyerowitz, are our adviser', they wanted my opinion on the enclosed draft of a cablegram to the Secretary of State the Right Hon. James Griffiths (who meanwhile had succeeded Mr. Creech-Jones), in which they protested against the Gold Coast Government's policy against Tekyiman. I consulted Mr. Bryden about it and then handed the draft cablegram to Dr. Rita Hinden, then Director of the Fabian Colonial Bureau, to take up the case and bring it to the notice of Mr. Griffiths. The Government's reply to the creation of the Brong-Kyempem Federation and to Dr. Hinden's letter to the Secretary of State was to suspend Nana from office for the third time. This time Nana did not care.

Three months later Nana received the reply to Tekyiman's Petitions to H.M. the King. In a letter, dated 25th July 1951, His Excellency the Governor of the Gold Coast informed the Tekyimanhene that 'the Secretary of State regrets that he has been unable to advise H.M. the King to take any action upon the Petition as he and his advisers, after the most detailed study and careful consideration' have reached the unanimous conclusion that he (the Tekyimanhene) had failed to establish a case for the return of the villages. The letter went on to say that it was hoped that the proposed modernization of local government would, to a

Epilogue

large extent, make the dispute with the Asantehene of much less significance, particularly as it was proposed that the nine villages would belong to the same District Council as the Tekyiman State. Furthermore the Government had appointed a Committee to study the situation presented by this dispute and to suggest ways and means of settling it.

I quote here extracts from the reply of the Tekyimanhene and his elders to the Governor's letter, because it shows better than anything else how the people felt about the rejection of their Petitions.

Para. 2. My Chiefs and Elders and people are unable to understand why the Petition and its Supplementary were dealt with at the level it was. The main Petition was based on the Treaty of June 5, 1897, between His Majesty the King's predecessor and my own predecessor as regards the State of Tekyiman. When upon presentation of the main Petition doubts were raised as to whether the nine (9) villages were in fact part of Tekyiman at the time of the Treaty and therefore covered by the Treaty: the Supplementary Petition was presented with evidence which left no doubt in the matter that at the date of signing of the Treaty in 1897, the nine (9) villages were part of Tekyiman. The question now is whether that Treaty is to be honoured by both the high contracting parties or whether by the law of nations it is permissible for one of the parties to hand over a part of territory covered by the Treaty to a third sovereign who was not a party to the Treaty.

Para. 4. As regards to the suggestion that the nine villages will, under the new Local Government project, belong to the same District Council as Tekyiman, and that they will by themselves constitute a District Local Council, my Chiefs, Elders and people cannot believe that Government seriously contemplates forming a Local Council for nine villages as dispersed as Tanoso is from Braman and Subinso, with Tuobodom and Boyem only five to eight miles from Tekyiman-city which is their natural tribal centre and with which they have geographical and economic as well as social interests in common.

. . . It will be wasteful and uneconomic for the nine villages whose population is only 8,918, compared to Tekyiman's 11,077 to be

formed into an independent Local Council. They would hardly be able to help themselves to any appreciable extent. The combined population of nearly 20,000 is in a better position to serve the needs of the whole of Tekyiman, the Tekyiman Local Council which shall include the nine villages to be part of the Wenkyi District Council.

The Committee to be appointed by the Government to study the situation, which the Governor had mentioned in his letter, was to be known as the Committee of Inquiry in the Dispute between the Brong-Kyempem Federation and the Asanteman Council formerly known as the Asante Confederacy Council. Its chairman was Nana Azzu Mate Kole, Konnor of Manya-Krobo, the king of a small state people mainly by Adangme in the south-eastern Gold Coast, who could be regarded as impartial.

In a letter dated 20th August 1951, the President of the Brong-Kyempem Federation, the Drobohene Nana Kofi Busia Gyinantwi III, approached me to give evidence on their behalf, which I had already promised Nana I would do. Here are the most important paragraphs:

We have written to the Chairman of the Commission of Enquiry into the Brong-Ashanti Dispute, demanding your presence at our next meeting as our witness, and we have asked him to inform us the time he will be ready to meet us again so that we can inform you to be present at the right time. A copy of this letter has been posted to you under separate cover.

. . . The Brong-Kyempem Federation looks forward to you as its God-sent deliverer. May the Lord give you the health and time to come over to save us from the Ashanti yoke.

Nana Mate Kole, whom I already knew, agreed to this with pleasure, but when the Government heard of it I was not allowed to come. After much delay the Report was handed over to the Governor in November 1952 and, although it was marked 'strictly confidential', Nana managed to send me a copy. The Report was sent off by Mr. J. H. Allassani, Assistant Secretary to the Prime Minister Dr. Kwame Nkrumah, and member of the Committee, with a letter in which he pointed out that the Committee's sympathies were with the Brongs. There are a few interesting sentences in this letter which are worth quoting:

. . . these people (the Brongs) have been regarded and treated with every possible contempt by Ashantis in the past. There is no gainsaying that the so-called historic unity of Ashanti has all along been a unity maintained by a strong suppressing hand at the sacrifice of the freedom and happiness for the non-Ashanti peoples like the Brong.

I believe that our bid to remove imperialism from our country and to bring freedom and happiness to our people must not be limited only to foreign forms of imperialism but also to local forms of imperialism. Freedom from fear within is as important to the happiness of men as freedom from fear without. To compel these people to continue to subject themselves to humiliation and exploitation from the Ashantis would be the saddest unkindness we could do to them. This is the reason why we have recommended that they should be given the Council which they have asked for.

A month later the Prime Minister, Dr. Kwame Nkrumah, visited Tekyiman to reopen the Tekyiman Native Courts which had been closed since Nana's first suspension from Office in 1947. He had a tremendous welcome from the people and Nana gave a speech in which he asked the Prime Minister to assist Tekyiman in regaining the nine villages. Moreover he begged for the Government's recognition of the Brong-Kyempem Federation. In return Nana, speaking for his people, pledged devoted loyalty to the Convention People's Party, the party which had brought Dr. Kwame Nkrumah into power.

My activities on behalf of Tekyiman ceased about that time. I was still consulted in the years following when difficulties arose but, gradually getting out of touch with the quickly changing conditions, I was less and less able to give advice. When Nana lost his land case with Wenkyi, first in the Supreme Court and then in the West African Court of Appeal, he brought the case to the Privy Council in London (1956), after Tekyiman people had been chased off the lost land by the Wenkyi. Thanks to Mr. A.

Epilogue

L. Bryden, the Privy Council Appeal Agent, I was present when the case was dealt with by the most eminent British judges, but owing to lack of evidence the case was dismissed. If I had been in Tekyiman at the time I could have collected the history of that strip of land; in London I could do nothing.

Nana wrote less and less after Mr. Afwireng had left; I did not know the new secretary. From Ankomah I received affectionate letters and also information when I got stuck with my material till he died;[1] Owusu supplied me with all the news till he got seriously ill. There was thus a long gap in the correspondence, but it was renewed when he recovered. The Tuobodomhene and the Offumanhene also wrote to me, mostly about their never-ending troubles.

In 1957 the Gold Coast ceased to be a British possession and became Ghana. The Nkrumah Government was not immediately able to restore the nine villages to Tekyiman; but in July 1958 it enlarged the Brong-Kyempem Federation; all the Brong states were united into a new Federation called Brong-Ahafo. When the reorganization was complete the Brong-Ahafo Federation was gazetted by the Government in April 1959 as the eighth region of Ghana.

The case of the nine villages was brought before the Brong-Ahafo chiefs; four of the nine villages, Tanoso, Tanoboase, Tuobodom and Boyem, immediately returned to Tekyiman (October 1958) and the Tuobodomhene and the Tanosohene, who had been suspended from office ten years earlier, were re-enstooled. The other villages followed one after the other. Nana should have been happy and celebrated the great occasion, but meanwhile new trouble had arisen—in Offuman and Tuobodom. When in 1935 the Ashanti Confederacy had been created by the Gold

---

[1] Ankomah was never reinstated as the Inspector of N.A. Police. For a while he was employed by Nana in the office but felt so humiliated, especially after he had been accused wrongfully, to have conspired against Nana, that he withdrew to his cocoa farm. When he got into debt he tried to sell his land, which however did not belong to him but to the Offuman Stool. The Offumanhene wished to help him but Ankomah refused, and managed to sell the land. Three days later the spirits of the Offuman chiefly ancestors slew him. He was brought with a high fever to Sunyani Hospital and died in 1954.

2. Brong-Ahafo and Ashanti Territories

Coast Government the Offumanhene sided with the Tekyimanhene, but one of the Offuman elders who owned most of the
land, went to Kumasi and swore an oath of allegiance to the
Asantehene. For this action he was rewarded with the chieftaincy;
that is to say, he became the chief of Offuman No. I whereas the
rightful Offumanhene was labelled by the Government as chief
of Offuman No. II. The Brong-Ahafo chiefs wished to cancel one
chieftaincy and for some reason or another supported the chief of
Offuman I. The case is still pending. With regard to Tuobodom,
well, it left the Tekyiman State and declared itself independent,
following a quarrel with Nana when the latter refused to pay the
stool debts of £11,000, a legacy of the usurper and his successor.

Epilogue

As a village of nine hundred souls cannot exist by itself, Tuobodom will have to return one day to Tekyiman.

Then in April 1961 pressure was put on to Nana by his own people to abdicate. Years of nervous strain had proved too much for him, and his health had suffered to such an extent that a long rest was necessary. His abdication was accepted by Dr. Nkrumah who, for Nana's services rendered to the Ghana Government, awarded him £5,000 and a council house in Accra. Nana's great service to Ghana had been to have created the Brong-Nkyempem Federation, which had made it possible for Dr. Nkrumah to break the power of Ashanti and to establish the Brong-Ahafo Federation of states.

All in all the Nana's Royal Ancestors in the sacred cave, whom Nana consulted about me in 1944, had made true prophecies. Thanks to my help, and to a lucky change in political circumstances, Tekyiman was relieved of its trouble with Ashanti and the Gold Coast Government. Furthermore, in writing about the Bono Kingdom in my four books, I could be said to have restored some of its ancient glory; and in a small way I have been responsible for the re-union of the 'Thousand Brongs' or Bono. Ashanti lost over half of its territories and the ancient Bono Kingdom was resurrected in modern form, for the Brong-Ahafo region covers approximately all the lands which were once under the suzereignty of the Bono kings.

Chronology

Tekyiman's Struggle for the Restoration of Nine Villages which they had lost to Ashanti

1740   The destruction of the Bono Kingdom (founded about 1298) by the Ashanti. Tekyiman, Bono's second largest town, becomes the capital of a small vassal state called Bono-Tekyiman; a nephew of the last King of Bono becomes its king.

Chief Baafo Pim, the traitor, is rewarded by the Ashanti with the Nkoranza State.

1810   Nkoranza rebels against Ashanti. Tekyiman is forced by the Ashanti to fight the war for them. Tekyiman troops take the King of Nkoranza prisoner and to revenge his predecessor's treason, sacrifice him over the stool of the last King of Bono against the wish of the King of Ashanti.

1818–19   The Ashanti–Gyaman war. Tekyiman is forced to send troops and seven powerful priests, chiefs of villages, to help Ashanti. After the victory parade the King of Ashanti, Osei Bonsu Panyin, punishes Tekyiman for having refused to hand over the captured Nkoranza king, by seizing the seven villages and the lands belonging to them.

1877–96   The Tekyiman–Ashanti war. Victory of Tekyiman. At the same time Ashanti is defeated by the British. The villages return to Tekyiman.

1897   Tekyiman's Treaty with Queen Victoria which guarantees them peace and protection.

Chronology

1935   The Gold Coast Government establishes the Ashanti Confederacy; former vassal states of Ashanti are invited to join. In November the Tekyimanhene is forced to join and has to swear an oath of allegiance. After he had done so the King of Ashanti, Nana Prempeh II, deprives Tekyiman of the seven villages—Tanoso, Tanoboase, Tuobodom, Boyem, Offuman, Nkyiraa and Branam—as well as two others—Agwaase and Subinso—which meanwhile had been founded on the lands of the former.
Protests by Tekyiman; the Gold Coast Government, however, refuses to interfere in the quarrel which it regards as an internal matter to be dealt with by the Ashanti Confederacy Council.

1944   Nana Akumfi Ameyaw III becomes King of Tekyiman. The Gold Coast Government creates the Tano-Subin administrative area which comprises the nine villages in dispute; they still have to pay taxes to Ashanti.

1947   Tekyiman's Petition to the Chief Commissioner of Ashanti requesting once more the return of the villages: it is refused.

1948   Letter to the Ashanti Confederacy Council, signed by the Queenmother of Tekyiman and all the elders and chiefs, informing Ashanti that their King will no longer attend the meetings of the Council. At the same time a letter is sent to the Governor of the Gold Coast telling him that the Tekyiman State has broken off all communication with the Ashanti Confederacy and from now on refuses to pay the one-third share to the Ashanti National Fund.
Nana Akumfi Ameyaw III is thereupon suspended from office together with his State elders.
Petition to the Governor asking once more for the return of the villages and to rescind the suspension order. Demand for a Committee of Inquiry into the Tekyiman–Ashanti dispute. Refusal by the Gold Coast Government.

1949   Nana Akumfi Ameyaw III's second suspension from

office. Tekyiman's Petition to His Majesty the King of
England.

1950   Supplementary Petition to H.M. the King.
Nana Akumfi Ameyaw's third suspension from office.

1951   The Domaa State and other Brong States secede from the
Ashanti Confederacy and join Tekyiman. They form the
Brong-Kyempem Federation.
Negative reply to Tekyiman's Petition to H.M. the King
of England.
The Gold Coast Government appoints a Committee of
Inquiry into the dispute between the Brong-Kyempem
Federation and the Ashanti Confederacy.

1952   The Prime Minister Dr. Kwame Nkrumah visits Tekyiman and reopens the Tekyiman Native Courts which had
been closed since Nana Akumfi Ameyaw III's first suspension from office.

1957   The Gold Coast ceases to be a British possession and
becomes Ghana.

1958   All the Brong states, former vassals of Ashanti and members of the Ashanti Confederacy, join the Brong-Kyempem Federation which is renamed Brong-Ahafo.

1958–9   The nine villages are restored to Tekyiman.

Index

237

Index

Index

Index

Index

Index

Index

DATE DUE

MAY 1 3 '67			